2 The Fires of Faith

312

432

451

520

Newsweek Books New York

Editor Friedrich Heer

622

794

800

2 The Fires of Faith

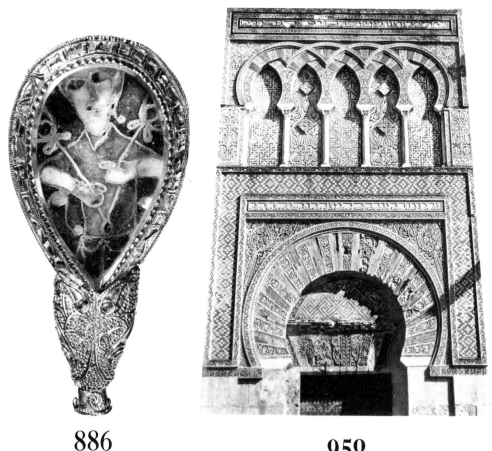

886   950   955

Library of Congress Catalog Card No. 74—98160
ISBN: Clothbound edition 0-88225-060-4
ISBN: Deluxe edition   0-88225-061-2

© George Weidenfeld and Nicolson Ltd, 1970
First published 1970. Second edition 1973.

Printed and bound in Italy
by Arnoldo Mondadori Editore - Verona

982

1066

1077

1100   **1194**   **1204**

Contents

Introduction

The title of this volume is not meant to imply that fires were burning continually from 312 to 1204. Yet fires there were: fires lit by zealous men that consumed the ancient gods, ancient cultures and eventually men themselves.

The rise of Christianity to its position as the official Church of Constantine's Empire was accompanied by fires in which the temples and other treasures of ancient cultures were destroyed—for example, the library at Alexandria. Then the Islamic fires from the desert seemed to consume the gardens of late antiquity, where vases and statues had survived from the age of Hellenism. And at the dawn of our own age, in 1204, the crusaders plundered and set fire to Constantinople and destroyed, for the time being at least, the Empire of the Romans. The Byzantine Empire and in particular Constantinople itself, with its glittering palaces, its baths, its art treasures and its luxury, was coveted as much by the tenth-century Ottonian Germans as by the Franks—the Latin Christians of 1204.

The fires of faith, the bright lights of destruction, the explosions of fanaticism, the everlasting wars and feuds that filled this era—was there even *one* year when there reigned a peace comparable to the *pax romana* that Augustus had envisaged or the *pax mongolica* that the great Mongolian khans created at the height of their power? All the undoubted devastation should not make us forget that the fires of faith brought life as well as destruction. The contents of this volume demonstrate that the dynamic forces that created the western world had their origin in these troubled centuries, and that the foundations of European culture up to the present day were laid over a thousand years ago.

We know both a great deal, and very little, about Constantine, to whom the Church owed its rise to power. Until 1969 the princes of the Roman Catholic Church—the Eminences, Excellencies, Cardinals and Bishops—bore the official titles of the higher bureaucracy of Constantine's Empire. The liturgical vestments of the clergy are still based on the robes of office of the imperial official. We know a great deal about Constantine, his life, his policy and all that this self-styled "thirteenth apostle" did for the Church. Yet we know little about his inner life. He was no doubt pious in his own way, like men who, since the earliest days of humanity, have waited in fear and hope for a sign from the Holy One.

St. Patrick's Celtic mission signified the beginning of a specifically *European* Middle Ages, with the activity of highly individual and highly individualistic monks and missionaries who traveled from island to island, farther and farther northwards, and then conquered the continent of central Europe and northern Italy in one great movement. Europe was becoming Celtic. In contrast to the centralism and uniformity of Rome, "Celtic" Europe was blessed with a multiplicity of highly independent personalities. These men from the British Isles thirsted after freedom; they had lively intellects and were fired with curiosity.

One, Pelagius, became the great opponent of St. Augustine, and the heresy of Pelagianism was considered a great danger by Rome for more than a thousand years. Pelagius saw man as a creature destined by God to freedom and reason, to shouldering the responsibility for what he did with his own life.

Carolingian civilization and the culture created by Charlemagne, his sons and his grandsons, which provided a broad and secure basis for European civilization up to the eighteenth century, would have been unthinkable without the gifted clerics from the British Isles. These clerics were the first *clercs* or intellectuals; they provided the officials and the school teachers for the whole of the European continent.

The Europe that was coming into being underwent a number of major invasions. The battle against the

Introduction

Huns on Campus Mauriacus near Troyes in 451 and the Battle of Lechfeld in 955 have a great similarity, indeed a close affinity, in that they were not, either of them, simply battles in which the West repelled the East—as they have too often been considered. On the contrary, these two great battles showed the extent to which East and West were interwoven. The frontiers were blurred; there were Eastern and Western troops, leaders and politicians in both camps.

The Rule of St. Benedict: possibly nothing has contributed more to the inner peace of Europe and the formation of an inwardly stable race of men than the Benedictine Order. Moderation, a wise balance between physical and mental activity, a renunciation of fanaticism in any form, including exaggerated asceticism: those were the maxims followed in the Benedictine monasteries that spread civilization throughout Europe in the "Benedictine centuries." The humanity of the Benedictines made an irreplaceable contribution to the turbulent, constantly warring Europe of their day.

Mohammed's *Hegira* or emigration (it was not a flight) from Mecca to Medina marked the beginning of the rise of Islam. A new world was created, a self-contained hemisphere reaching from Baghdad to Cordoba and even Toledo. For too long people saw only the "scourge of Allah" over the East; today we see the "sun of Allah" instead. Arabian doctors, technicians, philosophers, scientists and poets (and consequently Jewish ones, too, since the Jews were at the courts of the Arabian princes) created a civilization oriented towards Hellenistic antiquity in the Near East, without which European civilization at the height of the Middle Ages would have been unthinkable. The learned "disputation," the art of dialogue and verbal combat, was an offspring of the "world of the three rings" in the glittering Arabian civilization of the Spanish peninsula. Those three lights of the Christian Middle Ages, Albert the Great, Thomas Aquinas and Dante, were the spiritual inheritors of this Arabic-Hellenistic intellectual civilization.

The year 800 was a particularly important milestone, with the Carolingian Renaissance in the West paralleled by the Japanese Renaissance in the Far East. The political unity of Europe in Charlemagne's Empire was short-lived, but the social, religious and cultural foundations laid with the help of men from Spain, northern Italy, and above all the British Isles, lasted until the French Revolution and Napoleon, who considered himself a new Charlemagne.

What Charlemagne achieved for the Continent, Alfred the Great achieved for England. This truly great man, who won London from the Danes in 886, was the real founder of the English nation. Alfred also created the English navy as a political tool. He founded English literature, in the continuity of a tradition from Latin antiquity. The "scholar," and the essentially English type of education with its "open" tradition derived from ancient humanism (witness Thomas More and even J. H. Newman), were both offsprings of the erudition encouraged by Alfred the Great. Alfred himself translated into English Boethius' *On the Consolation of Philosophy*, which sought to offer mankind a *via media*, a "middle path" and a means of self-assertion between life and early death.

After the Battle of Hastings in 1066, Anglo-Saxon England was linked, through the Normans, to the Continent. An Anglo-French "western hemisphere" was created by the extensive possessions of the English kings in France. French was Richard Coeur de Lion's language, and the language spoken at the English court until the late Middle Ages.

In the "dark ages" of the tenth century, when the Continent was being invaded by Normans, Arabs and Magyars, and Rome seemed likely to collapse under the "pornocracy" of patrician families who used dagger and poison in their fight for the papal throne, Otto I brought about a unification of the ravaged German territories.

The kings and emperors of Otto's time became the great instruments of a reformation in Rome; and the monks of Cluny became their most powerful allies. With the unfortunate Henry IV began a two-hundred-year-long battle in which emperors and popes deposed and execrated each other. The battles over investiture that took place in Germany and Italy in the time of Henry IV and Henry V were destined to be repeated in England and France in the thirteenth and fourteenth centuries. From the protracted conflicts between emperors, kings and popes there developed on the one hand the world state (which then subjugated "its" Church once again), and on the other hand the imperial Church of the Pope. The papacy ultimately defeated the emperors and the Pope was proclaimed "true Emperor, lord over all kings and princes, and commander of the earth." It was not until the Second Vatican Council that the ideology, political aims and claims to power of the papacy were challenged as un-Biblical—mainly by theologians from countries that lay at the heart of the old Holy Roman Empire.

The twelfth century brought to Western Europe a flowering of culture to a degree unknown since the days of classical antiquity. Cities were constructed (chiefly at first in Italy), universities were founded, and the Gothic style was born. France or, to be more exact, the small area around Paris under the direct rule of the French kings, and Provence in the south—the cradle of courtly love, with its own language, a civilization focused on women and love that fostered a refined, cultured existence—became the cultural center of Europe, attracting students and teachers from all over the Continent.

This Latinized Europe of the West was, however, preparing for an explosive confrontation with the East. Nowadays we can define the "East" not only as Byzantium—the political civilization of the East Roman Empire, its intelligentsia, its bureaucracy and its education—but also as Byzantium's close allies, the Islamic princes with their lands in *Outremer*, the Holy Land. The Emperor in Constantinople sent his hearty congratulations to Saladin for his conquest of Jerusalem, the Holy City of Jews, Christians and Moslems. The "Franks" (the name by which western Europeans had been known for hundreds of years in the Middle and Far East), with their crusades, must be considered just as much a continuation of the Viking voyages as a prologue to the colonial expansion of western Europe.

Europe in the year 1200 knew little of events in other continents. Buddha existed in the West only in the legend of Baalaam and Josaphat—disguised as a Christian saint. Mohammed was thought of as a type of devil or antichrist, a fiendish deceiver. China, India and Japan were very remote. The conception of a wider world existed only in visions, dreams and legends. Nevertheless, southwest Europe was already assembling the force that—in the thirteenth and fourteenth centuries—was to send Franciscan monks to Africa, Asia, China, and deep into Mongolia.

This then was Europe—and the world—as it was forged in the fires of faith marking the tumultuous millennium that stretched from Constantine's vision on the road to Rome to the destruction of his city on the Bosphorus by errant crusaders.

FRIEDRICH HEER

In This Sign
Shalt Thou Conquer

The Roman Empire, at the end of the third century A.D., *was at the point of collapse.
Struggles among rival emperors brought frequent civil wars, while barbarian hordes threatened
the borders. Early in the new century, a soldier named Constantine proclaimed himself Emperor
and immediately set out to make good his claim in a series of campaigns that took him, by the
summer of 312, to the edge of Rome. Constantine had a momentous vision—a vision in which
he was told that he would conquer in the sign of the Cross, the symbol of the despised young
Christian religion. The warrior's subsequent victory at the Battle of the Milvian Bridge won
for Christianity an end to persecution and recognition as a legal religion.*

The third century of the Christian era was a grim, squalid age. For centuries the Roman Empire had maintained peace and fostered prosperity throughout the Mediterranean world, but now it was in decline. Stable central power had collapsed, as a succession of would-be warlords marched their predatory armies up and down the Empire, striving to seize power or to hold it against their rivals. Sometimes the legions actually put the Empire up for auction. At one and the same time there might be three or four self-styled emperors. None of them lasted long.

Meanwhile, the lot of the common man became ever more miserable and uncertain as cities were sacked, the countryside ravaged and wealth confiscated to pay the rapacious soldiery. Debasement of the currency and interruption of trade routes led to a galloping inflation. The urbane, sophisticated culture of the cities sank under a rising tide of philistinism and peasant brutality, as men jettisoned their intellectual baggage in the cheerless struggle for survival.

Faced with the uncertainty of life, people turned to magic and divination in attempts to penetrate the inscrutable will of the power that ruled the universe. Or they embraced religions that promised salvation in the next world to those who performed the right actions or held the right beliefs. A single, all-powerful god more and more replaced in men's minds the consortium of Olympians. Some called him Apollo; some, the Unconquerable Sun; others, Mithras.

Toward the end of the century, the successful soldier-emperor Diocletian tried to stabilize Roman society. To solve the problem of political power, he devised a cumbersome system of joint emperors, the junior succeeding the senior at regular intervals. To solve the economic problem, he tried to freeze all prices; predictably, it did not work. Neither did his arrangements for the succession to power; emperors would not retire at the appointed time—though Diocletian himself did—and rivals turned their armies against one another. Soon there were six or seven self-proclaimed emperors ruling in different provinces, and all seemed set for a return to the chaos of the preceding century.

One of these contenders for power, Constantius Chlorus, ruled in Britain and Gaul. He died in July, 306, in the legionary camp at York. His eldest son, Constantine, had the support of the army and came to terms with Severus, who ruled in Italy and Africa. Their plan to rule as joint emperors in the West was short-lived: in a few months Severus was eliminated by Maxentius, son of Diocletian's old colleague Maximian. Constantine felt his position threatened, and in any case he would never have been content to share power. In 307 he proclaimed himself sole legitimate Emperor in the West.

At first Constantine had to ward off German attacks on the Rhine frontier. After a year or two of marches, battles, sieges and skirmishes, he could be sure of his rear. In 310 he advanced into Spain, defeated Maxentius' forces there and gained control of the provinces. But this was not enough. The key to lasting and stable power lay in Italy, and above all in Rome. Constantine's army was by now a disciplined and confident force, accustomed to victory. In 312 its commander decided to put its fortune—and his own—to the ultimate test by invading Italy.

In the late summer of 312 Constantine marched his army across the Alps. It was not a large force, for he could not risk denuding the Rhine frontier of troops. Although Maxentius' army was many times larger, he was no soldier, and he waited irresolutely in Rome, plying the pagan gods with sacrifices and magic rites. Constantine, as always, was decisive, rapid and driven by an overmastering lust for power. Susa, at the exit from the Alpine pass, was taken by storm. Turin was entered after a cavalry battle. Without resting, Constantine pressed on to Milan. A few days to rest his tired but exultant troops—and he advanced on the strongly fortified city of Verona, which controlled the crossing of the Adige. Before

The gold *solidus* issued by Constantine the Great shows the Emperor adorned with a halo to indicate his hieratic status.

Opposite Constantine the Great, God's vice-gerent on earth; a contemporary Roman head of colossal dimensions.

13

A eunuch-priest of the cult of Cybele (*Magna Mater*), one of the many mystic religious cults prevalent during the early Christian period. He holds the symbols of fertility and is surrounded by the sacred implements of the cult; second-century bas-relief from Latium.

Below The four tetrarchs who succeeded Diocletian in 305 were the last rulers to persecute the Christians in Italy; fourth-century porphyry group from St. Mark's, Venice.

the city walls stood the main force of Maxentius' army in northern Italy. The battle was long and hard-fought, but discipline and leadership told. By evening the plain was strewn with corpses and Constantine held Verona.

The conqueror was now free to march on Rome. His route, through Bologna, across the Apennines to Florence, and southward through Etruria, was that followed today by the Autostrada del Sole. During his march south he had a portentous vision.

This was not Constantine's first vision. A few years earlier, in Gaul, Apollo the sun-god had appeared to him. More than most men of his age, Constantine was alert for the miraculous. Years later he recounted to Eusebius, the Bishop of Caesarea, what he had seen on the road to Rome that autumn day in 312. Eusebius recorded the story:

He called to God with earnest prayer and supplication that he would reveal to him who he was, and stretch forth his right hand to help him in his present dangers. And while he was thus praying, a most marvelous sign appeared to him from heaven. He said that about noon he saw with his own eyes a cross of light in the heavens, above the sun, and bearing the inscription BY THIS SIGN SHALT THOU CONQUER. At this divine sign he was struck by amazement, as was his whole army, which also witnessed the miracle.

The nature of Constantine's vision has been discussed for centuries. The most plausible explanation is that he saw a solar halo, which is sometimes cruciform. The inscription was probably the product of his own overheated imagination. Be that as it may, Constantine believed that the god of the Christians had revealed himself as the true god and had promised him victory.

As he slept in his tent that night, he dreamed that Christ appeared to him, displaying the same sign and commanding him to make a likeness of it and use it as his standard in battle. At dawn the next morning, he set his artificers to work to fashion the labarum, a Christian version of the traditional Roman military standard with the monogram of Christ set in a wreath surmounting it. It was an overt proclamation that Emperor and army were under the protection of the Christian god. Sure of his destiny, Constantine pressed on to Rome.

As his enemy approached, Maxentius at last bestirred himself. His forces outnumbered Constantine's, but army and populace alike were demoralized by famine and by the capricious barbarity of Maxentius' rule. And, finally, Maxentius was a poor strategist. Encouraged by an ambiguous oracle, which told him that the enemy of the Romans would perish, he stationed his army by the Milvian Bridge where the Via Flaminia crosses the Tiber, about two miles from the walls of Rome. The army thus had its back to the river, always an uncomfortable situation. To make supply and reinforcement easier, he constructed a second bridge of pontoons or boats close by the existing stone bridge.

On October 26, 312, Constantine reached his enemy's position. At once he began the attack, and Maxentius' ill-prepared and unenthusiastic forces

soon cracked. Constantine threw his reserves into the breach, and all along the line Maxentius' men, afraid of being surrounded, turned tail and ran. The rout was complete. Emperor and army fled back to the river, hoping to reach the far bank and the safety of the walls. But as Maxentius was crossing the bridge of boats, it collapsed. Rumor at the time said that, as a trap for Constantine, it had been built to break, but this seems like an explanation after the event. The fleeing soldiers panicked, and in the crush Maxentius was thrown into the river. The next day his body was found, and its head was cut off and carried on the point of a spear into Rome.

There was no further resistance to Constantine. Crossing the Milvian Bridge, he entered the city the next day by the Porta Flaminia, amidst the acclamations of Senate and people. He had united the whole western half of the Roman Empire under his own rule.

Equally important, Constantine felt that the god of the Christians had demonstrated his power by granting him the promised victory. Henceforth he was committed to the support of the Christian Church. And that Church, from being a repressed, poor, and occasionally persecuted minority of low social status, now found itself suddenly raised to the heights of power, prestige and patronage.

After a brief stay in Rome, Constantine returned to Milan. There he had a meeting with Licinius, who held the Balkan provinces. It was in their interest to make common cause against Maximinus, the ruler of Asia Minor and the East. Their alliance was sealed by the marriage of Licinius to Constantia, the sister of Constantine. At the same time the two emperors issued a joint edict on religious toleration, the famous Edict of Milan:

We resolve to grant both to the Christians and to all men freedom to follow the religion which they choose, that whatever heavenly divinity exists may be propitious to us and to all who live under our government.

Further clauses spell out the details of the program of toleration and order the restoration of Christian places of worship that had been confiscated.

The Edict of Milan marked the triumph of Christianity over persecution and put it on the same footing as other legitimate religions. It did not establish the Church as the official religion of Rome, but it was accompanied or followed in the next few years by a series of enactments favoring the Christians. Members of the clergy were exempted from costly municipal duties—and the wealthier classes, upon whom these duties fell, now began to become priests and bishops. Regular payments were made to churches from state funds. Sunday was proclaimed a holiday in the army: for some it was the feast of Christ, for others that of the sun god. The churches were recognized as legal institutions, able to receive legacies and administer property. The decisions of bishops were given the same validity in civil law as those of the courts. Freedom of pagan sacrifice was limited by legislation; some pagan temples were closed and their property sequestered.

Constantine and members of his family gave

The catacombs, galleries hewn out of underground rock, were used by Romans as burial chambers, and by the persecuted Christians for secret meetings and services as well as burials. This fresco from the third-century catacomb of St. Calixtus shows early Christians at prayer.

This early Christian inscription illustrates the symbolism of the early Church, a private code of supreme significance to secret worshipers. The fish represents Christ himself (probably with implicit reference to the miracle of feeding the five thousand) and the laurel leaves are the sign of his promised triumph.

15

The Milvian Bridge where, in A.D. 312, not two miles from Rome, Constantine fought his most crucial battle. Victory secured him control of the western half of the Roman Empire, but its most significant outcome was the confirmation of his prophetic vision of success and his new-found faith in the Christian God.

A relief from the Arch of Constantine showing the battle of the Milvian Bridge being joined between Constantine's army and the more numerous but demoralized forces that defended Rome under Maxentius.

lavishly for the building of churches all over the Empire. And when the Church itself split into factions, either because of the conduct of individuals during persecutions, as in Africa, or because of doctrinal disagreement, Constantine intervened. He organized synods and councils and put strong pressure on them to reach agreement, and in the last resort he used the arm of the civil power to enforce the decisions of the Church.

Although Constantine never wavered in his espousal of the Christian cause, he was not baptized until 337, when he was on his deathbed. Such deathbed baptism was common at the time: by making it difficult to commit a mortal sin between baptism and death, salvation was guaranteed.

Constantine, who held absolute power in a violent age, had sinned much; his hands were stained with blood, not least with that of his son Crispus, accused by the Empress Fausta of an attack on her virtue. Fausta herself was the next victim, charged with false accusation, and while the true facts of the case

are lost, the executions in both cases were by Constantine's order. His approach to Christianity was gradual and idiosyncratic. In 312 he probably knew little theology and less about the history and organization of the Church. Years later—we do not know exactly when—he was able to preach an Easter sermon in which he touched on many of the thorniest problems of Christian doctrine. He was fond of referring to himself as the bishop of those outside the Church. What he presumably meant was that by guiding the Roman state along Christian lines he ensured divine favor and protection for the Romans as a whole, including those who did not accept Christianity.

Constantine's conversion has fascinated historians and psychologists for centuries. Yet, all is still not clear. The difficulty is twofold. First, the world of ideas of the early fourth century is strange to us, and many of the key facts are unknown. Second, there is the problem of entering into the mind of this unusual man—unusual to his contemporaries as well as to us. Ill-educated but fond of the company of scholars; gentle and humane, yet never hesitating before a battle—or an assassination; superstitious and otherworldly, yet a realistic administrator and a bold and decisive reformer—Constantine was a man of many parts.

Today we know more about the fourth century than scholars did a generation or so ago. And it may be that we have a deeper understanding of psychology in general and religious psychology in particular than they had.

One long-held view can be rejected out of hand. According to this theory, Constantine's conversion was entirely a matter of policy, carefully and cynically calculated, and designed to win for him the support of a numerous and important group in the society of the time. But the Christians were neither numerous nor important, and this was especially true in the western half of the Empire.

It is true that Christians were more numerous in some of the eastern provinces. But in 312 the eastern

provinces were not Constantine's problem, and even there Christians were far from forming a majority. It is unlikely that Christians—however we define them —formed ten per cent of the population of the Empire. As for their importance, there were upper-class Christians, of course; but the bulk of the Christian community seems to have belonged to what we call the lower middle class of the cities and towns—traders, artisans, small landowners and petty "rentiers," whose influence on the course of affairs was negligible. Nowhere were the country people Christian. And the army, whose support was crucial for Constantine until the last of his rivals had been eliminated, was and long remained solidly pagan. If Constantine's conversion was a matter of calculation it was an ill-considered one, and with no real bearing on his success.

Constantine was evidently a religious man—in the terms of the early fourth century—in that he was anxious to identify the Supreme Power that ruled the universe and to put himself in the right relation with it. He was also an ambitious man, one determined to concentrate the imperial power in his own person and then pass it on to his sons. He did not seek the personal indulgence that power permits. He was no Maxentius, unable to see beyond extortion and debauchery. He was, in fact, rather austere in his personal life. For him, power meant the ability to impose order upon chaos, to tidy up the appalling mess of the Roman Empire. He wanted to find God, but not in any spirit of humility; he was a man fully conscious of his mission and of his ability to

This roundel from the Arch of Constantine incorporates material taken from an earlier sarcophagus.

accomplish it, if only the power that ruled the universe would help him.

The war with Maxentius had been a desperate gamble. As Constantine marched through Etruria to the decisive conflict at the Milvian Bridge, he must have anxiously hoped and prayed for a revelation. In these circumstances it is not surprising that one was vouchsafed him. He had Christians in his entourage, among them his mother Helen, who was later canonized as a saint. Repudiated by his father for the sake of a dynastic marriage, she was a devout

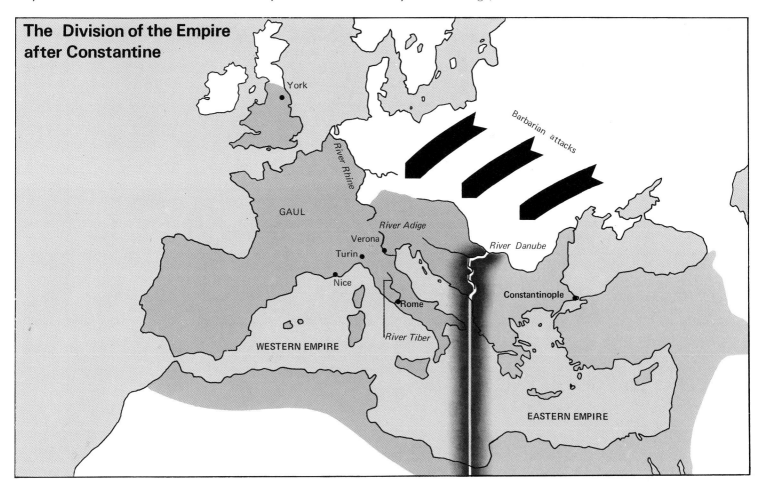

The Division of the Empire after Constantine

Christian who in her old age made a pilgrimage to
the Holy Land and there, it is believed, found the
True Cross. The god of the Christians was to Constantine one of the candidates for Supreme Power in
the universe. In a state of emotional exaltation, he
took a natural phenomenon for a divine sign. That
his revelation was corroborated by a dream that
night also need surprise no one. What confirmed
Constantine in his assurance not only that the
Christian god was the true god, but that he, Constantine, was his chosen vessel, was the victory a
few days later at the Milvian Bridge, a victory that
changed the shape of the world.

Constantine lived and reigned for twenty-five
years after 312. In 324 he invaded Licinius' territory, confident that he had the protection and support of the Almighty. A naval battle in the Bosphorus
and a land battle at Chrysopolis on the Asiatic shore
sealed Licinius' fate. Once again the god of the
Christians had given victory to his servant, and
Constantine now held the whole, reunited Empire.

It was then that Constantine refounded the
ancient Greek city of Byzantium, calling it the city of
Constantine—Constantinopolis—and designating it
the second capital of the Empire, the new Rome. No
doubt Constantinople lay on one of the main military roads of the Empire, leading from the Rhine
and Danube frontiers to the Persian frontier. No
doubt, too, that the economic and demographic
center of the Empire lay in its eastern provinces. Yet
it was not these considerations that led Constantine
to found the new capital and to enrich it with the
spoils of the Empire. He said himself that he gave the
city its name by the command of God. It was to be
the first wholly Christian city in the world, adorned

with magnificent churches built by the Emperor's
command, and containing no pagan temple. Constantine surely intended it as a symbol and a memor-
ial of his final victory—won close by—and of the
accomplishment of his great design.

Meanwhile, faced in the East with a split in the
Church on doctrinal matters, Constantine had once
again intervened. The Council of Nicaea in 325,
at which the Emperor himself presided, defined the
beliefs of the Church. The Emperor ordered that
they be adhered to and put the full weight of the
State behind the Church authorities in dealing with
recalcitrants. To Constantine it seemed his obvious
duty to ensure that worship was conducted in a
manner pleasing to the Almighty. Thus, though the
majority of Romans were still pagans, though Constantine himself still retained the old pagan office
of *pontifex maximus*, though pagan symbols still
appeared on the coinage, a further step was taken
towards the fusion of the Roman State and the
Christian Church.

With the vast mass of bullion that his victories had
given him, Constantine issued a new gold coin of
guaranteed purity, the solidus. This, together with
the peace of a united Empire, ended the inflation
and encouraged trade and industry.

The administration of the Empire was radically
reorganized. Civil and military power were rigidly
separated; a mobile strategic reserve was created;
and a new hierarchy of officers of state, responsible
to the Emperor himself, was established.

Constantine had his sons, Constans and Constantius, brought up as Christians; unfortunately they
became religious bigots. Later they were appointed
junior co-emperors, and arrangements were made

for them to succeed their father on his death. All did not go exactly according to Constantine's plan, but a major struggle for power was avoided. Until 350 Constans ruled in the West and Constantius in the East. From 350 until his death in 361 Constantius reigned as sole Emperor, like his father before him.

As Constantine, at last baptized and a full member of the Christian Church, lay on his deathbed on Whitsunday of 337, he could reflect that he had solved the constitutional, military and economic problems of the Empire and that he had given it a new capital and a new religion.

We might put the emphasis differently today. The Roman Empire Constantine knew soon crumbled. In 410 Alaric the Goth sacked Rome. Soon the western provinces and even Italy itself became barbarian kingdoms. But the eastern provinces, Greek in speech and Greco-Oriental in thought and feeling, survived. With its capital, Constantinople, the Eastern Roman Empire for a thousand years preserved the cultural heritage of Greece and the political heritage of Rome.

Constantine's other innovation is still with us, and without it European civilization would be unrecognizable. It was Constantine who launched Christianity on the path to power. In the half-century between the battle at the Milvian Bridge and the death of Constantius, the Christian Church changed decisively. From being a persecuted, inward-looking minority, it became a confident, sometimes arrogant majority. Not only were Christians far more numerous in 361 than in 312, but they now counted their adherents among the influential upper classes; they had taken over and adapted the intellectual heritage of Greece and Rome; their churches were the most magnificent buildings in the cities and their bishops were the leading citizens. The Church had acquired prestige, riches, power and a network of communications extending to every village of the Empire. Julian the Apostate's attempt in 361–63 to put back the clock failed.

There was nothing inevitable about this. Christianity had a missionary dynamic, but so had other religions. Without the support of a successful ruler, it could not have become the commanding ideology of the Empire. We need only glance at Rome's neighbor Persia to be convinced. There Christians were an active, occasionally persecuted minority. And this they remained until they were overwhelmed by the Arab conquest. No Emperor ever paid much attention to them, let alone gave them his passionate and powerful support.

As we survey the history of the Middle Ages, the Renaissance and modern times, almost everything that we see—from the great cathedrals of Europe, the iconography of our art, and the imagery of our literature, to our systems of education, law and philosophy—owes much of its shape to Constantine's vision on the road to Rome and his victory at the Milvian Bridge.   ROBERT BROWNING

The Emperor Constantine being blessed by Christ is the scene depicted on this sixth-century, late-Byzantine ivory plaque. Constantine's claim to divine authority directly given by Christ was acknowledged by the Pope in Rome and transmitted to a long line of Byzantine emperors.

Below The church of St. Irene in Constantinople was founded by Constantine, and is one of many churches in the city formerly known as Byzantium which Constantine renamed when he chose this meeting-point of Europe and Asia, overlooking the Bosphorus, as the Empire's new capital.

The fourth century, which opened with the triumph of Christianity in the Roman Empire, closed with the beginning of the Dark Ages. Leaders of the barbarian tribes, massing outside the Empire's frontiers, had already infiltrated their agents into the high places of imperial politics. The old order of Roman imperial administration, already severely weakened in the late third century and only partly restored by the reforms of Diocletian, was gradually disrupted during the years following Constantine's death. Thus, the gulf between the East, where the imperial system continued, and the West, where conditions of virtual anarchy came to prevail, can be clearly seen. The breakup of the West into a number of smaller units was already in prospect. The main subject of this passage will be events in Europe and the Eastern Roman Empire, but at the same time things were happening outside Europe—in some cases parallel to European history, in others, dramatically different from it.

The World of the Orient

In the Far East, the once-great empire of Han China had fallen apart in the early third century, and China was long to remain in a state of political turmoil. Then came the establishment of the Tsin dynasty in the year 265, and about this time a new force was beginning to make itself felt in northern China. During the fourth and fifth centuries, meanwhile, the Tsin were to extend their power into the southeast, and a new era in Chinese social and cultural history was inaugurated.

At first the Tsin power in the north had been severely curtailed by the incursion from beyond the frontiers of Hunnic tribes from central Asia. A number of warring barbarian dynasties were established in the north, but they were supplanted in about 430 by the new northern Wei dynasty.

The great unitary Chinese empire seemed a thing of the past. Despite the turmoil that preceded the foundation of the Tsin, the so-called age of the Three Kingdoms in the third century was regarded by succeeding generations as an age of chivalry, commemorated in the great *Romance of the Three Kingdoms*. Moreover, despite the continuation of civil war and foreign invasion, the fourth century witnessed a revival of cultural life and significant technical advance. The

Taoist stele ; northern Wei period.

native Chinese religious philosophy of Taoism enjoyed a new vogue, and the pacific cult of Indian Buddhism made considerable advances. It may well have been in a spirit of resignation that people in the war-torn land of China sought refuge in the Taoist ethic, one that rejected personal striving and endeavor and held that it was the function of the ruler to provide the minimum of good government necessary for peace and order. The tenets of Confucianism, based on a fully administered and well-ordered state, were in full retreat.

It was not for many centuries to come that the links of trade between China and Europe were to re-establish a degree of contact between the two civilizations. But it is important to notice that, although remote from one another, both Europe and China suffered the same scourge in the depredations of the Huns. Failing in their attempt to overrun the whole of China, these nomadic warriors retreated to the steppes of central Asia, from which in the fifth century they were to descend on Europe.

The hordes of nomadic barbarian tribes known collectively as the Huns were the scourge of civilization in several areas during the fourth and fifth centuries. Roughly contemporary with their attacks on China were their invasions of northern India, which became intensified during the fifth century. But at first these troubles on India's northern border did not seriously disturb the course of a period of peace, prosperity and unity that may justly be regarded as the golden age of ancient Indian civilization. It was

the age of the Gupta dynasty, which established itself in the north in A.D. 320, just four years before the Emperor Constantine asserted his sole rule over the whole Roman Empire.

In the first fifty years of their dynasty, the Guptas unified the whole of north and northwest India and were soon to gain the homage of the states of the south. The climax of this age of unity and cultural advance came in the reign of Chandragupta II (380–415). The prosperity of his empire is described in the diary of the Chinese Buddhist monk Fa Hsien, who was in India from 405 to 411 to research and collect Buddhist and other religious texts. Chandragupta and his successors promulgated a code of law for the whole subcontinent, and sent embassies as far afield as Rome. This was also a golden age for the arts; it witnessed the beginnings of

Painting of a Boddhisattva from the Ajanta caves.

the mural paintings in the Ajanta caves and the career of the Sanskrit dramatist Kalidasa.

Just as China had been subject to the religious influence of Indian Buddhism, so during the fourth century was her civilization also enriched by contacts with Persian as well as Indian traders. Like India, Persia enjoyed a period of great power and prosperity during the fourth century, under the rule of the Sassanid dynasty. Ever since

The Sassanid King Peroz (459–84) hunting.

the founding of their power and the capture of Ctesiphon in 226, the Sassanids had successfully established their ways throughout Persia and had extended their influence beyond their frontiers, even defeating the armies of Rome. During the reign of Shapur II (309–79), Persia continued to offer a major threat to the eastern frontiers of Rome, which suffered another major reverse when the Emperor Julian the Apostate was defeated and killed in battle in the year 363. The conflict between the two empires, which was centered upon the border state of Armenia, was temporarily resolved by the partition of that country in the last decades of the fourth century. The Armenians had accepted Christianity and consequently were subject to persecution by their Persian rulers, a pretext for the intervention of eastern Rome in the future.

The first century of a Christian Empire

When Constantine followed up his victory at the Milvian Bridge with the Edict of Milan, a new era in European affairs opened. As we have seen, the edict did not make Christianity the official religion of the Empire; but the sturdy and well-organized Christian Church achieved a new status that it fully exploited during the coming century. Constantine used the growing power and influence of his new ally to further his own ends. He saw his own authority encompassing ecclesiastical affairs. After his victory over the ambitious Licinius, which made him the sole arbiter of the Empire, he had convened the Council of Nicaea, the first general council of the Church, which decided many important matters of faith and Church administration. Ex officio, the Emperor had always held the office of *pontifex maximus*, the ultimate authority in the

The deification of the Emperor, from an ivory panel.

As the Church emerged from the shadows of governmental disfavor with the Edict of Milan, it revealed a bewildering number of conflicting views on the nature of the faith and, above all, on the nature of Christ. The most general view was that Christ, despite his human manifestation, was of the same substance as the other members of the Trinity, a mystic and indivisible unity. Yet it was the opinion of an Alexandrian priest named Arius that God the Father had created Christ, the Son who, although the first being of creation, was not equal with the Father. The Arian heresy, perhaps the most serious threat to the faith of Christendom before the Reformation, spread so widely in the eastern parts of the Empire that it endangered civil as well as religious peace. It was to meet this

Fresco from Dura Europos, Syria, one of the earliest surviving Christian churches in the Near East.

religious affairs of the Empire, and Constantine had no intention of surrendering this important attribute of his predecessors. Yet by linking the hierarchy of the Church to that of the civil administration, Constantine not only reinforced the one by providing it with a powerful spiritual ally, he also strengthened the other by giving it influence beyond its spiritual concerns.

Yet it was in the spiritual field that the Church really exercised her power. By the end of the century it had almost usurped the ancient authority of the imperial *pontifex maximus*. The climax came in the reign of the Emperor Theodosius, who was forced to seek public absolution from St. Ambrose in the cathedral of Milan.

Three points had been at issue: who was to be the final arbiter in matters of faith, Church or Emperor? If Church, was the claim of the bishops of Rome to supreme authority in the universal Church to be allowed? And finally, how was faith to be defined? The Church was involved in a struggle for power with the Emperor, but it was also at odds with itself.

Coin of Theodosius.

threat that Constantine had convened the Council of Nicaea and it was there that Roman Catholic orthodoxy found its champion in the figure of St. Athanasius. But although Nicaea proclaimed the Trinitarian doctrine, Arianism remained strong throughout the century; the barbarians adopted it as they came within the orbit of the Empire, and even some Emperors were among its adherents.

Throughout the centuries of religious dispute, the bishops of Rome held firm in their opposition to Arianism. As early as the reign of Pope Julius I (337–52), they were pressing their claim not only to seniority among the patriarchates of the Church, a claim by the city of St. Peter that was not denied by Antioch or Alexandria, but also to the supreme authority in matters of faith. Their claim was strengthened during the reign of Pope Damasus I (366–84) when Valentinian I, the Emperor of the West, decreed that all religious disputes should go to the Pope, and still more significantly when Theodosius as Emperor in the East officially con-

demned Arianism and made belief in the equality of the members of the Trinity the test of orthodoxy.

With Theodosius' decree "De Fide Catholica" of 380, the doctrinal position of Rome was vindicated by imperial authority. But the Church in the West did not in any way accept this as vindicating imperial claims to authority over it. On the contrary, St. Ambrose preached openly that the Emperor was in the Church, and not above it. When, therefore, Theodosius found himself excommunicated for his brutal repression of the citizens of rebellious Salonika, he was obliged to make formal public confession of his "sin" before he could regain admission to the sacraments.

In matters of doctrine and, quite sensationally, in matters of Christian discipline, the Western Church had by the end of the fourth century made good even its most grandiose claims. Although the Arian heresy survived for centuries in the barbarian kingdoms, it had

been branded as heresy and the Roman position had been upheld. Later, in the Middle Ages, the popes of Rome were to find their position threatened by the secular power, but that position and its authority had been unequivocally stated as early as the fourth century. And in the generation of upheaval and turmoil that followed in the West, the spiritual rulers at Rome were to be the only unbroken link with the glories of the imperial past. Thus, when new kingdoms emerged after the barbarian invasions, they received their Christianity, their passport to the new Roman civilization, from the Church. They found themselves confronted by a sophisticated and mature diplomatic and political body in the papal chancery. A body that so controlled the "commanding heights" of civilization could hardly be seriously challenged on its own ground.

Under Gregory I the temporal power of the popes was firmly established. One of his greatest successes was the conversion of England, which Gregory entrusted to St. Augustine. But the light of faith had never, in fact, been completely extinguished in Britain, and the Celtic Church, which survived in Ireland, Scotland, Wales and Cornwall, represented a tradition dating from the first or second century. The Celtic Church kept faith and learning alive, and Celtic culture flourished at a time when civilization seemed, in many places, to be in retreat.

Crucifixion scene from the great Roman church of St. Sabina.

Mission to Ireland

In the spring of 432, Laoghaire, ruler of a petty kingdom in northern Ireland, gathered his court near Tara to celebrate the annual rites of his pagan religion. The Christian missionary Patrick appeared in the midst of the gathering, confounded the King's magicians with a miracle of fire and—on Easter Sunday—converted Laoghaire. Patrick went on to strengthen the fledgling Christian Church in the Emerald Isle and to establish a religious tradition that was to endure for centuries. As Continental Europe slipped into the Dark Ages following the collapse of the Roman Empire, it was the monks of Ireland who kept alive the flame of faith and who—as missionaries—brought that faith back to the lands where it had been lost.

According to the annals of Ireland, St. Patrick arrived there in 432, and died three decades later, in 461. His mission to Ireland had been prompted by a series of dreams or visions, which strengthened an earlier resolve to dedicate himself to God's service. His great work, the *Confessio* (written about 450), is his spiritual autobiography, his account of his dependence upon God for his ability to carry out this resolve. We gather from Patrick's own words that the journey of 432 was made with a set purpose, the evangelization of Ireland. He recognized to the full his natural disabilities, such as teaching and writing in a tongue not his own. But outweighing all these was his unshakable belief that God had dedicated him to be a bishop to the Irish.

When St. Patrick went to Ireland he knew very well what kind of country he was going to. Years before, when he was only sixteen, he had been carried off from his father's home in Bannavem (either in Britain or Gaul) by pirates and taken to Ireland. There he was bound to a master, Miliucc, whose flocks he tended for six years. Then in response to a dream, he traveled two hundred miles to the coast and escaped by ship. He eventually reached his own family, but soon, in another dream, a man named Victoricus appeared to him with letters from the Irish begging him to return to them. Accordingly he set out once more for Ireland.

Patrick appears to have landed on the east coast. But we must leave the saint's own narrative at this point, for he tells us little about his practical life and his work, though we learn something of the insults that he had to endure from unbelievers, something of his converts, and of the sons and daughters of Irish chieftains who, at his urging, became monks and virgins of Christ. Otherwise, he speaks merely of journeying through many perils, even to outlying regions beyond which no man dwelt, and where no one had come to baptize, or ordain clergy, or confirm the people. The *Confessio* concludes with a pious hope that on this account he should never part with his people, and a prayer for perseverance in whatever he should have to endure.

The rest of our information comes from Muirchu, a seventh-century chronicler. Patrick resolved, as his first act, to go to his former master Miliucc with an offer to pay him the ransom that would have been due to him if Patrick had not escaped, and also with the hope of converting him. Muliucc, however, heard of his coming and, the chronicle says, set fire to himself and his house and all within it.

As the Feast of Easter was now approaching, Patrick proceeded on foot to the Plain of Tara, where King Laoghaire and his court were celebrating the great heathen feast of the druids. On his arrival Patrick kindled a fire by miraculous means, confounding Laoghaire's magicians and throwing doubt on their ancient traditions. The king marched out from Tara and summoned Patrick to appear before him. But Patrick, according to the legends, brought a great darkness over the land and the frightened king feigned conversion and returned to Tara. The next day, Easter Sunday, Patrick entered the hall of the king's palace to preach the Gospel, and emerged victorious from all contests with the druids. Patrick then threatened the king with death unless he truly believed. On the king's compliance, Patrick granted him his life, but because of his obduracy he prophesied that none of his seed should be king thereafter.

It is clear that the Easter ceremony is the climax of Muirchu's traditional narrative. The conversion of the king of Tara was, in his view, the apotheosis of Patrick's evangelization of Ireland. Along with it, he laid great emphasis on the keeping of Easter, and on the transition from the heathen to the Christian ceremony. The conversion of Ireland and the adoption of the "Patrician," or Roman, Easter are evidently held to be one and the same thing.

The Tara episode is followed in Muirchu's chronicle by a series of miracles much more briefly told, including the story of the bestowal of the land of Armagh on the saint, and ending with the story of the choosing of the little boy Benignus as Patrick's successor. Most of Book II of the chronicle is devoted to accounts of the saint's death, tidings of

An inscribed stone at County Kerry in Ireland, one of several examples of monuments of pagan Druidic ritual which have been adapted with Christian symbols by early Christian worshipers for their own use.

Opposite A cross from the illuminated manuscript of the Lindisfarne Gospels which shows the force of the Irish Christian mission started by St. Patrick.

Above left A portal dolmen, a monument which would originally have been covered in earth to form a chamber. This one, near Ardara in Donegal, is typical of the Druidic monuments St. Patrick would have encountered in Ireland.

Above right Croagh Patrick, the hill where St. Patrick worked as a shepherd after he was brought to Ireland as a prisoner.

Below The Gallarus Oratory, made of unmortared stone, is still watertight, though probably 1200 years old. It is one of the best preserved early church buildings in Ireland.

which he was said to have received from an angel, and which he sent to Armagh, "which he loved beyond all other places," summoning men from there to assist him to his last resting place. Patrick is believed to have died in 461, and to be buried at Saul, near the present city of Armagh.

Muirchu's *Life* is a chronicle in the form of a biography, but a comparison with Patrick's own *Confessio* reveals at once the tendentious nature of the former document, and above all the change in the gentle and noble picture of Patrick himself to a wonder worker who indulged freely in curses and vengeance.

Muirchu's information about Ireland at that time concentrates on the "high-kingship" because, at the time he was writing, Tara was the political center of Ireland. King Laoghaire was the eldest son of Niall Noígiallach, who had made himself master of the north of Ireland by conquering the ancient

kingdom of Ulad, which had formerly stretched across northern Ireland from Antrim to Donegal. But in Patrick's time, Ireland was divided into a number of *coiced* or small kingdoms, and there was no "high-king." Niall is believed to have conquered the Ulad and destroyed their capital, Emain Macha, which was only two miles from Armagh. He presumably made Patrick his chaplain there, but one can only speculate on the sequence of events that led to this, since he could hardly have liked or trusted Patrick. Niall had raided often in late Roman Britain, and his mother's name was Cairinn (from the Roman, Carina). Late Roman political influence may have helped place Niall in his advantageous position in central Ireland, and may also have influenced the appointment of Patrick.

With Niall we enter a new phase of Irish history, just as with Patrick we enter a new phase of Irish religion. The two came about simultaneously. Niall must have been a very able politician to create and retain his central position, and to retain, in that age, the loyalty of his sons. His influence grew and by degrees he acquired the midlands. His policy can be traced in the work of Muirchu, and in that of another chronicler, Tírechán of Armagh. Under Niall the influence of Patrick's work grew also.

Patrick was not the first to introduce Christianity into Ireland. According to Prosper of Aquitaine, a fifth-century theologian, Palladius was sent to the Irish as their first bishop by Pope Celestine in 431. Little is known of Palladius, but he probably worked in Wicklow in the south of Ireland. Muirchu tells us that his efforts met with little success, that he eventually left, and died in the land of the Picts (Scotland).

The centralization of episcopal authority in the see of Armagh is one of the first signs of Patrick's Roman influence. In Gaul the bishops were centered in the principal towns of the provinces. But in Ireland, where Roman influence was less direct and up-to-date, the bishops were stationed in the monastic centers, the only places of civil organiza-

North Africa and challenge Rome

involved in the complexities of Irish clan politics. In the end it was this very clannishness that enabled the Irish to retain their strong identity as a nation throughout the centuries that followed.

The early history of Scotland

We have seen how St. Columba established an outpost of Irish Christianity on Iona in the sixth century. The island was part of the Scot kingdom in northern Britain that had been founded by settlers from Ireland itself. The original inhabitants of Scotland—the Picts—are one of the more shadowy peoples

Pictish stone slab from Scotland with figures of warriors.

of European history. It seems likely that they settled in the country before the arrival of the Celts in Britain and had received Christianity during the fifth century at the hands of St. Ninnian. At the time the community of Iona was founded, the land we now know as Scotland was divided among several kingdoms: the Picts to the northeast; the Scots; the British in Strathclyde to the southwest; and the Angles in Northumbria to the southeast. During the ninth century a new power established itself in the Hebrides and the mainland districts of Caithness and Sutherland. This was the Norse earldom of Orkney, which all but destroyed the Pictish kingdom. As a result, before the middle of the century the Scottish king, Kenneth I MacAlpin, was able to extend his control over what remained of the kingdom. It was with his house and its successors that the future of Scotland was to lie. In the tenth century they succeeded in winning the lowland areas of Lothian and the Tweed frontier from the English King Edgar. In the early eleventh century, Kenneth MacAlpin's succes-

sors acquired the whole inheritance of the last of the kings of Strathclyde. The power of the earldom of Orkney had gradually been eroded, so that by the end of the eleventh century only the isles and the northeasternmost tip of mainland Scotland was controlled by the Norwegian rulers.

The Vandals in Africa

In 451 Europe was confronted by the menacing power of the central Asian steppes that had so long affected her destiny indirectly. Fear of the Huns had been the force that had driven the first wave of German invaders into the Roman Empire during the fourth century. Gradually, their long trek westwards was to lead the two great confederacies of the Goths to set up kingdoms in the old lands of the Roman Empire. The stories of these kingdoms will be the theme of a later chapter.

The first Germanic kingdom to be established within the Empire was, however, that of the Vandals. They had been settled on the Danubian frontier as early as the third century and had, in the figure of the noble Stilicho, given Rome one of her greatest statesmen. However, Stilicho, like the Roman Aetius after him, was to fall victim to the murky intrigues of the court of the later Western Empire. Among other charges against him was one of having invited the barbarians into the Empire in the fateful year 406.

Crossing the Pyrenees

It is true that the Vandals were among the group of tribes that crossed the Rhine in that year. Unable to find territory in Gaul, they continued to move west, crossing the Pyrenees three years later. In Spain they lived on uneasy terms with the Empire, to which they made nominal allegiance, and with their barbarian neighbors, the Visigoths. However, they were even at this stage showing abilities in seamanship that were later to make them the first barbarian naval power in the Mediterranean. In 429, under pressure from the Visigoths, they were led by their king, Gaiseric, to Africa.

Here again we find contemporaries charging the imperial commander of the province, Boniface, with collusion. But the charge can almost certainly be discounted, and the defeat of Boniface himself was

Mosaic monument to early Christian martyrs in North Africa.

so complete and so rapid that history, as distinct from scandal and rumor, has been denied the opportunity of fabricating any

real explanation of this supposed treachery. Within five years the imperial government had been obliged to recognize the *de facto* power that the ruthless leader of the Vandals had won for himself in Africa. During his long reign of fifty years, Gaiseric (*d.* 477) not only established a kingdom in Africa, but became a menace to Mediterranean shipping, and seriously threatened the Eastern Empire. In 455, he sacked Rome with legendary brutality. He defeated all attempts to overthrow him and concluded a peace with the Emperor in which Zeno recognized the barbarian power in North Africa and Sicily, Sardinia, Corsica and in the Balearic islands.

The Vandals remained a ruling minority in Africa, settling on the estates of dispossessed Romans. They retained their ancient customs and traditional method of mounted warfare, but gradually succumbed to the unaccustomed life of southern luxury. The Roman citizens of the former province retained their own law courts and continued to serve in the main offices of the civil administration. But in one crucial respect the life of the conquered population was frequently one of bitter oppression. Like Germanic peoples elsewhere, the Vandals were Arian Christians. Persecution of the Catholics, by fines, confiscation and outright cruelty, recurred throughout the Vandal period.

The Moorish onslaught

After Gaiseric's death, Vandal power in Africa was under increasingly severe attack from the Moorish tribes of the interior. Although toward the end of the period some rapprochement was achieved with the Eastern Empire, and the persecution of Orthodox Christians ceased, the last Vandal king, Gelimer, renounced the alliance. The kingdom fell prey to the armies of the Emperor Justinian under the command of Belisarius.

The incursions of Attila were among the more sensational events in the history of Europe during the fifth century, but his Hunnic ancestors had long before set in motion a train of events that had far-reaching consequences for the Empire in the West. The century of Vandal rule in Africa was paralleled by the Ostrogothic domination of Italy, and outshone by the enduring state the Visigoths established in Spain after the Vandals left.

Seal of Alaric II, powerful king of the Visigoths.

29

Ireland before the coming of Patrick

According to the most ancient traditions of Ireland, her history had been linked to that of the Mediterranean world long before the coming of St. Patrick and the religion of Rome. Even after St. Patrick, the history of the country was to remain the preserve of an oral tradition handed down by a

Minstrel harp from a Viking burial.

class of minstrels or bards. In western Europe these minstrels were the latest heirs of an heroic Iron Age society, of which the earliest example known to us was the Greece described by Homer. At the time of Patrick's mission, Ireland was ruled by Celtic kings and her society was by then entirely Celtic. Yet the picturesque and misleadingly precise lays of the bards not only traced the descent of every one of these kings back to the most remote past (genealogies which, after the acceptance of Christianity, were to stretch back to Adam), but also told of four conquerors who had preceded the Celts.

Their origins and their destinies must necessarily be classed as obscure, but we are told that when the original settlers of the island were defeated by the seafaring Fomors, many of them fled to Greece. The next race of invaders, the Tuatha De Danann (in whose name there might be a fossilized form of "Danai"—one of the names by which the ancient Greeks were known), made use of magical powers to assist them in their conquest. However, these arcane skills were not proof against the Milesians —according to the legend the last

conquerors of the island and, if so, a Celtic people. The Milesians, whose name also has an attractively Mediterranean flavor, originally came from Spain. This tradition is neither inherently absurd nor lacking in some archaeological evidence. It is now fairly generally accepted that Phoenician traders from the Mediterranean reached Cornwall in their quest for tin— sufficient indication of the skills of the early seafaring peoples. And more direct links between Ireland and Spain itself may be seen in the remains of megalithic monuments in these two countries, as in other parts of coastal Europe.

Whatever their origins, the Celts were well established in Ireland at the time of the Roman conquest of Britain. Their numbers were swelled by the arrival of small groups of refugees fleeing before the invading army. We know from the account of his son-in-law, the historian Tacitus, that the Roman

Early Celtic head from England, dating from the time of the Roman occupation.

general Agricola had contemplated the conquest of the island—not, it appears, because of military necessity nor in the hope of material gain; but rather as a tactical move of psychological warfare against the Britons themselves, to impress on them the omnipotence and ubiquity of Roman arms. But the demonstration was never made. The conquest of Ireland by Rome, if so it may be termed, did not come until four centuries later, when she received her religion and first literate culture at the hands of a Roman missionary.

During the intervening period, there is evidence of trading with the Empire and also of some raiding by Irish adventurers. Yet for the

Stone font in the Greenan mountains, Ireland, for centuries the seat of the Kings of Ulster.

most part these centuries were spent in the internecine warfare between seven kings who divided the country among them. During this period the most powerful house attempted to make good their claim to be High Kings.

In many ways Ireland was remarkable among the countries of western Europe in the early Middle Ages, especially for the survival of an ancient Iron Age culture, complete with the institution of kingship. But more important still is the early sense of a unity of culture that surmounted the political divisions of the country and was expressed in the use of a common language and a common legendary tradition. It was this tradition that was so important a feature in the success of missionaries of the fifth century.

Ireland after Patrick

The brilliant story of Christian culture in Ireland and its importance to the civilization of medieval Europe has been touched on. The talents of the Irish in the humane arts were not, however, matched by an equal skill in the business of politics. When the Norse invaders fell upon the country at the end of the ninth century, the Irish were unable to dislodge the intruders. Nor could they sink their differences in order to form an effective counterbalancing power. The reason may perhaps be found in the continuing clannish structure of Irish society. Despite the temporary unifying effect of the reign of Niall the country continued to be divided into warring territories.

The Norsemen brought not only destruction to the thriving cultural

life of the island, but also a new principle of social organization in the towns that they founded— such as Limerick, Wexford and Waterford—and the trade that they conducted. Furthermore, the Norsemen, engrossed in their trading activities and with their overseas territories in Man and the north of England, never seem to have concerned themselves with the outright conquest of Ireland. Thus, unlike their neighbors in England who, in the eleventh century, surrendered independence for a strongly unified state, the Irish were free to continue their interclan rivalry until, during the twelfth century, they too felt the weight of Norman conquest and entered into a tragic period of foreign oppression.

Only once did the situation seem likely to alter. In the early years of the eleventh century, Brian Boru, King of Munster, usurped the high kingship and united the country. On the historic field of Clontarff, in the year 1014, he defeated a great army composed of the Vikings of Dublin, of Man and the Isles, and their Irish allies. The power of the Vikings in Ireland was broken. But in the same year Brian Boru, who had described himself proudly as *Imperator Scottorum*, and who seems to have tried to modify the fragmented nature of Irish society, was killed. The Norsemen's influence was now limited to the important but no longer menacing trading communities. The petty kings and great families of Ireland resumed their age-long struggles, which even the first impact of the Norman conquest in the 1160s did not check. Even the Normans, who never conquered this turbulent country, soon found themselves and the decision of the Council of Nicaea, was upheld by Bishop Wilfrid of Ripon, and that of the Celtic Church, which preferred the older practice of reckoning Easter in the same way as the Jewish Passover, by Colman, Bishop of Lindisfarne. Oswiu and his people decided in favor of Wilfrid and Rome. In 669 Theodore of Tarsus, consecrated Archbishop of Canterbury by Pope Vitalian, arrived in England. During his archiepiscopate the unity and organization of the Church of Canterbury was secured.

The death of St. Columba did not at all mean that the sanctuary of Iona came to an end. On the contrary it continued to flourish under a succession of Columba's collateral descendants for several centuries till the time of Adamnan; but the gradual extinction came with the repeated incursions of the heathen Norsemen, who sacked it time after time. In 802 the monastery was burned and in 806 some sixty-eight monks were slain. In 825 the whole community perished. At last in 849 the sacred relics were transported to the new church at Dunkeld by Kenneth MacAlpin.

Iona was not the only sanctuary destroyed by the Norsemen. In Ireland, especially, the destruction was great, and traces of heathenism did not finally disappear in Ireland until the end of the ninth century. Monasteries such as Clonmacnois, which had been founded in 548 and which had been virtually a university, were pillaged of their treasures. There was a wholesale evacuation of monks to the Continent, some carrying their books with them but far more carrying with them, as more easily portable, the Latin learning that, especially since St. Patrick's day, they had been quietly absorbing in their monastic libraries. In this matter, Ireland's loss was a gain for Europe. Many a Continental library has been enriched by manuscripts salvaged from the Viking period in Ireland, and by the learning of her refugee monks.

Among the most famous of the scholars who left Ireland for the Continent at this time were Sedulius Scottus and Johannes Scottus. Sedulius was a member of the court of King Charles the Bald at Liège, and may have been a member of a mission of Irishmen that is known to have come in the middle of the ninth century to the court of Charles the Bald from Maelsechlainn, the Irish king. He was one of the most learned men of his time—poet, scholar, scribe, theologian and courtier. He was a precise Latin scholar, and there are hints of Irish sources in some of his writings and some slight knowledge of Greek.

Even more remarkable was Johannes Scottus Eriugena, "John the Irishman." Little is known of his origin or of his early life, but he was also a member of the palace school of Charles the Bald. He must have arrived there at least as early as 845, and remained at least till after 870, probably as a teacher. His learning was wide and precise, including Latin and Greek—the latter a rare accomplishment of his day. Among his many writings, the greatest is the *De Divisione Naturae*.

"It is impossible for the Classical scholar to exaggerate the significance of the part played by the Irish in the work of preserving Classical literature," says Norden. From the earliest period one has only to think of St. Gall and Bobbio, and during the ninth and tenth centuries there had been hundreds of refugee monks who sought the retreats offered by the Irish monasteries of Péronne, Laon, Reims, Fulda, and Würzburg. In the eleventh century Ratisbon was founded by an Irish monk from Donegal on his way to Rome. From Ratisbon foundations were made at Würzburg and Nürnberg, and even at distant Kiev a monastery was founded which lasted till the Mongol invasion in 1241. For three hundred years these abbeys kept in touch with Ireland and drew their monks from them.

NORA CHADWICK

Above The Ardagh Chalice, the most famous piece of early Irish Christian metal work, is of beaten silver decorated with gold and enamel. Among the remarkably delicate engravings are the names of the Apostles and animal symbols. It probably belonged to an eighth- or ninth-century church.

Left The Book of Durrow is the earliest fine illuminated manuscript and it represents in its maturity of style the highest point of artistic achievement in the Irish illumination tradition, particularly in the pages illustrating the symbols of the Evangelists, like the one shown here, in mellow colors.

The Scourge of God

*Attila, the legendary "Scourge of God," was the force that—curiously enough—helped to hold
the tottering Roman Empire together for a few more years. Halfway through the fifth century,
the Empire was defended by an array of feuding barbarian tribes enlisted as mercenaries.
These tribes were united by a common fear of the Huns, who had left Central Asia to invade
India, Persia, Central and Eastern Europe and were now threatening the West. Aetius,
commander-in-chief of the Roman army, knew the Huns well and their leader, Attila, in
particular—the Roman general had once been a hostage in the Huns' camp. Aetius also knew
that the real danger to the Empire came from within, from its disintegrating society.
When Attila invaded Gaul, Aetius checked him at a battle fought southeast of Paris.
But the Roman "victory" brought only a temporary halt to the inevitable fall of Rome.*

On the battlefield of the Campus Mauriacus—to the west of the old Gallo-Roman town of Troyes, some ninety miles southeast of Paris—two armies faced each other in the year 451. In retrospect they might be seen as the forces of two contrasting worlds: Asia against Europe, the civilization of the plains against that of the towns, pagan barbarism against the Christian heritage of Greece and Rome. But this assessment would be superficial.

Arrayed behind the Hun, Attila, was a horde of tribes more or less under his command: not only his own people but also Ruli, Heruli, Gepidae, Ostrogoths, Lombards and others. Opposed to him in defense of the Roman Empire was the last of the great Romans, the nobleman Aetius. Among his forces there were hardly any Gallo-Romans, but a mixture of barbarian peoples whose loyalty was not to be relied on: Franks, Burgundians, Alans, Sarmatae, Visigoths, and even a number of Britons who had been recruited indiscriminately along with the very Germans who had driven them out of their own island territory. What is more, the Visigoths under King Theodoric could well find themselves confronted by their kinsmen, the Ostrogoths, under the command of a Hun. Attila had defeated the Visigoths in a previous battle; he treated the Ostrogoths as run-away slaves. Aetius' forces had only one common bond: their fear of the Huns who had driven them from the steppes of Russia and the plains of Germany and forced them into Gaul.

The defense of the Roman Empire at this time was entrusted to the very people who presented the greatest threat to its peace. Barbarians were enlisted as mercenaries—first in small groups, then whole peoples at a time. German soldiers reached the highest ranks. Both the Vandal Stilicho and later the Sueve Ricimer were to command Roman armies.

Unfortunately, these dangerous allies expected regular payment, which the Empire was no longer in a position to supply. Some of them revolted, and

demanded lands off which they might live; the Visigoths, who had put themselves at the service of the head of the Eastern Empire in 376, ravaged certain Greek provinces and Italian towns under their chief, Alaric. In 410 they sacked Rome herself before crossing the Alps and finally settling in Aquitaine.

In 407, a particularly violent wave of tribes had broken on Gaul. The Alans, Sueves and Vandals had been driven from Persia by the Huns and had made their way across Europe. The Alans had ended up as scattered communities on both sides of the Pyrenees; the Sueves were eventually to establish a kingdom in the region of the Douro in the north of what is now Portugal, while the Vandals made their way from Spain to Africa, where they were to dominate the Maghrib for more than a century.

Peoples who had previously been living between the Elbe and the Rhine followed the example of these enterprising invaders, and ventured forth in their turn. Burgundians, Alamani, and Ripuarian Franks established themselves on the left bank of the Rhine and acquired the status of federate territories. At the same time Angles, Jutes and Saxons were gradually occupying the eastern parts of Britain, from which the kingdom of England was later to emerge.

Behind these German tribes there were the Huns, or rather the various peoples of Hunnish stock who had left their native steppes of central Asia to invade India and Persia on the one hand, and central and eastern Europe on the other.

As soon as he learned that the Huns had crossed the Rhine, Aetius hastily assembled an army from among the barbarian tribes established in Gaul for half a century. This army clearly lacked unity, as Aetius was only too well aware: although there were many reliable troops, the loyalty of the Alans under their king, Sagiban, was not to be relied on.

Attila himself, ruler of the people who occupied the vast plains between the eastern Alps and the

A portrait of Theodosius the Great, ruler and defender of the Eastern Empire from Constantinople.

Opposite An ivory diptych in Monza Cathedral traditionally said to represent Aetius, the defender of Gaul, his murderer the future Valentinian III and the princess Galla Placidia. (Some scholars prefer to identify the portraits as the Vandal Stilicho and his family.)

The weapons of barbarian warriors; a two-edged, gold-handled sword found in France and probably made by a Byzantine craftsman, which tradition attributes to King Theodoric; a silver Moldavian helmet, possibly Hunnish; and the boss of a shield.

Urals, was not interested in territorial gains but rather in military victories; above all he was a man drunk with power and greedy for fame. However, he must not be thought of simply as a brute or a hardened fighting man who never got down from his horse and who ate his food raw. He was a skilled politician and was gifted with a lively intelligence, to which was allied a certain cruelty. He did not conquer merely in order to possess but fundamentally to assert his own greatness and extend his dominion.

The Roman Empire fascinated this barbarian; in fact, he might well have wished to be a Roman. He exchanged ambassadors and hostages with Constantinople, as a guarantee of the mutual desire for peace. He lived in a palace whose rooms, although of timber, boasted rich carpets and where the pleasures of the Roman bath were enjoyed. He held court in the Roman manner, reclining on a state couch, and presided over brilliant banquets at which a wealth of gold plate was to be seen. His chancellery was managed by Roman scribes, and one of his secretaries, the poet Orestes, was to become regent of Italy and father of the last Western Emperor, Romulus Augustulus.

Overweening ambition was the dominant trait in Attila's character. Shortly after the death of his uncle, King Rugila, Attila had his own brother Bleda assassinated so that he should be sole ruler. But this empire was only a brief episode in the history of the Hunnish tribes. In 445 Attila renewed his advance towards the Mediterranean.

Whether war or diplomacy would be required for this advance, the king of the Huns cared little—so long as he was the master. But this crafty Oriental knew when to make a strategic withdrawal. On one occasion he had brought pressure on the Eastern Emperor at Constantinople, Theodosius II, to pay him tribute money. But when the feeble Theodosius was succeeded by a more energetic man, Attila turned his attention to Rome.

On this occasion he came in the guise of a friend, but one whose friendship was mixed with impudence. He demanded the hand of the sister of the Emperor Valentinian III, for whose dowry he thought that half of the Western Empire would be appropriate. Valentinian showed this suitor the door.

What then was to be the next step for a man who was to become the legendary "Scourge of God"? After his repulse by Constantinople and his humiliation by Rome he simply went to seek his fortune elsewhere. In the spring of 451 he was on the banks of the Rhine where he became involved in the internal quarrels of the Ripuarian Franks, and announced that he was going to punish his fugitive slaves, the Visigoths, who were for the time being peacefully installed in Aquitaine.

The man who was governing Gaul at that time probably knew Attila better than anyone else. Aetius, who was the son of a noble family, had in fact spent part of his youth as a high-ranking hostage at the court of Rugila. Attila had been his companion. He understood, better than anybody else, the nature of the Huns. Surrounded by terrified barbarians who trembled at the Huns' approach, only Aetius understood Attila's character. To him fell the task of defending Gaul.

He appreciated the warlike qualities of the Huns. As a nobleman and commander-in-chief of the Roman army, Aetius had enlisted Huns for his personal bodyguard and his picked troops; and it had been with the help of Hunnish auxiliaries that he had subdued the Burgundians in 435.

Aetius realized that Attila was more concerned with his reputation than with acquiring territories for which his nomadic horsemen would find no use. He also knew that Attila lacked persistence. Treves, Metz and Reims were burned, and Attila's hordes passed some distance from Paris, where St. Geneviève urged the people to remain calm and not to flee. In May of 451, Attila besieged Orléans, whose bishop, Aignan, was able to escape in time to seek help. It was at this juncture that Aetius called up the federal troops based in Gaul and marched on Orléans. Thereupon Attila retreated. Once more, in the face of firm resolution on the part of his enemies, he decided to abandon his original plans and explore fresh fields.

At the Campus Mauriacus, however, Aetius caught up with Attila at last. The carnage and ferocity of this battle were to become legendary. Theodoric, the king of the Visigoths, was killed in the fight, but the battle was indecisive: neither the troops of Attila nor those of Aetius were overwhelmed. Attila, however, had been halted in his tracks, and this was sufficient: he had not wished to fight and so once again he turned back and recrossed the Rhine without hindrance. Aetius could easily have pursued the retreating Huns and harassed them, but in fact he did nothing. He made no effort to exploit his victory and he even sent home the barbarian contingents that made up his army.

A great deal of criticism has been directed at this strange decision, which left at the gates of the Roman Empire a potential invader who might at any time renew his attacks. Was it want of resolution? Aetius was not lacking in decisiveness, as his brilliant campaigns in Africa bear witness. It has sometimes been thought that the earlier friendship of the two opponents and their youthful comradeship may have influenced his decision, but it is scarcely likely that Aetius would have let such a sentiment come before the interests of the Empire.

Nor must one forget that Aetius had a profound knowledge of Attila's character: he was ambitious and arrogant, but in the last resort he was less of a menace than his people had been three centuries earlier when they had established themselves north of the Black Sea and dominated all who had not fled. Aetius alone realized that the fear of the Huns was out of all proportion to the real danger they posed.

He also knew that the greater danger that threatened the West was an internal one; the break-up caused by the rivalry of peoples who had only recently established themselves, and the collapse of Roman hegemony. For many years he had fought all over Gaul against the banditry of the Bagaudae, and had kept guard on frontiers that he had no choice but to entrust to the federate peoples. It was only the fear of the Hun that gave these groups a certain degree of cohesion.

The defeat of Attila could only lead to the outbreak of quarrels and revolts among the very people who were defending the Empire. It would therefore be better to leave a man like Attila on the other side of the Rhine, so as to keep the federate peoples in a state of vigilance. This would ensure internal peace and security from external attack. Fear of the Hun was to serve Aetius' purpose in his relations with the Burgundians, Visigoths and Franks.

As always, when checked in one direction, Attila decided to try his luck elsewhere. In 452 he invaded Italy; Aquileia, Pavia and Milan fell into his hands. The Emperor Valentinian III was jealous of Aetius' prestige, and instead of calling upon him for help, fell back on Rome where he proceeded to negotiate with the Hun. Pope Leo I intervened, and a payment of tribute was agreed upon. Attila had humiliated the Western Empire and he retired satisfied.

The death of the king of the Huns in 453 was also the death knell of the dominion that had been founded on his extraordinary character. The subject peoples revolted, and the Huns themselves split up. It was the end of the Hunnish threat—and also the end of the Western Empire.

In spite of Aetius' efforts, the unity of the western world was shattered. The Roman Empire had survived many other revolts, but the object of almost all of these was to usurp power at Rome and acquire the universal domination that went with the title of Emperor. From this time onwards, national wars were to be the common lot of Europe.

There was no central authority that could withstand the forces of disintegration. Valentinian killed Aetius—who he realized would eventually supplant him—only to be assassinated in his turn. In Gaul the Visigoths and the Burgundians gained their

A mosaic from Carthage, c. A.D. 500 shows a Vandal landlord newly settled in as owner of the estate left vacant by a retreating Roman.

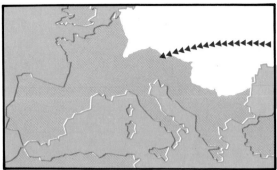

Barbarian Invasion of Europe

Huns
► In the first century they conquered parts of Germany. They provoked the Vandal invasion in 406; tried to invade Gaul in 451 and Italy in 452. Their attacks faded out in the late-fifth century.

Vandals
► Associated with other barbarian peoples, they set up an independent kingdom in Spain, after 410. They were driven out by the Visigoths in 430, when they crossed over to Africa. From this part of Africa now called Tunisia they dominated the whole of the western Mediterranean for a century.

Visigoths
► Settled in Illyria in 400 and invaded Italy in 410. They sacked Rome but failed in their attempt to conquer Italy. They settled in southern Gaul from 410 to 415. From there, in 80 years they conquered Spain and south-west Gaul as far as the Loire.

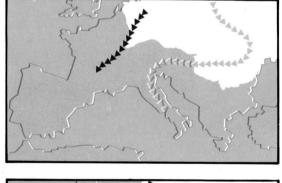

Ostrogoths
► Tried in vain to settle in Italy, after their entry into the Empire in 378. Installed after 450 in Illyria they eventually reached Italy where their king, Theodoric, created a mighty barbarian kingdom at the beginning of the sixth century.

Burgundians and Alemans
► Fought among themselves. Fleeing from the Alemans, the Burgundians installed themselves in Savoy after 440. Their kingdom slowly spread towards the Massif Central and the Durance until the end of the fifth century.

Franks
► Divided into very different groups. They only started moving south after 450. But they played a very big part in the Roman army.

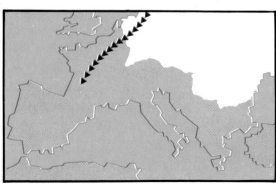

Extent of Roman Empire

independence and their kings promulgated laws which were binding on the Romans who were now under their authority. They had already forgotten that they themselves were intruders. On the northern frontier the Franks began their slow progress towards Belgium. Soon, the last Emperor in the West, Romulus Augustulus, was to be dethroned by the king of the Heruli, Odoacer. The Ostrogoths, who had formerly been subject to the Huns, made an incursion into Italy at the instigation of the Eastern Emperor, but were eventually to found an independent kingdom.

As soon as Attila disappeared from the scene, a whole new world appeared. The Visigoths, the Burgundians and other federate peoples who had been called to defend Rome had in fact been defending their new lands and their future kingdoms. From this time onward, the West was no longer Roman; it was barbarian, and the barbarians were well aware of it.

They did not, however, make a clean sweep of the civilization that they had found in the Roman Empire. In varying degrees they had all felt the same fascination as Attila. The Ostrogoth Theodoric modeled his administration on the same lines and with the same framework as that of Rome, and staffed it with Romans. He proceeded also to surround himself with men of letters, of whom the most famous was Cassiodorus. The Visigoth Ataulf had donned the woolen toga of the Romans when he married the Roman princess, Galla Placidia, to the sound of a wedding hymn. When his successors were driven from Gaul by Clovis, they established at Toledo a brilliant court. One of Ataulf's successors became a composer of hymns.

Throughout the entire West it was Christianity, the religion of the Romans, that gradually prevailed over that of the invaders, which was either German paganism or Arian Christianity. Mixed marriages, which increased enormously in course of time, were to eliminate many of the differences between Roman and barbarian families.

The Germanic peoples had added their social and cultural heritage to that of ancient Rome, and it would be unjust to ignore it. They contributed a different conception of society and the family, based on the hereditary principle, the contractual obligations of the craft unions and the vested security of public authority. It was due to the influence of German ideas that over part of Europe the conceptions of royal power, class structure and the disposition of property slowly evolved over a thousand years. Although they did not despise the written word as a means of administration, the barbarians made the verbal communication, as evidence or declaration of intention, the fundamental basis of the western juridical system. Because they were warriors and nomads they accepted the idea that service in the army carried greater prestige than work in the fields. The medieval lord was to imitate the German warrior, and not Cincinnatus.

They introduced new technical processes into Europe, notably in metalworking, both for armor

and for jewelry. They also widened the range of artistic conception with their own sources of inspiration and choice of themes.

At the end of the fifth century Clovis extended the kingdom of the Salian Franks in the northern half of Gaul, at the expense of the remaining Roman territory and the other Frankish tribes. In 507 Clovis also subdued the Visigothic kingdom of Aquitaine, and some years later his sons annexed the kingdom of Burgundy. Already, however, the Franks were divided among themselves and engaged in internecine strife. Neustria, Austrasia, Burgundy and Aquitaine were continually engaged in hostilities until the accession of the Pepin dynasty at the end of the seventh century. Either in concert or separately, the Franks joined issue against the peoples of Germany, in particular the Thuringians and Bavarians.

During the same period the Anglo-Saxon kingdoms all aspired to dominate Britain. The fortunes of war gave pride of place first to Kent and then to Northumbria and Mercia.

Within the boundaries of barbarian Europe itself, hostilities were engaged in with equal ardor. Britons and Anglo-Saxons were so antagonistic that missionaries had to be sent from Rome to evangelize England. In Italy, the partial failure of Justinian's attempt at reconquest left unprotected both the citizens of Byzantium and the last arrivals from the German migration, the Lombards, who had established themselves in the north and center of Italy in the middle of the sixth century.

Europe then remained divided. The unity that Charlemagne succeeded in achieving was to last only the length of his reign, and the coronation of Christmas A.D. 800, marks a summit rather than a beginning. The Church itself reflected the political fragmentation. The authority of the Pope seldom prevailed, and the religious synods brought together only the bishops of a single province or kingdom. The Latin language survived and was generally adopted, but each group modified it in its own way. In fact, there was only one unifying factor to act as a link between the Empire of Constantine and that of Charlemagne: the Christian faith. JEAN FAVIER

Above A mosaic in the church of St. Appollinare Nuovo in Ravenna, a church founded by Theodoric, King of the Ostrogoths, and decorated with scenes of his life. This one shows his royal palace.

Left The mausoleum of King Theodoric of the Ostrogoths at Ravenna.

Bottom left A gold lamina plaque from the crown plate of a helmet bearing the representation of King Agilauf the Lombard receiving the homage of his people.

Ironically, the victory on the Mauriac Plain sealed the fate both of victor and vanquished. After his death in 453, Attila's empire broke up not only as a result of the feuds among his heirs but also because of a successful rebellion among his German subjects. For the victorious Roman general, Aetius, the outcome of the battle was still more directly catastrophic. He fell victim to a palace conspiracy of enemies who feared his immense prestige. The Emperor Valentinian III is said to have boasted of the disposal of this powerful and popular rival to a favorite courtesan. Her laconic reply was: "You have cut off your right hand with your left."

With the sack of Rome in 455 by the armies of Gaiseric the Vandal, the weakness of the Western Empire was fully revealed. Thereafter the influence of barbarians in the imperial court, which had been considerable, became supreme. From his victory over Vandal armies in 456 to his death in 472, the Suevian general Ricimer was arbiter of the fortunes of the West. Beyond the Alps, only the territories of Syagrius in northern France remained under Roman rule, and these constituted, because of their isolation, a virtually independent kingdom soon to be destroyed by Clovis. During the brief reign of Majorian (457–61), the best traditions of the Empire were revived by that competent and conscientious ruler, but his growing prestige was a threat to Ricimer, who had him deposed and murdered. For another fifteen years the fiction of a Western Emperor was maintained. But in 476 the auspiciously named but pitiable figure of Romulus Augustulus was wiped

out by the soldiers of Odoacer, another successful German soldier who, like Ricimer, succeeded in wielding the real power in the West.

In the East, thanks to the determined efforts of the emperors, the influence of barbarians in the armed forces and the capital itself was held at bay. Despite the abortive expedition sent by Leo I against the Vandals in 468, the integrity of the eastern half of the Empire was largely maintained. Leo's son-in-law and successor, Zeno, was at first obliged to accept the *coup d'état* of Odoacer; later, he cleverly diverted the Ostrogothic tribes in the Balkans by commissioning them to put an end to Odoacer's regime in Italy.

New Powers: the Visigoths in Spain

It was the Visigothic army that, at the battle of Adrianople in 378, defeated the Emperor Valens; it was the Visigoths under Alaric who sacked Rome itself in 410. Yet, ironically, three centuries later it was the Visigoths who were virtually extinguished in their attempt to defend their Romanized Christian traditions against the invasions of a new wave of barbarians.

By 415, Alaric's successors had led the Visigoths through Gaul to Spain. There, in a series of campaigns fought ostensibly on behalf of the imperial power at Rome, they drove out the earlier Germanic settlers and returned most of the Iberian peninsula to imperial rule. As a reward for their labors, and lest they should become too powerful, they were settled in the large territories of southwest France, later to

be the semi-independent duchy of Aquitaine.

This Visigothic kingdom, free from all allegiance to the Roman Emperor, expanded dramatically. Under its great King Euric (c. 420–486), it extended from the Loire to Gibraltar. It comprised the whole of southern France west of the Rhone and all of Spain save the tiny states of the Basques and the Suevic kingdom to the northwest. It was this mighty power, with its capital at Toulouse, that was overthrown by Clovis and his Frankish army at the Battle of Vouille in 507. As a result, the Visigoths were, for the rest of their history, confined to Spain, except for a small stretch of territory on the southwest Mediterranean coastline of Gaul. Yet, reluctant to recognize the completeness of their defeat at the hands of the Franks, the Visigoths did not move their capital from Toulouse to Spain until as late as the 540s. The savior of the Visigothic cause in France had been Theodoric, the Ostrogothic king of Italy, who viewed with disquiet the rapid rise to power of the Franks. In addition, Theodoric also acted for a time as regent of the French Visigothic kingdom and did much to lay the foundations of its future.

Visigothic inscription from eastern Spain.

A vital part of the Visigoths' barbaric past, which was in part the cause of their ultimate downfall, was the principle of the elective monarchy. The principle indeed underlay the kingship of all the European post-barbarian kingdoms; but the internal division and weakness caused by elective monarchy were particularly serious in the exposed peninsular kingdom. The success of Justinian's Roman armies in Spain was facilitated by

the divisive rivalry for the Visigothic throne during the middle of the sixth century. The natural preference of the Romano-Iberian population for the religious orthodoxy of the Byzantine Empire as opposed to the Arian Christianity of their conquerors strengthened the Byzantine position, as did the conversion of the Suevi in the northwest to Catholicism. Yet despite this religious antipathy among the subject population, the great Visigothic king Leovigild, who finally established the capital at Toledo, was able to recover much of the territory lost to Rome. Furthermore, Leovigild lessened the effects of the religious conflict by passing legislation in favor of mixed Arian-Catholic marriages. His successor, Reccared, took the process to its logical conclusion: he presided over the third council of Toledo in 589 which, by a majority decision, proclaimed orthodox Catholicism the state religion. Yet the effects of the Arian period continued to be felt.

The king still possessed a decisive voice in religious affairs, a feature of Spanish life that remained prominent. Indeed, in the sixteenth century the notorious Spanish Inquisition was, in effect, an agent of royal policy. Under the Visigoths the regular councils of Toledo formed the great council of an almost theocratic state.

It was one of the great achievements of the Visigoths that, after their acceptance of Catholicism, they succeeded in welding into one people the diverse races of the Iberian Peninsula. A major reason for their success was the immensely significant legal code promulgated by King Recceswinth in the 650s. The code, written in Latin, was not only the first major legal code to be issued by one of the successor barbarian kingdoms, but it also, most significantly, unified into a single legal system the Roman and Visigothic laws of the two populations.

The Ostrogoths in Italy

The Italy St. Benedict knew was that of Theodoric the Ostrogoth, the barbarian ruler who most truly and splendidly continued the traditions of the ancient Rome that he had displaced. Theodoric's exact status within the political environment of the late antique world is not absolutely clear. In a letter written to the Byzantine Emperor Anastasius, he acknowledged the Emperor's seniority and admitted

German warriors of the period of the invasions.

The sixth century—in the West a period in which the seeds of a new type of monastic and Church-oriented culture and a fragmented political system were being planted—was for the Eastern Roman Empire and its Persian rival an age of great splendor. Despite the closing of Plato's academy at Athens by Justinian in 529, the tradition of lay classical learning was never broken. Moreover, the Arab civilization emerging in Egypt, Syria and Persia continued and even developed that tradition. The ease with which the Arabs overthrew Persia and conquered great tracts of territory from Rome was largely the result of the fierce religious ardor of their new Moslem faith; but there were also weaknesses within these great empires, to which we now turn.

The Age of Justinian

The Eastern Roman Empire was not unscathed by the turmoil of barbarian invasions, but whereas the Western Empire ceased to exist as a political entity, the East recovered. After a period during which the barbarians in the service of the imperial army had dictated events in Constantinople, there followed the reign of the Emperor Zeno. Although orthodox himself, he was willing to attempt a compromise with the powerful monophysite heresy, a heresy that denied the dual nature of Christ as man and God and claimed that he had only one nature—the divine. Zeno's successor, Anastasius I, restored the failing finances of the Empire and laid the foundations of the greatness of the sixth century. But his monophysite tendencies were marked. His successor, the aging but well-entrenched chief of the imperial guard, Justin, permitted no half measures; his persecution of the monophysites was total; he launched the edict against pagans and heretics that so angered Theodoric, an Arian. But if he was sound on religion, Justin was also very much a soldier and aware of his own limitations. He was virtually illiterate, and he increasingly entrusted the government to his nephew, Justinian, who succeeded him as Emperor in 527.

It was not at all clear to the people at the time that the might of Rome was finally a thing of the past. None of the intruding barbarian kingdoms had produced valid new systems of administration,

Justinian. Mosaic from St. Apollinare, Ravenna.

and both Theodoric and the Frankish ruler Clovis had accepted imperial insignia of office. When Justinian came to the throne, the Ostrogoths in Italy were facing difficulties after the death of Theodoric, and even the Franks were showing signs of chronic internal divisions. Throughout the Mediterranean world, in fact, the upstart regimes seemed ripe for conquest.

Only with the wisdom of hindsight can we see that the universal Roman Empire of antiquity had been irreversibly split and that the populations of Italy, Africa and Spain neither needed nor wanted the government of a distant capital with its dying ideals. Nevertheless, by the end of his reign Justinian, thanks to the talents of brilliant generals like Belisarius and Narses, had not only checked the Persian advance but also had made the Mediterranean once again a Roman lake.

Vandal empires crumble

First to go was the Vandal kingdom of Africa, Sardinia and Corsica; shortly after, Sicily was taken from the Ostrogoths. The conquest of Italy itself was to be delayed, largely by intrigues at the court against the generals in the field. Finally, in the middle of the sixth century, the Roman armies succeeded in recovering southern Spain from the Visigoths. Within its own terms, Justinian's policy, no matter how heavy the drain on the Empire's resources, was successful. However, it must be realized that within a century of Justinian's death the ill-defended Danubian frontier, his major strategic blind spot, had

been breached by Slav and Avar invaders. While they were conquering a large part of the west Balkans, most of Justinian's Mediterranean territories were also being lost. The most complete reversals, of course, were due to the astonishing advance of Islam.

Besides making notable territorial gains, Justinian, drawing again on the wealth of the imperial treasury and imposing increasingly heavy taxes on the old and newly conquered lands, put through a vast

Interior of Hagia Sophia, Constantinople, now a mosque.

program of public works that glorified Rome, Orthodox religion and himself. Chief among these were the church of San Vitale at Ravenna and the great cathedral of Hagia Sophia at Constantinople, one of the most remarkable achievements in the whole history of architecture. The jubilant Emperor is reported to have ridden his horse up the main altar of the basilica and cried out: "O Solomon, I have outdone thee."

Dissension and weakness

It is in the nature of empires to decay. Yet whatever the strictures of later historians, there is no real doubt that for half a century, thanks to the ambitions and qualities of Justinian, the Empire in the East enjoyed one of the most brilliant epochs in the history of empire.

Empress Theodora, from St. Vitale, Ravenna.

But the cracks in the structure were never far below the surface, and they found expression in religious differences. The Emperor as head of both Church and State had to ensure both religious uniformity and the loyalty of heretical territories. Justinian's attempts to strike an acceptable religious compromise led him eventually into heresy himself. Heresy was adopted in frontier religions such as Syria and Egypt as a mark of their opposition to the central government; in its struggle for independence against Constantinople, the patriarchate of Alexandria adopted monophysitism, and the divisions rent even the capital itself.

Opposed to the Orthodox Emperor was the party of Justinian's wife, the beautiful Theodora, who supported the monophysite cause. The factional politics of the late Roman imperial court have given us the phrase "Byzantine politics" as a synonym for intrigue and corruption. Procopius, whose official history is our best source for the period, also wrote the scandalous *Secret History*. In it, himself a representative of the old aristocracy, he attacks the upstart Emperor and his wife, whom he slanders for her humble origins in the world of the actors employed by the circus. Yet Theodora was a woman of courage and political acumen. In a regime where the popular voice was excluded from constitutional expression, the rival sporting factions of the Blues and the Greens of the Hippodrome, focused ostensibly upon the chariot races, acquired some of the characteristics of political parties. The Blues were the party of the Emperor and Orthodox in religion; the Greens were the party of the Empress and were junction in the monasteries that continued to multiply in Western Europe. It was only by a gradual process—the reverse of Gresham's monetary law—that the practical and spiritual excellence of the Rule gradually won for it first a wide popularity and later an exclusive superiority. At last Charlemagne, who was not in fact a great patron of monks, could ask if there were any other rule; and his son, Louis the Pious, endeavored in 817 to impose Benedict's Rule as the sole code for all monasteries of his empire.

Henceforward, save in the Celtic regions, Benedict's Rule was indeed the only rule for two hundred years (800–1000), and when new orders came into being in the eleventh century, most of them—including the greatest, that of the Cistercians—followed the Benedictine Rule while modifying it variously in practice in the direction of austerity, hermit life, or of a wider activity. During the same period the Rule was followed by all organized women religious. So wide was the extension of the monastic order that the years between 600 and 1150 have been called the Benedictine centuries, and it is undoubtedly true that in that epoch almost all the monks followed the Rule and that the particular qualities of the Rule impressed themselves on all monks and, through them, on the whole Western Church. What then were those qualities?

The first, perhaps, was its simplicity. Granted that the monastic life is a valid form of Christian dedication, then the Rule appears as the simple application of the teaching of Christ to that life. Flexible discipline, absence of distractions, and the elementary Christian duties of prayer, self-control, service and mutual help make up the Rule. Such an existence, lived in the spirit of St. Benedict, has the regularity and variety for a successful integration of body and mind.

Beyond and above this are certain positive qualities. It is a rule of life. In contrast to so many religious ordinances, the mention of death is rare, and there are no directions for the last moments and burial of the monk. Benedict is dealing with life, and beyond life with the reckoning that is the sole but solemn sanction proposed again and again as a warning to his all-powerful abbot. Next, there is the stress on mutual love, aid and service. Though the monk has left "the world," he has not left his fellow Christians, and his love of God can be fulfilled and tested by his love of his brethren, who may be frail or unattractive in body or spirit.

Though Benedict did not envisage any external work for others, his monks were, in fact, agents of great power in the development of medieval Europe. As a large majority of the trained and educated minds of Europe were to be found in the monasteries, a majority also of the leading bishops and counselors of emperors and kings were of their number. Inevitably, also, monks were almost the sole missionaries. Most of the priests outside the abbeys were tied to their rural churches as the appointees of the local landowner or group of urban citizens. They were also, for the most part, either married or living a family life with a consort recognized by conven-

An illustrated manuscript on music written at Monte Cassino. The monasteries, under Benedict's guidance, became the repositories not merely of religious documents, but of secular learning also.

tion, if not by law. It was left to the monks of Ireland, Scotland, England and Germany—Columbanus, Aidan, Boniface, Willibald, Anskar, Suitbert and the rest—to carry the Gospel to central and northern Europe. Gradually the monks gave to the whole Church their devout practices and spiritual outlook. Their liturgical arrangements were adopted by the secular clergy and by Rome herself. Lay devotions reflected monastic practice, since to that age the monastic way of life seemed the only perfect form of Christian life. The monks of St. Benedict, in fact, without conscious effort, brought the attributes of monasticism to the whole Western Church. Of the great saints and writers between 1000 and 1200, the majority were monks: Gregory VII, Anselm, Bernard, Abelard, Suger, Eugenius III, Ailred, and a hundred others.

All these were sons of St. Benedict, following the Rule that they had learned by heart as novices and heard each day in their chapter-house; the very name, chapter-house, was taken from the chapter of the Rule read publicly there daily. Throughout their lives they remembered well the passages in which Benedict exchanged the language of the legislator for that of the experienced father of a family, and set out counsels of justice and moderation, humanity and gravity, reminding them that the service and love of Christ must be their only aim, and God's judgment the only criterion of their action. Although historians have not mentioned this, it may well be that the greatest achievement of the Rule of St. Benedict was to give to adolescent Europe a message of fairness, of human feeling, and of civilized and Christian behavior. Such counsels, given to the moulders of opinion and the governors of Europe in the centuries when Western civilization and thought was coming to maturity, were an influence second only to that of the Gospel in furthering the spirit of tolerance and fair dealing as part of the Christian life.

DAVID KNOWLES

43

A page from the eleventh-century manuscript of St. Gregory's *Life of St. Benedict* written at Monte Cassino, showing the death of the Saint.

Right A monk engaged in his lonely task of manuscript writing; an illustration from a manuscript dating from the period of St. Benedict's life.

Rome, throughout its centuries of dominance, had been the only center of government and administration, of economic and financial life, and to it all talent had flowed. Both literally and figuratively all roads led to Rome, and in the later centuries of her Empire all methods of government, all articles of commerce, from cooking-pots to mosaics, from villas to ampitheaters and forts, were standardized in Rome, blueprinted and mass-produced throughout the provinces. It was this fact that had made the spread both of Christianity and monasticism physically possible.

After the transfer of the capital to Constantinople, and especially after the invasions around 400, all centralizing influences weakened and broke down. Fragmentation replaced consolidation, and the main unit of existence was the self-supporting village or estate. To such a world the monastery of the Rule was perfectly adapted. A compact economic unit, almost entirely self-contained and self-supporting, with its food cultivated by its inhabitants, and with domestic animals, arts and crafts within its ambit, it had a small surplus for market with which to buy a few necessities, such as metalware and salt.

The monastery was also self-contained in its life. The monks lived, prayed and studied in their monastery, and worked in its sheds and gardens. They had no employment or office that took them away from their enclosure, for this, as the Rule said, would be altogether harmful for their souls. They could indeed be sent on errands, to market or on the business of the house, but this was only infrequent, and not to be spoken of when accomplished. They had no superior beyond the abbot, and no alliance with any other community. In the background was the protective and punitive jurisdiction of the bishop, but this was rarely felt as long as all went well.

It was a microcosm of ages and types. Recruitment was of two kinds, the one of adults—some of them possibly clerics or monks from elsewhere, but others

from the illiterate native peasantry—the other of children, offered to God by their parents, to be educated in the monastery and then normally to become monks. All ages were therefore present, and all classes from the educated and well-born to the illiterate Goth and ex-serf.

There is no hint in the Rule, as there is in the contemporary scheme of Cassiodorus, a Roman monk who founded monasteries on similar lines, of the function of monks in copying manuscripts and preserving classical literature; but the provision for reading—both private and liturgical—presupposes books, and books presuppose literacy and writing, just as the presence of children made education necessary. If the Rule did not prescribe teaching and learning, it certainly did not forbid them. The careful copying and composition of books, with their lavish binding, ornamentation and illustration, both for the liturgy and for the library, inevitably developed. No doubt many of these activities and tendencies were already present in monasteries in different degrees when Benedict wrote, but in later ages without the Rule all would have depended upon the abbot—who might countenance or command either a stricter, more penitential life with longer prayers, or a less well-knit and self-contained regime.

Contrary to the venerable myth of Benedictine history that pictures the Rule spreading far and wide almost at once, it is certain that its influence was not widely felt for a century. A generation after Benedict's death, Monte Cassino was sacked by the Lombards, in 581, but the story of a group-migration to Rome and the foundation by Gregory the Great of monasteries observing the Rule has no sure authenticity. Pope Gregory indeed knew the Rule and wrote an account of St. Benedict, but there is no other mention of the abbot's name till a century after his death. Such evidence as exists seems to establish that for almost two centuries the Rule was only one of several, used either separately or in con-

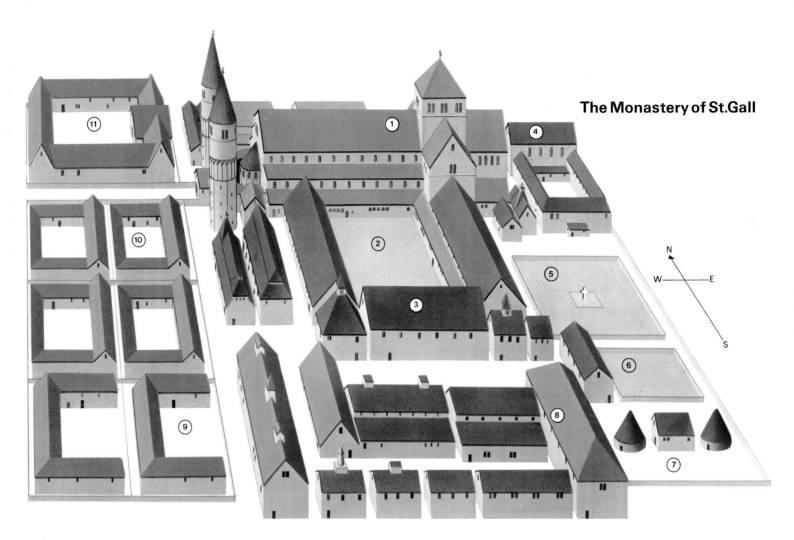

1 The basilican church, with transepts, square tower, an apse at either end, and two detached conical towers at the west end.
2 The cloister, surrounded by monastic buildings; dormitory to the east (*right*) and cellar to the west (*left*).

3 The refectory on the south side of the cloister, parallel with the church.
4 To the east of the church are two cloisters belonging to the novices quarters and the infirmary.
5 The monastic cemetery with a cross in the center.
6 The vegetable garden.

7 Enclosures for poultry.
8 The buildings far south of the church (in the foreground) include the kitchen, bakery and brew-

house, the press, the barn and other workshops.
9 Enclosures for horses and cattle.
10 Further farm quarters.

11 Important buildings including the school, the *scriptorium,* the guest's house and the abbot's house.

while armies were fighting for the control, or the destruction, of Rome. He, along with others of the same historical period, is one of the group known familiarly to historians as "the founders of the Middle Ages." Heirs themselves to the legacy of the past, they transformed and reinterpreted its treasures into a form acceptable to the world that was coming into being. Thus, Benedict summed up in simple form the monastic teaching of Egypt and Asia Minor, already latinized by Cassian. He incorporated the Roman tradition of firm but just government, and gave the entire inheritance to an institution that was to be of great significance for almost a thousand years of European history.

It also happened that in so doing he gave to that institution a viability that it had not hitherto possessed and ensured to it a particular character, both material and spiritual, that was essential to its survival. During his lifetime, the final disintegration of the Roman Empire of the West was taking place.

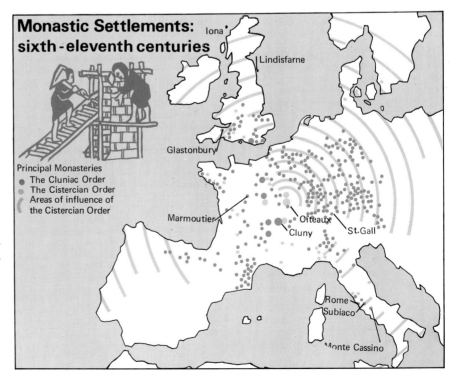

Monastic Settlements: sixth - eleventh centuries

Principal Monasteries
● The Cluniac Order
● The Cistercian Order
◗ Areas of influence of the Cistercian Order

Iona
Lindisfarne
Glastonbury
Marmoutier
Cîteaux
Cluny
St. Gall
Rome
Subiaco
Monte Cassino

The monastery buildings at Monte Cassino, the church in the background. These buildings were completely restored after their destruction by the Allies during World War II.

Subiaco, the small group of monasteries some thirty miles east of Rome, where Benedict was Abbot and from which he drew the monks who followed him to found Monte Cassino.

course of the monk's activities, both external and spiritual. The Rule provides for patriarchal government, which entrusts full authority and responsibility to an elected abbot. The adherents to the Rule are to remain in one place, be obedient and practice monastic virtue. The main function of the monks and the focal point of the community is the Divine Office or succession of services, which inspires the work, study, prayer and meditation with which the rest of the day is occupied. Goods are held in common but there is no specific vow of poverty—a feature of immense importance for the performance of the works of mercy. In addition, room is found for brief but profound instructions that combined common sense with spiritual wisdom. Of this life the abbot and the Rule were the two pillars, and the vow of stability (remaining in one place), which Benedict instituted, gave strength to the whole.

There is no autograph or nearly contemporary copy of the Rule but, as might be expected, the extant manuscripts are very numerous. They probably exceed in number those of any other ancient writing save the Bible. The oldest known manuscript is English, probably from Worcester, written about 700 and now in the Bodleian Library at Oxford. This, however, is not the most trustworthy text. That distinction is acknowledged by modern scholars to belong to manuscript 914 of the ancient library of St. Gall in Switzerland. The distinguished palaeographer, Ludwig Traube, showed in 1898 that the St. Gall manuscript was written about A.D. 817. It is a close, if not an immediate, copy of the manuscript brought from Rome to Charlemagne in 787 to be broadcast throughout his empire. Charlemagne's text is thought to have been a faithful copy of the original. It differs considerably from the smooth "vulgate" text, which removed the vernacular Latin forms and constructions of the original, and became standard from early times to the present day.

Until about 787 the forms and machinery of the decayed imperial system had continued to function, however weak and disfigured they may have been. When the young Benedict was a student at Rome, Boethius, the philosopher and friend of Theodoric, was writing his theological and philosophical treatises and planning to translate the whole of Plato and Aristotle into Latin. For the Roman Church, a golden age of liturgy and musical creation and legal study was just ending. Fifty years later, all this had vanished. Rome still survived, but the old official, educated class was gone, and the papacy and clergy had begun to fill the administrative void. The Rome of the popes had succeeded the Rome of the emperors, and the old literary education and thought had ceased to exist in Italy.

The life of St. Benedict spanned this unique historical divide, and the Rule was actually written

Scene of chariot races in Constantinople.

monophysites. The two parties were generally rivals, but they united in the famous Nika riots in 532. Justinian would have fled before the fury of the mob, but Theodora and the generals held firm and order was restored.

Corpus Juris Civilis

For subsequent generations this intense, confident and vital period presents a barely credible amalgam of the most diverse elements. But there can be no doubts about its achievements: its greatest monument, the *Corpus Juris Civilis*, a codification of all Roman law, was to exert an immense influence on the West and has remained the basis of all systems of Roman law in Europe today.

After Justinian's death, the Empire's external enemies made severe inroads. The slow but sure progress against these threats by the emperor-soldier Maurice was brought to an end by the usurper Phocas in 602. His overthrow of Maurice served the Persian emperor as a pretext for several highly successful campaigns of conquest, supposedly to avenge his former protector. The Avar advance gained a fresh impetus. In 610 Phocas was replaced by Heraclius, but the counter attack could not be launched for another decade. During this period the Persians took Jerusalem, capturing the most sacred relic of Christendom, the True Cross.

The end of an Epoch

Heraclius began a triumphant but arduous campaign of reconquest which ended in 627 with the capitulation of Persia, Rome's ancient enemy. During the war, the city of Constantinople itself had withstood siege by both the Avar and Persian forces. But the very year in which Heraclius set out upon his epic campaign, 622, was also the year of the Hegira. Islam thus arose at a time when both Emperor and Empire were exhausted by the depradations and exertions of the previous generation; the hard-won provinces—with them the great Greco-Roman cultural centers of Caesarea, Antioch and Alexandria —were soon lost to the lightning conquest of Islam. The importance of this conquest in shaping the brilliant culture of the Arab World can hardly be overrated.

The Byzantine Era begins

It is usually from the reign of Heraclius that historians date the beginning of the Byzantine Era as distinct from the age in which the Eastern Empire is regarded as merely the continuation of Rome. In social affairs the change is marked by the restructuring of the provinces so that the civil and military authorities, separate since the time of Diocletian, were merged under the military authority. At the same time, something similar to the later European system of feudal land tenure was introduced; each province supported a body of troops and the soldiers received grants of land on condition of military service. Greek rather than Latin became the official language of the Empire; Egypt, Syria, Spain and North Africa were lost and the possessions of the "Roman" Empire in Italy itself were greatly reduced. After the time of Heraclius, in fact, the Eastern Empire took on its medieval aspect.

The last glories of the Sassanids

In the fifth century the Persian Sassanid rulers, the weak and in-effective successors of Shapur, were forced to pay tribute to the northern barbarian kingdom of the Hephta-lites. To this external enemy was added a subversive religious doctrine, preached by Mazdak, who derived many of his ideas from the teachings of Mani, which also had revolutionary social implications of common ownership of property and of women. The doctrine, which struck at the very roots of the hierarchical and aristocratic system of society, was nevertheless taken up by King Kavadh I, possibly as a welcome weapon against the overpowerful nobility and as a counter-balance to the influence of the Magi, the Zoroastrian hierarchy at court. In fact, Kavadh laid the foundations for a revival of the Persian power by combating the anti-monarchist powers within the state, reforming the conditions of peasant life, and restructuring the administration for more effective

Ruins of a Persian Zoroastrian temple.

exercise of royal power. His son, Chosroes I (531–79), brilliantly extended the achievements of his father's reign, and led the newly confident empire in triumphant war against its enemies: the Heph-talite kingdom was crushed; the northern frontiers were secured against the Huns; while to the south he even brought Yemen under Persian rule. Against Rome, Chosroes was able not only to invade the Syrian provinces of the Roman Empire, but even to sack the mighty city of Antioch. Pretexts for the dispute between these ancient enemies were never lacking. The Christian kingdom of Armenia was a constant source of irritation to the Persian emperors, and both empires maintained client Arab princes in the buffer zone on their Syrian frontier; the internal disputes of these could always be seized upon at will as a *casus belli* by either of the great powers. Nor was the confrontation one between the simple opposites of Christian and infidel; monophysitism was strong within the Armenian church and the Arab tribes of Syria, so that the crucial matter of religious unity was inevitably intertwined with the vexing problem of political allegiance.

After the glorious reign of Chosroes I, symbolized by the rich and splendid monuments and palaces of his capital at Ctesiphon, whose ruins are still to be seen today, there followed a period of civil disturbance and rebellion. It was not until the accession of his grandson, Chosroes II, supported by the Byzantine Emperor Maurice, that the greatness of the Persian Empire seemed to have returned. Yet, exhausted by the ambitions of Chosroes II, crushed by the defeats inflicted by Heraclius and weakened by renewed civil war and internal dissension, the once mighty Persian Empire fell an easy prey to the armies of Islam, which captured the fabled wealth of Ctesiphon in the year 637.

Ruins of the Arch of Chosroes and palace at Ctesiphon.

45

The Flight to Medina

Hoping to find a more receptive audience for his message, the prophet Mohammed fled from his native Mecca to the neighboring city of Medina. This event of 622, the Hegira, marks the beginning of the new Moslem religion and the beginning of a dynamic new civilization in the Middle East. Mohammed himself proved to be both an inspired religious leader and an astute politician, creating a theocracy and presiding over it as Allah's Messenger. He also was a military leader: Mecca was soon brought into the Moslem orbit and at Mohammed's death in 632 the entire Arabian Peninsula was his. But it remained for his successors, the caliphs, to impose Islamic rule over much of Asia and Africa and to bring a frightening challenge to Christian Europe.

The Moslem era begins in A.D. 622, the date of the Hegira, Mohammed's emigration from his home town of Mecca to the neighboring city of Medina. In fixing the date for the initiation of the Moslem era, Caliph Omar, successor to Mohammed's first Caliph, Abu Bakr, is said to have hesitated between choosing the Hegira, the date of Mohammed's birth, or the date he first accepted the vocation of prophet. When Omar chose the first alternative he no doubt had good practical reasons: the date of the Hegira was better fixed in men's minds than the less spectacular moment when Mohammed was finally convinced of his divine mission, a date that was, in any case, altogether dubious.

Yet the Caliph may also have been quite conscious of the fact that it was the Hegira, even more than the first appearance of the angel Gabriel to Mohammed, that marked the historical epoch of the rise of Islam. In Mecca, Mohammed—a tradesman and previously a caravan leader—had gathered around him a considerable number of followers. Yet, faced with the resistance of the leading families, he was unable to attain political power—despite the fact that the visionary side of his character went hand-in-hand with a genius for affairs and a mastery over men. Having become familiar with Judaism and Christianity, he felt it was his prophetic mission to warn his pagan compatriots of the coming day of judgment and urge them to turn to the one true God—and the ethical duties imposed by him upon man—before it was too late. To the astute politicians of Mecca, Mohammed might have appeared as an impractical dreamer or, as they less politely put it, a madman.

Latent in Mohammed were immense political gifts, which found only limited scope in the role of venerated head of a small and persecuted religious community; of these immense gifts his later career as the founder of a powerful religious state in Medina bears eloquent witness. Having failed to satisfy his political aspirations in Mecca, Mohammed cast about for more promising fields of action in the neighboring town of Taif and among different

Bedouin tribes, but without avail. His chance came from the great oasis of Yathrib, north of Mecca, the center of which was also called Medina, i.e. "the city." The oasis was inhabited by several tribes that followed the Jewish religion, and by two others, the Aws and the Khazraj, that were pagans and warred among themselves.

Some Medinians came in contact with Mohammed, and in 621, during the pilgrimage to the pagan sanctuaries near Mecca, a number of them met Mohammed on a mountain pass outside Mecca and accepted his main religious teachings. In the course of the next year, more Medinians adhered to the teaching of the prophet, and at the next pilgrimage the Medinian contingent included a considerable number of Mohammed's followers. At "the second treaty of the pass" they agreed that Mohammed would come to Medina and that they would give him full protection.

After this agreement was reached, Mohammed's Meccan followers began to slip away from the city and find their way to Medina, in anticipation of the eventual emigration of their Prophet. Their empty houses, with their doors thrown open by the wind, made—so the traditional account says—a sad impression upon the Meccans who passed by and expressed their grief at the disruption caused by Mohammed in the life of the city. At last, of the Moslem community only Mohammed himself, his cousin Ali, and Abu Bakr (who was one of the Prophet's oldest adherents and was particularly close to him), and their womenfolk, remained.

By September, 622, Mohammed himself was ready to escape from his native city. The Meccans obviously did not relish the idea of the persecuted community of Moslems finding a new home in Medina and possibly causing trouble to them. Therefore they were determined to prevent Mohammed from leaving and joining his followers in Medina; he had to flee. Although the word Hegira (or, to render the Arabic more exactly, *Hijra*) does not mean "flight," as it is often translated, but rather

A tile from Asia Minor with a view of Mecca, the shrine of the prophet Mohammed's birth place and holy center of Moslem belief.

Opposite The mosque in Cairo, the earliest surviving example of a place of Moslem worship.

"emigration," the circumstances of Mohammed's emigration justify our speaking of his flight.

One September day Mohammed informed Abu Bakr that he was to accompany him. His cousin Ali would be left behind to look after the womenfolk. Abu Bakr took with him all the money he had, amounting to five or six thousand *dirhams*. (*Dirham* was the name of the silver coins current in Mecca, no doubt mainly Persian pieces with the image of the Persian king; the Meccans minted no coins of their own. A *dirham* would be about four grams of silver.) He also arranged with one of his sons to come every day to their hiding place in order to bring news from the city, and ordered a freedman of his, Amir the son of Fuhayra, to graze some sheep in the desert in order to provide fresh milk and meat every night.

The two fugitives left Abu Bakr's house by a back door and hid in a cave of Mount Thawr, an hour's journey to the south of Mecca. This was in the opposite direction to that of Medina, and thus they hoped to evade search parties who would look for them on the road leading north. Mohammed and Abu Bakr remained in the cave for three days, living off the milk and meat of the sheep brought nightly by Amir, and other food brought from Mecca by a daughter of Abu Bakr. In later times, many legends were woven around the stay in the cave, in marked contrast to the sober realism of the earlier accounts, the essential truth of which is confirmed by Mohammed's own reference to the cave in a passage of the Koran (9:40): "If you do not help him, yet God had helped him already when the unbelievers drove him forth the second of two, when the two were in the cave, when he said to his companion, 'Sorrow not; surely God is with us'."

The rulers of Mecca promised a reward of a hundred camels for the return of the fugitives. After three days, when the hue and cry had died down, the two men set out on their journey. The practical Abu Bakr had arranged every detail. He had previously given two camels to a Bedouin called Abdullah, son of Arqat, who was to serve them as guide. The Bedouin now appeared riding his own camel and bringing the two camels for Mohammed and Abu Bakr. Abu Bakr's daughter also arrived with provisions for the journey. The freedman Amir rode behind Abu Bakr on the same camel and served Mohammed and Abu Bakr on the way.

The three men thus made their way through the desert to Medina, after a detour that brought them to the shore of the Red Sea. After a journey of four days, they arrived at Quba, near Medina. Mohammed remained in Quba, as the guest of a local man, for two to four days, or longer according to some accounts. Those days were perhaps spent in making the last negotiations with the various sections of the population of Medina, so that Mohammed would be able to enter the city itself as a guest protected

The rocky terrain between Mecca and Medina across which Mohammed rode on his camel with his companion Abu Bakr to found a new religious state.

by the whole Medinian community. At last (according to the most widely accepted version, on Friday September 28, 622) Mohammed left Quba and, riding on his camel, proceeded to Medina.

In one version of the legend, the various clans of Medina through whose quarters Mohammed made his way vied with one another in offering the Prophet hospitality. But Mohammed left it to the divinely inspired decision of his camel to choose for him the place where he would stay. On the spot where the camel stopped, the place of worship—mosque—was to be built. It was a covered space with a courtyard. Rooms for Mohammed and his four wives adjoined the courtyard, and the land was bought from the guardian of the orphans to whom it belonged.

Mohammed was thus established at Medina and the opportunity was given to him of proving himself as a statesman, as he had earlier proved himself a religious leader at Mecca. He proved equal to the task, and during the remaining ten years of his life accomplished deeds for which his first fifty years had scarcely prepared him; those latent powers rose to the occasion. The Prophet was armed, and he showed, in addition to his gift of spiritual leadership, the great astuteness and lack of scruple of the politician.

First he firmly established his position as the political head of the community: strict obedience "to God and his messenger" was demanded. The

The birth of the prophet Mohammed as it is shown in the *Universal History* of Rashid ud-Din.

Left A scene showing the revelation brought to Mohammed by the Archangel Gabriel, from Rashid ud-Din's *Universal History*.

Below The Dome of the Rock, Jerusalem, the first monument of Islam, built *c.* 691 on the site of King David's altar, the spot from which Mohammed is believed to have ascended to heaven.

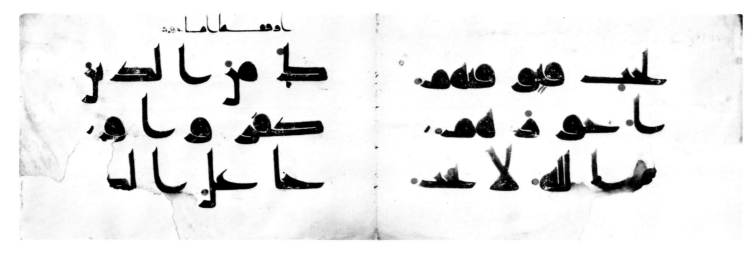

An extract from a parchment Koran, one of the earliest copies in existence of the prophet Mohammed's teachings, the first piece of written Arabic literature.

messenger, Mohammed, became the actual ruler of a theocracy.

During the first years following the Hegira, the war with the Meccans took up most of the energies of the new Moslem state. But opportunities to get rid of the Medinian opposition, branded as the "hypocrites," and the Jewish tribes, who were either expelled or massacred, were not missed.

Soon, however, Mohammed's ambitions went far beyond defending the Moslem refuge in Medina; his new aim was to subject the Arabian peninsula to his rule. Mecca itself was conquered in 630, eight years after the Hegira. Although Mecca's pagan sanctuaries were incorporated into the system of the new religion, and Mohammed's birthplace with its holy Kaaba became the religious center of Islam, the capital remained at Medina. The Bedouin tribes were subdued by force or diplomacy; and by paying the "alms-tax," these nomads acknowledged

the supremacy of the Prophet, even if their religious fervor left a great deal to be desired. Thus, within ten years, the anarchic tribal society of the Arabian peninsula was organized into a semblance of a nation—in itself a stupendous achievement.

Did the Prophet's ambition embrace even wider horizons? Had he, whose mission had originally been the call to preach to the Arabs, hitherto deprived of prophets, come to think himself the bearer of a message to mankind at large? And if so, did he contemplate, as a corollary, the conquest of lands outside Arabia, after having conquered Arabia itself? Before his death in 632, there were skirmishes on the frontier region between the Hijaz and the Byzantine Empire, but it is uncertain whether they were considered as the preliminaries of any large operations. In general, it is difficult to give any definite answer to the question about the Prophet's views of the outside world. If he had any extensive

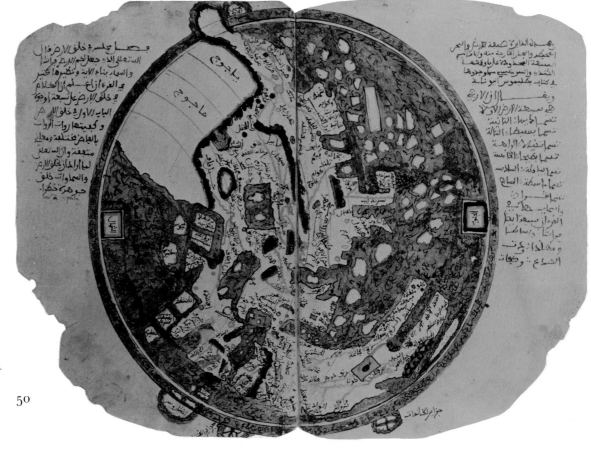

A thirteenth-century Moslem map of the world by Ibn Said. The spread of Islam was accompanied by the introduction of classical and medieval learning to the Arabs.

50

plans, he died without having the chance of embarking on their execution. It was his successors (or Caliphs) who founded the Islamic Empire and governed it first from Medina, then from Damascus, and then from the newly founded Baghdad.

The Islamic conquests—whether they were planned by Mohammed as a further step in the succession of events inaugurated by the Hegira, or were rather the result of chance successes being exploited and then energetically directed by the Caliphs of Medina—changed the face of a large part of the earth. Within a few years the Persian Empire of the Sassanids was overrun and such important provinces of the Byzantine Empire as Syria and Egypt (followed soon by North Africa) were incorporated into the Islamic Empire. At the beginning of the eighth century, a second wave of conquests added Transoxania, the Indus valley in the east and Spain in the west. They gave Islam roughly the geographical extent it maintained until the eleventh century. (At that time small losses of territory in Spain and Sicily were compensated by large increases in central Asia, India and Anatolia.) Provinces that had formerly belonged to separate states and civilizations were now united within a new empire that developed its own civilization. The political and cultural map of western Asia and the Mediterranean basin had been remade.

For a century and a half, the new Islamic Empire was a centrally governed state, headed by the Caliph, Mohammed's successor as political ruler, but not his successor as prophet. Even after the caliphate began to disintegrate, it still remained a powerful structure for another century, and its ghost haunted the Moslem world long after its real might had disappeared. The office of Caliph was a peculiar creation of Islam: it grew naturally out of the particular circumstances in which the Moslem community found itself after Mohammed's death. In contrast, administrative methods were largely taken over from previous empires, and the bureaucratic system continued the secular traditions of the conquered lands.

The basis of the new Islamic civilization was provided by the economic and social unity of the world it conquered, and this unity lasted even after the disappearance of the political state. Commercial traffic passed easily through the vast tract of land between Transoxania and Spain, and the same (or almost the same) currency was employed; this greatly promoted trade—and with goods traveled social and cultural patterns. Not only merchants but also learned men traveled from one end of the Muslim world to the other and spread a common form of education and culture. Islamic civilization did not grow out of nothing, it assimilated elements of different character.

The Islamic religion itself, the main cementing factor in the new civilization, owed a great deal to preceding religions, chiefly Judaism and Christianity. But the borrowings were used in an original manner and the new religion was more than a new combination of existing elements. Both religious and secular literature was expressed in the Arabic

language, and while the vernaculars of the different provinces survived in spoken use, everything—from the simplest letter to the highest literature—was written in Arabic. The Koran, containing the text of the prophecies pronounced by Mohammed in Mecca and Medina, was the first piece of Arabic literature committed to writing, but it was not this fact alone that gave the Arabic language its religious significance. The whole many-branched theological literature created by Islam was in Arabic and was carried by traveling scholars all over the Islamic world.

Secular literature was in the first instance based on the traditional oral literature produced by the tribal society of pre-Islamic Arabia. Its traditional heroic lyric poetry and prose stories were adopted by Islamic civilization; after having been the functional expression of tribal society, this whole literature—reduced to writing by philologists—became the foundation of the humanistic education of urban Islamic society, in the same way as Homer had been the bible of Hellenism. In the Islamic period there developed a courtly urban poetry which, however alien in spirit to the ancient poetry of the desert, was in its style deeply indebted to it. Thus the legacy of

Mosaics from the Great Ummayad Mosque at Damascus, eighth century. The Mosque was formerly a Christian church and still earlier a pagan *temenos*. The most notable mosaic shows the region now Damascus.

51

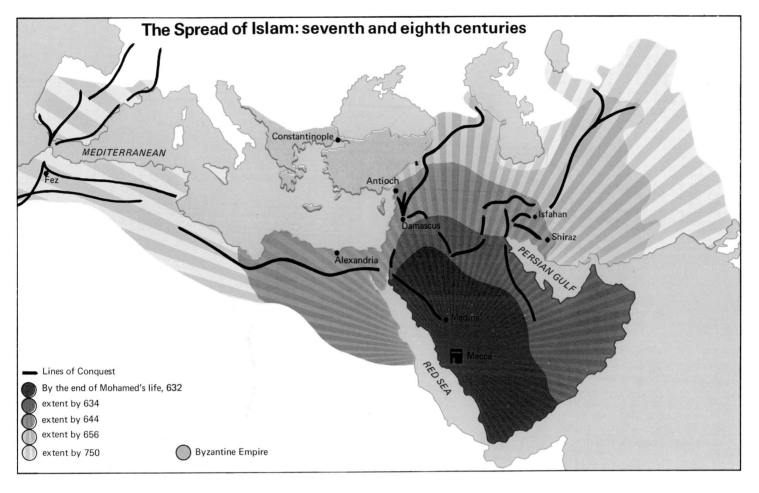

The Spread of Islam: seventh and eighth centuries

MEDITERRANEAN

Fez

Constantinople

Antioch

Damascus

Alexandria

Isfahan

Shiraz

PERSIAN GULF

Medina

Mecca

RED SEA

— Lines of Conquest
By the end of Mohamed's life, 632
extent by 634
extent by 644
extent by 656
extent by 750

Byzantine Empire

pre-Islamic tribal Arabia was one of the component elements of Islamic civilization. The other elements came from the ancient civilizations of the territories incorporated into the empire.

The Persians, with an imperial history of more than a thousand years, possessed a strong national sentiment. This tradition had been closely, but not inextricably, connected with their national religion, Zoroastrianism; and even after their conversion to Islam, the Persians did not renounce their attachment to their secular national traditions. While using Persian as their vernacular, they too wrote in Arabic and adopted the Islamic culture expressed in Arabic; but they introduced into that culture many elements of Persian ideas on statecraft. It was mainly government officials of Persian extraction who were responsible for the promotion of Persian ideas within the world of Islam. Some scientific

Right The Great Mosque at Kairouan, one of the oldest Islamic buildings and the first important one in North Africa.

treatises were also translated from Persian into Arabic; and so were some Indian books, either directly, or through Persian mediation.

In the scientific field, however, the main contribution came from Greco-Roman antiquity. The Christian subjects of the Islamic Empire were in the possession of a large body of scientific and philosophical literature, either in the original Greek or in Syriac translations. (Syriac was the Aramaic dialect used as a literary language by many Christians in the eastern provinces of the Roman Empire, as well as in Persia.) Christian translators rendered these books into Arabic, in which form they became available also to the Moslems, who never mastered either Greek or Syriac. At first their interest in Greek science was mainly practical: they needed physicians to cure them and astrologers to advise them how to arrange their affairs under the most favorable influence of the stars. But soon science and philosophy attracted them for their own sake. Nor were they satisfied with passively studying the writings of the ancients—but reorganized and sometimes even improved upon them.

In general, it would be as wrong to consider the Islamic civilization a mere juxtaposition of existing elements as to consider Islam a mere adding up of Judaism, Christianity and Arabian paganism. By a strange alchemy, the old elements were so fused together and transformed that something quite original resulted. Thus, while Islamic art owes a great deal to the traditions of the previous civilizations, it has a strong character of its own. One of its most individual aspects springs from the prohibition placed by Islam on iconographic representation, with the result that this is virtually nonexistent.

It is obvious, therefore, that Islamic civilization did not come into being in one moment. Nor was it static; it remained—as does everything in history—in continuous flux. The re-emergence of Persian as an Islamic literary language in the tenth century, for example, tended to give the eastern part of the Islamic world a character different from the

western part, where Arabic was used exclusively. The foundation of the Islamic Empire—a direct or indirect consequence of Mohammed's Hegira—gave rise to a new civilization. Islamic religion is still very much alive. It is, however, more than doubtful whether Islamic civilization still exists; but for twelve hundred years or so it has undoubtedly shaped the life of a considerable portion of the human race.   S. M. STERN

The Great Mosque of Shah Abbas at Isfahan, showing the rich detail of seventeenth-century faïence work and decorative vaulting.

Overlooking the walls of Fez to the crowded city beneath, typical of the Moslem cities of north Africa.

The siege of Byzantium

During the seventh and eighth centuries, while Europe was in the turmoil of the conflicting dynasties that had succeeded the first generations of barbarian invaders, events of immense importance were taking place on the southern shores of the Mediterranean.

Within a hundred years the armies of Islam had taken the legendary city of Samarkand in the East, while in the West they touched for a moment the banks of the Loire. The successor of the Prophet Mohammed was not to sit on the throne of Constantine until another eight centuries had elapsed, but throughout the seventh and early eighth centuries the threat to Byzantium was a serious one.

By 717 the Arab armies were actually at the gates of the imperial capital. Twice the siege was withstood; twice the Byzantine fleet proved its superiority and the armies of the new faith were driven back.

But although they escaped military conquest, the Byzantines did succumb to the influence of the religious philosophy of their enemies. Within ten years of the first siege of Constantinople, the Emperor Leo III issued the first "iconoclastic" decrees against the

Coin of the iconoclast Byzantine Emperor Leo.

worship of images. For close to a century the Church in the East prohibited images of the saints—the descendants of local deities that Christianity had displaced—and permitted only the barest decoration of its places of worship. The puritanic zeal of Islam infected its rival; and the Emperor Leo, determined to withstand the attack of the infidel, did not hesitate to emulate his virtues. For, like Christianity, the faith of Islam claimed universality; like Christianity, it was exclusive.

Islamic beliefs

Islam, however, differed from Christianity in two important respects. First, belief in a unitary God was absolute and uncompromising —to a Moslem, the Christian doctrine of the Trinity and the inummerable local cults of patron saints inevitably appeared as a thinly veiled polytheism. In the second place, although Islam worshipped one god, Allah, and believed that the full revelation had been given only to Mohammed, his Prophet, it nevertheless recognized parts of the Christian and Jewish canon that Mohammed himself had accepted. This fact reinforced the universal claims of Islam. It may have also been a factor in the welcome that the conquering armies found among the subject populations of the Byzantine and Persian empires.

The faith of the conquerors was not entirely alien and, still more important, they allowed their new subjects to retain their own religious practice only on condition of the payment of poll and land taxes. As we have seen in both the Roman and the Persian empires, religious heresy was often connected with political separatism; for many a provincial of the Near East, oppressed both by heavy taxation and religious discipline from the central government, the armies of Islam appeared as the scourge of God for the sins of an irreligious emperor, or even as their liberator.

The birth of Arab civilization

After the first astonishing wave of Arab conquest had spent itself, the conquerors consolidated their position in their new empire by taking on many of the ways of the Persian monarchy which they had displaced. Already by the time of the fourth Caliph, Uthman, the early ideals and puritan zeal were beginning to fade, and the Caliph was using the semi-sacred office to which he had been elected to buttress his own position and that of his family. In 656 Uthman was assassinated and there followed a disputed succession that was to cause a schism in the faith of Islam which has not been healed to this day. Uthman was succeeded by Ali who, as son-in-law of Mohammed, had been expected by many to follow the prophet himself. In turn, Ali too was overthrown and the new

Decoration from the Ummayad Palace near Jericho.

Caliph, Muawiyah, is generally regarded as the founder of the Ummayad dynasty which held the Caliphate for the next hundred years. While the great body of Islam, the Sunnites, accepted the succession of the first four Caliphs and the laws and traditions (or *sunni*) of the early period, a minority of sectarians (*shiites*) hold that ever since the murder of Ali, the line of the Caliphate has been in the hands of usurpers.

The Dome of the Rock

Under the first Ummayads, the Arabs rapidly enlisted the services of the subject populations and assimilated their skills. Although few monuments survive from this period, they include such architectural achievements as the Dome of the Rock in Jerusalem.

This famous mosque is built over the spot where, according to Arab tradition, Abraham led Isaac to the sacrifice and where Mohammed ascended to heaven. Completed in 691, the Dome of the Rock was built on the orders of Abd al Malik, one of the greatest of the Ummayad Caliphs. He gave a new durability to the empire by introducing a standard coinage, reorganizing the government, improving communications within the empire and making Arabic its official language.

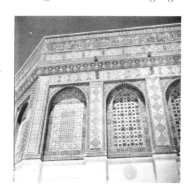

Detail of tiled panels on the Dome of the Rock, Jerusalem.

Although his own campaigns against Islam's external enemies were inconclusive, Abd al Malik prepared the ground work for the resurgence of the eighth century.

The great Oriental civilizations

The art of the early Islamic potters gives the clearest possible evidence that Persian and Arab artisans were very strongly influenced by the high-glazed porcelain wares brought along the trade routes from T'ang China. The T'ang dynasty, established in 618, just four years

A T'ang vase with dragons decorating the handles.

before the Hegira, reached the summit of its glory and power during the seventh century. The short-lived Sui dynasty had reformed the administration and radically improved communications, but the T'ang built on these foundations a brilliant and impressive edifice. T'ang armies extended Chinese power over the neighboring territories of Korea, Manchuria,

dynasties—unifies the nation

Mongolia, Tibet and Turkestan; the art of the potter was brought to the level of high art; and T'ang scholars and poets produced an unequaled flowering in literature.

In the early decades of the dynasty, the influence of Indian Buddhism, which had been a part of Chinese religious life to greater or lesser degrees for centuries past, was powerful. It is from a Chinese Buddhist monk that one of the most interesting documents of the medieval world has come down to us. This is the *Record of the Western World* by Hsuang Tsang, who spent some twenty years researching in Indian Buddhist libraries during the first half of the seventh century. But, although Buddhism retained an important position even under the later T'ang, it was to suffer periods of proscription, and pride of place went to the social and ethical code of Confucius. The Confucian code, with its stress on the right ordering of social relationships, became the official religion of the empire, a role for which it was ideally suited.

The first century of T'ang China was not only a period of foreign expansion but also one of ordered administration, in which centralized government was conducted by a class of officials recruited by a system of examination for merit—a system that was not to be emulated in the West until the nineteenth century. Like all great empires, of course, that of the T'ang was subject to the laws of decay; and already by the middle of the eighth century, the barbarian Uigurs had succeeded in wresting from the Empire considerable tracts of territory on the borders, a situation that was seriously compounded by local rebellions during the ninth century.

Chinese head of a Boddhisattva; seventh century.

Like his homeland of China, the India that Hsuang Tsang visited was enjoying a brief but glorious period of political unity and cultural advance. Under the rule of Harsha, who reigned from 606 to 647, virtually the whole of northern India was brought under the rule of a single government with its capital at the town of Kanauj. Harsha was himself a poet and philosopher. In early life he accepted the tenets of Hinduism, but was converted to Buddhism and became its devout and generous patron. The great Buddhist convocation held at Kanauj in 643, attended by some twenty kings and princes, not only symbolized the king's devotion but also his power. But, after the death of Harsha, India gradually split up again into a series of warring states.

The rise of Japan

We need hardly be surprised that these giant empires of the East enjoyed such comparatively brief periods of unity. The areas that they attempted to control were immense; communications, unless constantly tended, fell rapidly into disorder; and the frontiers were under recurrent attack from barbarian invaders from central Asia. For the much smaller political units of Europe, the road to unity and stability was a long and difficult one. It is therefore all the more interesting to find in the history of at least one empire of this period that the ambitions of the central government were not beyond the possibilities of the situation and its abilities were commensurate with the problems. Although the mountainous geography of Japan encouraged internal divisions, and although these divisions threatened the unity of the state from time to time, nevertheless, from the middle of the sixth century, Japan was to display considerable resilience and survival power as a political entity.

Invasion of Korea

As early as the fourth century, we have records of Japanese expeditions against the mainland kingdom of Korea. At that time much influenced by the culture of China, Korea was to remain an important bridge for the transmission of Chinese influence to the island state. Even before the fourth century, this influence had been felt. The

Japanese probably had knowledge of the Mandarin Chinese system of writing at a very early date and from the fourth century onwards—after what must have been a Herculean feat of adaptation (the two languages are in fact unrelated; Chinese is monosyllabic while Japanese is richly polysyllabic)—the Japanese chancery was using a system of script derived from the Chinese system. The process of assimilating and adapting Chinese culture continued. Thousands of Chinese and Koreans came to settle in Japan, so that by the end of the seventh century a large number of the leading families of the Japanese aristocracy could boast of a mainland ancestry. From China too, in the fifth century, had come the religion of Buddhism. Although it never fully displaced the native Japanese cult system of Shinto, Buddhism quickly gained influential supporters, among them Crown Prince Shotoku Taishi (*d.* 621). Shotoku is remembered also as the creator of the first truly centralized Japanese administration, which took as its model that of China.

A recurrent feature of Japanese history is the ascendance of the powerful clans which, while recognizing the imperial house, sought to control the effective power of the state. Later, it became common for the emperor to turn over all but his ceremonial functions to another member of the imperial family. This person in turn deputed effec-

Japanese mask of the Nara period.

tive executive authority to ministers of state.

The first important clan to win the ascendance in the state was that of the Soga; but in the middle of the seventh century they were displaced by the Fujiwara family, under the leadership of the great Fujiwara Kamatari. He consolidated and improved on the achievements of his predecessor, Prince Shotoku. And, modeling his work almost slavishly on the example of the T'ang, he set up a centralized administration. In the early eighth century a capital city was built at Nara, which was to emulate the splendors of Ch'ang 'an, the city of the T'ang emperors. But at the end of the century the capital was moved to Kyoto, or Heian-Kyo as it was called, marking the beginning of a new age of elegance and courtly civilization.

Japanese Buddhist triad from the ancient temple of Horyu-ji; seventh century.

55

Japanese Renaissance

Since the sixth century, Japan has been ruled by a hereditary imperial family. At first the Japanese court modeled itself on the Chinese, in its principles of politics, ethics and religion, in its writing system and in its entire culture. It was not until 794, when the capital was transferred from Nara to Heian (modern Kyoto), that Japan started to develop a national culture of its own. About the year 1000, the Lady Murasaki Shikibu wrote the world's first novel, The Tale of Genji, *a masterpiece of literary invention that mirrored the life of the brilliant Heian court. In painting, architecture and the decorative arts as well, there were signs of a growing culture that was remarkably refined, advanced for its time and—most important—essentially Japanese in character.*

Tamon Ten, one of the four guardian demi-gods from the Kaidan-in Temple; an eighth-century statue in clay painted in brilliant color.

Opposite The gateway to the shrine of the vixen at Kyoto. The city boasts many such shrines, all of them restored at a later date.

Throughout Japanese history, legitimate authority has resided in the hereditary imperial family which has been on the throne since the sixth century, but power lay in the possession of land. Despite seventh-century measures designed to assert the imperial title to all land, powerful families amassed vast estates and in the course of time won immunity from tax assessment. It is an ironical fact that the power of the Fujiwara clan lay in precisely this kind of tax immunity, for eventually it fatally weakened the imperial (and hence the clan's) authority. Respecting the hereditary principle that was deep-rooted in all Japanese society, the Fujiwara never attempted to usurp the title of Emperor but instead acted as regents. The Emperor gave legitimacy to their regime and was also the fount of honor from which they could draw the titles and offices to reward their family and supporters.

This acceptance of a higher if usually ineffective legitimate authority by the real rulers of Japan was of immense importance in the country's history. In all states and at all times palace politics have been important, but in Heian Japan they were virtually the sole activity of the regime. Some of the regents were gifted administrators concerned with the public interest; but their supremacy rested on their adept manipulation of palace politics and a subtle and deep understanding of the intricacies of social and human psychology. Thus the most powerful men in Japan were long devoted not to the administration of the state but to the maintenance of their power base in a court society that had increasingly little contact with the country over which in theory it ruled.

For most of the ninth century the Fujiwara were merely the Crown's most powerful ministers, but from about 900 to 1068 their power was virtually supreme. For the next seventy years the "cloistered" emperors largely bypassed their Fujiwara ministers; finally, the family was displaced by the military clans that they had called to their aid. Yet even during the ascendancy of the Fujiwara, administration was often threatened by turbulence in the provinces, only suppressed because the leading military families were willing to support the regency.

Thanks to external peace, the Empire had no effective standing army, and there was no force to stop the encroachments of the great landowners; thus, by the end of the ninth century most of the country was virtually controlled by vast tax-immune manors. Among the many causes of this process, two were particularly important. First was the oppressive labor tax, which led many poor men to commend themselves to their more powerful neighbors. Second were the large tax concessions granted by the government, theoretically for a limited period, to those who undertook the development and cultivation of new land necessary to feed a growing population. But not only did the government find itself powerless in the long run to recall these concessions, but the landowners, from the greatest to the least, "reclaimed" vast tracts of poor or uncultivable land for the sake of the tax concessions. Here again the little man, conscious of his weak claims to this kind of land, commended himself to a more powerful neighbor, paying him an annual rent for protection against the central authorities. It was in this environment of insubordination and lawlessness that the great military clans were born. The central power was obliged to recruit its own provincial governors and police forces from the local nobility and even to call in their aid on occasion to suppress rioting in the capital.

Fujiwara power depended on the marriages they arranged for their womenfolk, and even at the height of their ascendancy the great regents were to base their claim to power first and foremost on their relationship to the royal family. In 986, Fujiwara Yoritada, father-in-law of the emperor who died in that year, resigned as regent. Since his daughter, the widowed empress, had produced no heirs, he could no longer claim connection with the royal family. Such an act, incomprehensible in Chinese terms, seems almost inevitable in Japan, where respect for the hereditary principle was total.

The Phoenix hall, a building of wonderful proportion forming part of the temple of Byodo-in, one of the loveliest Japanese architectural monuments. The temple was originally a villa, built on the outskirts of Kyoto for a wealthy member of the Heian court.

Portrait of Fujiwara Mitsugo. The Fujiwaras rose from the status of courtiers to enjoy supreme power during the tenth and eleventh centuries.

And now we have come to the crucial weakness in the attempt of medieval Japan to graft on to its body politic the principles of Chinese government. Codes embodying these principles were issued and successively revised from the seventh century onward, but realities and the system were out of touch. In Chinese politics the idea of absolute hereditary right was overruled by the doctrine of the mandate of heaven; any new imperial dynasty was vindicated by success—thus it proclaimed the support it enjoyed from the heavenly powers. For the Chinese, the guiding principle of state, as of human life, was that of *Li*, the traditional proprieties by which the harmony between heaven and earth and hence human happiness and political stability were possible. In this system a prime duty of the Emperor was to maintain the correct ritual conduct of his duties and the due observance of *Li*. The Japanese adopted this idea as well as a rigid hierarchy of administration designed for a state where central authority was exercised; it was wildly unsuitable for a country where central authority was virtually unknown. Moreover, the Japanese were unable to take over the one thing that turned the Confucian doctrine of *Li* and the well-ordered state into practical politics— namely, appointment to office on merit and public examination. With such a civil service, the Chinese Emperor could afford to believe that the stability of his power rested on his harmonious balance of the eternal principles of *Yin* and *Yang*.

The Japanese administration—divided between the bureau of Religion and that of State, in which the former was the senior—was dominated by the rulings of its own bureau of *Yin-Yang*, but the men who acted on these rulings were usually well-born courtiers and nothing else. It is important to remember when reading the description of Heian society that follows, that despite its elegance and formality it was surrounded by disorder and danger. Even within the court itself the veneer was thin, and we learn from the diary of Lady Murasaki that the boorishness of Michinaga himself broke through the polite code of etiquette over which he presided. His predecessor was so confident of his position that he would appear in the presence of the emperor stripped to his undershirt for comfort in the heat of midsummer. And this in a society where both men and women dressed with meticulous care, wearing many layers of garments, each chosen for its color, so that even the fringe of the sleeve of an undershirt might be admired! The Heian court was uniquely sensitive to all aspects of human life: to etiquette, to dress, to learning and to the true movements of the heart itself. A lover was expected to conduct his courtship in delicate verses of his own composition and apt quotations from the Chinese classics.

The upsurge in the vitality of native Japanese arts is well illustrated by the architecture of the new capital at Heian. The gridiron pattern of the town plan of Nara had been closely copied from that of the T'ang capital of C'hang-an in China, while the architecture was also essentially Chinese. The rooms were paved in stone, the ceilings supported by painted wood pillars, and the roofs were of semi-translucent glazed green tiles. At Heian a tradition of native Japanese domestic architecture asserted itself. The pillars and other woodwork were in unpainted dark wood, the roofs were covered with strips of bark from the *hinoki* cedar tree, while the floors were of wood raised on stilts above the ground, the court returning to the traditional Japanese habit of sitting not on chairs but on rush matting on the floor.

Heian architecture had other distinguishing features. A noble family was housed in a complex of buildings. The *shinden*, or chief pavilion, was surrounded by a number of lesser ones, linked to one another and to the central one by corridors or bridges. The whole was set in a formal park. The garden itself, which at first contained miniature replicas of beloved landscape scenes, came to be subject to strict laws so that it became an object not only of esthetic but also metaphysical contemplation, being viewed from a window and not entered.

Within the interior of Japanese houses, rooms were defined by sliding doors. Free-standing folding screens were also used to vary the space or were placed between the participants in a conversation where etiquette forbade that one should look on the other. The young Genji, in Lady Murasaki's novel, might not see the face of his adored lady until late in a courtship. On one disastrous occasion the lady was so shy that eventually one of her maids answered Genji's gallantries from behind the screen of honor. Delighted by the sweet voice, he pressed his suit; when he eventually did see his princess he was horrified by her plainness!

Genji, however, would at least have been able to entertain himself with the works of the finest painters and poets of the court, for the screens and partitions were decorated with exquisite painting and calligraphy. The artist's inspiration was often a verse or line from Chinese and, later, even Japanese literature. This would be inscribed in a cartouche within the borders of the painting—thus, to the beauty of the painting was added the literary beauty of the text and the quality of the calligraphy. The native Japanese poetic form of the *waka* gradually supplanted Chinese forms. The subject matter also changed: from dealing with idealized landscapes with craggy mountains, so favored by Chinese artists, poets turned to scenes in which undulating hills are decorated with the beauty of the flowering cherry tree and the purple-leafed maple. The subject matter became more urbane and the figures of Chinese legend were displaced by daily scenes in the life of the Japanese aristocracy or of the common people.

It is possible that Lady Murasaki based her description of the early morning in a village on a screen painting rather than her own actual observation of such a scene—the bleacher at work with his mallet or the threshing mills as they begin to grind into action at the beginning of a new day. One tenth-century court poet wrote a series of screen poems on the occupations of the twelve months, or on the character of the four seasons. Other poems were devoted to the description of famous provincial beauty spots; of famous travelers on the road; of the life of the peasants or of nobles indulging in some typically courtly diversion such as hawking or

admiring blossom on the trees. Painters delighted to set people in their landscapes, and in her diary Lady Murasaki records that one of the princesses at the court loved to go out to see the sun go down or the moon fade before the onset of the sun at dawn, or to follow a nightingale through the woods. Indeed, it is remarkable that in a society so essentially wedded to the urbane pleasures of the court and the delights of the capital, city life as such provided poets with little inspiration. Nevertheless, verses survive that poignantly tell of the pains of exile from the capital, for throughout the Heian period exile was the standard punishment for subversion, or even political failure.

Hand in hand with the brilliant flowering of the arts encouraged by the building of the new capital, and with the development of a more truly national style in painting—the so-called *Yamato-e* or "Japanese painting"—went a rise in the status of the painters themselves. Toward the end of the ninth century we find for the first time records of the names of the artists; among the most famous is perhaps Kanoaka—traditionally believed to have been the first to paint real as opposed to imaginary Japanese landscapes.

With the invention of a type of syllabary script in the late eighth and ninth centuries it became comparatively simple to write Japanese. The result was not only that poets tended to abandon Chinese, but they moved toward the development of a prose literature—novels, memoirs and diaries. Great statesmen left diaries written in Chinese, which was

The sophistication of calligraphy was an important aspect of the cultural renaissance fostered by the Fujiwara dynasty from their court at Heian.

An illustration from *The Tale of Genji*, perhaps the world's earliest novel, written *c.* 1000 by Lady Murasaki to mirror Heian court life.

59

to remain the language of scholarship for centuries to come, but it is in the Japanese novels and memoirs that the brilliant, sensitive—if somewhat artificial—society of Heian Japan lives. These early Japanese works, which are among the most delightful books in world literature, range from the fairy-tale atmosphere of the *Taketori monogatari*, which tells how five noblemen and then even the Emperor himself attempted to woo a beautiful girl only to find that she was a spirit whose home is the moon, to the truly ardent *Genji monogatari*, or *Tale of Genji*. The genre of prose romance reached its highest flowering in the hands of female authors at the beginning of the eleventh century. In addition to the work of Murasaki Shikibu (who wrote a fascinating diary as well as her famous novel), there was the diary of the poetess Izumi Shikibu, recounting her numerous amorous affairs, and the *Pillow Book (Commonplace Book)* of Sei Shonagon, another lady at the court.

Thanks largely to Chinese influence, divination and oracles became a central part of Japanese life. The bureau of *Yin-Yang* and its offices was consulted not only on the auspices for the ceremonies of state, but also by the nobility on the most detailed aspects of life. For the people as a whole there was a large and profitably employed class of diviners and soothsayers. Perhaps the strangest of a mass of superstitions was the belief that the spiritual powers walked abroad and that it was unlucky to cross their "directions." Indeed, the world was so thick with dangers that it was safest of all to stay at home. Yet even in this state of total withdrawal, called *monoimi*, one could not be certain of safety indefinitely—on every sixtieth day, the Day of the Monkey, danger could be avoided only by staying watchful all night

and residing in a neutral place. In the year 1104, the cloistered Emperor Shirakawa spent the Night of the Monkey in his carriage at one of the gates of the city—returning to his palace only at daybreak. If a man had to go out on an inauspicious day, he might wear a ticket, called an *imifuda*, in his hat, to warn people with whom he came in contact that they should not approach him. The Japanese delight in ceremonial and display of all kinds was so great that we have contemporary records of great occasions where some of the spectators present arrived wearing their *imifuda*, anxious not to miss the ceremony and protecting themselves against the powers of evil in this way. Some of the most magnificent displays were those put on by the Buddhists.

Buddhism came to Japan during the seventh century. Its immense influence at the capital in the Nara period may have been a factor determining the move to Heian. But Buddhism was to have a deep and lasting effect on Japanese culture. Its broad and non-exclusive nature enabled it to accommodate the local spirits and gods of the Shinto cults as the protectors of the Boddhisatvas of Buddhism, and the old faith held its own as an essential part of the religion of the state and the people.

In the early ninth century the sects of Tendai and Shingon arose, both modifications of sects already established in China. The center of Tendai Buddhism was the monastery of Enryakuji, built on Mount Hiyiei overlooking Heian. It was as dangerous to the life of the capital as anything that may have happened at Nara. As the century progressed, both sects became increasingly esoteric, and during the late tenth and eleventh centuries they were to some extent displaced by the cult of the

Below left Layout of the temple at Todaiji at Nara pre-dating the renaissance of Heian court culture.

Below right The statue of the Shinto goddess Nakatsu Hime Zo wearing the robes of a court lady, at the Hachiman-gu shrine in Nara.

Above An eleventh-century Buddhist monk on horseback.

Left The great Buddha in the temple of Byodo-in. The sculptor devised the system of assembling pieces of carved wood.

merciful Buddha Amida. This cult revolved around belief in immediate rebirth in the paradise of Amida and a very simple devotional system based on repeated invocations of the name of Buddha.

Perhaps the most influential of all the precepts of Buddhism was the belief in reincarnation, and above all the idea of Karma, roughly to be described as the belief in the unavoidable cause-and-effect relation between past, present and future, and the conviction that man's life was affected at every turn by events in his own past lives. Such a belief squared well with the strong streak of fatalism in Japanese thought, and the quietistic aspect of Buddhism constituted a welcome contrast to the violence of life itself. Yet the Buddhist monasteries were far from quietistic in their contacts with the world at large. Rich and tax-exempt, they soon recruited immense bodies of fighting men. These armed "monks" enjoyed a semi-religious status somewhat analogous to the lay brothers of Western monasticism, and their rioting came to be a constant threat to the capital. The civil authorities often showed understandable reluctance to proceed against them.

There were many occasions in the history of Western monasticism when its representatives fell far below the high aspirations of their vocation. But only very rarely do we find accounts of the outright hooliganism that was a recurrent feature in the history of the monasteries around the Japanese capital. Of course, the proximity of Japanese Buddhist monasteries to the cities was an important fact in their development. Nevertheless, at the other extreme, we find examples of asceticism and piety among Buddhist monks which more than equal the most exalted achievements of the West.

It is above all this contrast between extremes that strikes us so forcibly about the society of medieval Japan. A civilization of remarkable sensibility and esthetic achievement was born in a country not remarkably rich in natural resources. Its court was governed by elaborate and elegant ritual and an exquisite awareness of the nuances of social convention and human sensitivities. Yet, as minor but revealing episodes from the history of the period show, the physical conditions of life were often uncomfortable, and the brutal and coarse facts of human nature often broke through the façade of etiquette. In comparison with the situation in Europe during the eleventh century, and indeed for generations to come, however, the civilization of this Oriental culture is breathtakingly advanced.

GEOFFREY HINDLEY

61

Japan during the Heian Period

For some three and a half centuries after the founding of Kyoto, Japan had an imperial court and administration devoted to a refined culture that has shaped the character of the people down to this century. Power was in the hands of the Fujiwara family who intermarried with the imperial house and provided "regents" for a line of boy-emperors, most of whom abdicated voluntarily when they reached adulthood. The Emperor became an idealized figure, protected from the corrupting effects of actual political rule. The sensitive, stylish yet formal spirit of the Heian period under the Fujiwara, who enjoyed their greatest ascendancy from the mid-tenth to the mid-eleventh centuries, is fully embodied in the literary masterpiece *Genji Monogatari* written by a court lady, Murasaki Shikibu, in the early eleventh century.

In sharp contrast to the delicate, almost effete life of the capital was the life on the great semi-independent estates. The large landowners gradually acquired exemption from taxation; thus developed a feudal system with parallels to that in Europe.

As the Fujiwara began to lose their grip on events, civil war broke out between rival factions of the family. In the twelfth century they called two of the powerful military provincial families to their aid. Not surprisingly, when the smoke cleared after a long period of near

anarchy, the Fujiwara found that they had been entirely supplanted by their military advisers. In 1166, the Taira family seized power and for the first time in three centuries Japan witnessed political executions; some twenty years later, the Taira were overthrown by the great Minamoto Yoritomo, and in 1185 Japan came under a government controlled by the military. The age of the tea ceremony was succeeded by the age of the samurai: the struggle between the Taira and the Minamoto launched the great period of Japanese chivalry. The principle of military control of the government was to remain at the heart of the Japanese administrative system for another seven centuries.

The Lombards in Italy

Only six years after the founding of Kyoto had marked the beginning of a new epoch in Japan, a still more dramatic turn of events gave new style and pretension to the more backward if perhaps more vigorous civilization of the West. In terms of territorial power, Charlemagne had just claim to the title of Emperor. In a real sense he controlled most of Christian Europe, and the rise of the Frankish power and the house of Charlemagne himself will be an important theme in what follows. But first we must look at events in Italy after the fall of the Ostrogothic kingdom in the sixth century.

Like all the barbarian invaders of the later Roman Empire, the Lombards had originated in north

Germany. By the middle of the sixth century they were established in a territory comprising parts of modern Austria and Hungary, where they acted as the allies of Justinian, assisting the imperial armies against another Germanic tribe, the Gepids, who threatened the Danubian frontier. In the late 560s, however, they abandoned their allegiance to the Emperor and crossed into northern Italy where they established themselves within a generation. The capital of the new Lombard state was at Pavia, in the region still known as Lombardy. To the south, the two powerful Lombard duchies of Benevento and Spoleto maintained their independence of the Byzantine emperors and, for a long time, of the Lombard kings of the north as well.

The three Powers

During the seventh and eighth centuries, Italy was divided among three main powers: the Lombards in the north and central areas; the Roman papacy, at first acknowledging imperial suzerainty but soon acting with increasing independence; and the Byzantine exarchate at Ravenna, with additional strong Byzantine presence in the southernmost part of the peninsula and on Sicily.

The Lombards were at first a ruling warrior minority, distinguished from their subjects not only by race and language, but also by religion—those who did adopt Christianity chose Arianism. The independence of Spoleto and Benevento is to be explained not only by their geographical remoteness from the capital but also by the Lombard social order in which the local leaders, or dukes, enjoyed a considerable authority over their following. Indeed, after the death of Alboin, the leader of the original invasion, Italy was ruled for ten years by thirty-six dukes. But the pressures of Byzantine and Frankish armies compelled a return to kingship. Thereafter, the state became increasingly unified, with a system of royal ministers in the provinces. In the middle of the seventh century a code of laws, written in Latin and reflecting both Lombard and Roman practices, was published. Despite the continuing separateness of the Lombard warrior-aristocracy, the increasing influence of late Roman ideas in art and administration is observable. Most significant of all was the gradual ousting of

Jeweled book cover of the great Lombard Queen Theodolinda.

Arian Christianity in favor of Catholicism, and the intermarriage of the Lombard and Roman populations.

The height of Lombard power and prestige came during the reign of Liutprand (712–44), who extended the conquests of Byzantine territory still further and asserted northern Lombard authority over the duchies of Benevento and Spoleto. During his reign, the great Lombard historian Paul the Deacon began his famous history, the earliest of a German people by a German writer, which ends with the reign of Liutprand.

Liutprand's successors, in an attempt to remove the alien corridor between the two halves of the Lombard domain, moved against the lands of the papacy and the remaining territories of the exarchate of Ravenna. But the papacy called in the assistance of its powerful Catholic "sons," the Frankish kings.

On the first occasion of a papal

Contemporary portrait of the commander Minamoto Yoritomo.

Rare example of Lombard art prior to the conquest of Charlemagne; three female saints from a church at Cividale.

Frankish hordes. The disintegration of Europe begins

The iron crown of Lombardy, one of the most sacred relics of imperial history.

summons, Pepin the Short compelled the Lombards to abandon their conquests and confirmed the papacy's possession of these lands. From this so-called Donation of Pepin may be dated the existence of the papal states as a separate and autonomous territorial unit. Some twenty years later, the Pope called on the aid of Pepin's son Charlemagne. In 774, after his defeat of the Lombard armies, Charlemagne was himself crowned king of Lombardy with the iron crown. From this time on, the successors of Charlemagne were to claim imperial rights in Italy, which was to lead them into many exhausting and largely fruitless expeditions.

Rise of the Franks

While the sun of imperial Rome in the West was setting over the walls of Ravenna, and while the popes at Rome were maintaining themselves as best they could between the Arian heretic king of Italy on the one hand and the claims of the Byzantine Emperor on the other, a new power was rising north of the Alps early in the sixth century. This was the Frankish kingdom of Clovis and his descendants. With his victory at Soissons over Syagrius in 486, when he was only twenty, Clovis had effectively put an end to the last vestige of Roman rule in Gaul. Over the next twenty years, this leader of a once insignificant tribe overthrew the most powerful barbarian kingdoms, defeating in turn the Thuringians, the Alemanni and above all the Visigoths at Vouille in 507.

In the long vista of history, perhaps the most important event in Clovis' reign was his conversion to Catholic Christianity. By this act he won the support of the indigenous Romano-Gallic population, the support of the Church and the title of consul from the Emperor. In return, Clovis himself protected the Roman Church in Gaul. In the years that followed his death in 511 the Frankish kingdom—although divided among his four sons—continued to expand. The kingdom of the Burgundians, between the Rhone and Loire, was conquered; the duchy of Bavaria acknowledged Frankish suzerainty; and at this early date we find the Franks making expeditions into Ostrogothic Italy as allies of Justinian.

Charles Martel

In the early seventh century a new power structure emerged in Gaul, one dominated by the western kingdom of Neustria, the eastern kingdom of Austrasia, the semi-independent kingdom of Burgundy and the duchy of Aquitaine. In the last twenty years of the century, Austrasia and Neustria—although nominally ruled by descendants of Clovis, the notorious "do-nothing" kings—were united under the effective rule of Pepin of Heristal, the chief minister or "mayor of the palace" of the king of Austrasia. He was succeeded by his illegitimate son, the great Charles Martel (the Hammer). Martel was not only the ruler of the two northern Frankish kingdoms but also received the submission both of Aquitaine and Burgundy.

At this point the impetus of the second wave of Islamic conquest was by no means spent. Even after the crushing defeat that the Frankish army under Martel inflicted on them at the battle of Poitiers in 732, the Arabs might still have posed a severe threat had it not been for their own internal dissensions. In addition to his achievements as a soldier, which included the pacification of a number of Germanic tribes on the right bank of the Rhine, Charles Martel did much to unify the Frankish kingdom, both by eliminating the worst excesses of the nobility and asserting the influence of the state in the affairs of the Church. In many ways he laid the foundations for the achievements of his son, Pepin the Short, and his grandson, Charlemagne.

Although Charles Martel did not assume the title of king, the fiction of the Merovingian rule was already difficult to support during his rule. Ten years after Martel's death, Pepin the Short had his deposition of the last of the Merovingians and his own coronation confirmed by the Pope—in return for helping the Pope against the Lombards in Italy. Half a century later, Pepin's son was to accept the consecration of the Church for a still greater honor, that of Emperor, on the fateful Christmas Day of the year 800.

Figure of Christ from a casket of Frankish workmanship; seventh century.

King Pepin III crowned by a divine hand.

63

A Crown for Charlemagne   800

At a solemn moment during the celebration of Mass in Rome's St. Peter's Basilica on Christmas Day of the year 800, Pope Leo III stopped and turned toward the large man kneeling in front of the altar. Then, in a dramatic gesture that has been the topic of countless historical arguments since, Leo crowned Charles, King of the Franks, as the new Emperor of the Romans. The coronation apparently took even Charles by surprise; and it probably displeased him as well, since it seemed to imply that he received his power from the Pope. Indeed, this may have been Leo's aim, for only a year before he had been driven out of the city by a rebellious population and he was now eager to reassert his authority. Whatever Leo's motives, his action was of momentous significance—in creating a European Christian empire, in continuing the division between East and West, and in sowing seeds of conflict between Church and State.

On Christmas Day in the year 800 Charlemagne heard Mass in St. Peter's in Rome. As he knelt at prayer, Pope Leo III placed on his head a gold circlet in token of an imperial crown and the Romans proclaimed him Emperor· "To Charles Augustus, crowned by God, the great and peace-giving Emperor of the Romans, life and victory!"

Charlemagne the Frank was a huge man, six feet and four inches tall, and broadly built. He spoke quietly, and was a cheerful, talkative man who enjoyed the debating matches that were popular among the Germanic races. He drank sparsely but ate a great deal, and detested wearing fine clothes made of silk. He favored the shirt and linen tunic of the Franks over tight hose, and in winter a cloak made from the skins of otters or rats. He wore a blue serge cloak and carried a short sword with a hilt of silver or gold. Charlemagne loved hunting, riding and swimming; he loved women, too. Apart from those he was wedded to by Christian marriage, he had some wives under Germanic folk laws and four concubines. Charlemagne valued culture, and the learning of the clerics—he himself understood Latin but probably could not write, since it was only with difficulty that he could form the letters of his name for a signature.

Charlemagne wanted to see ancient Rome reborn in his capital city. In Aix, near the famous hot springs, the imperial chapel was built as an octagon, probably modeled on the Church of the Holy Sepulcher at Jerusalem. Apart from the cathedral and the *sacrum palatium* where the Frankish king intended to live, there was a third building, named the "Lateran." Aix, like Constantinople, was to be a second Rome.

Pope Leo III was made aware of this great project of Charlemagne's when he fled from Rome to the town of Paderborn in Germany in the summer of 799. The people of Rome had driven him out and he sought help from "the protector of the Romans,"

Charlemagne. Rome (*Romanitas*) and Christendom (*christianitas*) were identical to Charlemagne, and for him both concepts were religious. However, "Rome" and "Christendom" had totally different meanings for the Pope and for the Emperor in Constantinople. The latter considered himself to be the only legitimate Roman Emperor, and his Greek Orthodox Church the only true one. The Pope for his part saw himself as the successor of St. Peter, and therefore the one true Roman. His concept of Rome was implicit in his attempt to renew papal Rome as the axis of the Christian world.

Charlemagne's plan to turn Aix into a second Rome could only alarm the Pope, and probably was the basic reason for the coronation of A.D. 800. The idea of transferring the papacy from Rome to Aix must already have taken shape by 799. Once in Aix the Pope would have been only *primus inter pares*, the first of the imperial bishops, in the world's eyes.

At the imperial coronation on Christmas Day, A.D. 800, at least four opposing claims came into conflict: the claims of the Franks, the papacy, the people of Rome and Byzantium. Historians always have and probably always will argue about the correct interpretation of this event, which was both political and religious, and embodied both a sacred and a political constitution for Latin Europe and the West. The argument arises from the conflicts that existed at the time. Charlemagne remained the short-term victor. For him, as for his Franks, his subjects in Lombardy, and the Anglo-Saxons, Irish and Spaniards who were his ideological allies, the imperial coronation of A.D. 800 was a coronation at the hands of God Himself. Charlemagne the king and priest was the successor to the priest-kings of the Old Testament "after the order of Melchisedech." Charlemagne, the "new David," was enthroned in Aix on a sacred imitation of King Solomon's throne. He also saw himself as the successor of Justinian, carrying out and adding to the latter's enactments.

The throne of Charlemagne in the minster at Aachen, seat of Carolingian pretension and a focal point of the cultural heritage of Western Europe.

Opposite Charlemagne the Frank, crowned Emperor of the Romans on Christmas Day, A.D. 800; a late-ninth-century bronze statuette portraying the ideal of the monarch as soldier and judge.

A warrior nobleman of the ninth century, one of a class whose power Charlemagne increased and upon whom his government depended; a fresco in the Oratory of St. Benedict.

Below The Frankish talisman worn by the Emperor Charlemagne is a phial mounted in gold and precious stones which probably contained relics sacred in primitive Frankish ritual.

Right Charlemagne in the ceremonial dress of the Roman Emperors, a ninth-century statue at Müstair church, founded by Charlemagne. The Carolingian sculptor probably used a late antique model for the details of imperial dress in an effort to represent Charlemagne's ideal of a revived Roman Empire.

had been transferred from Constantinople to Rome.

Leo's coronation of Charlemagne, which surprised and embittered the latter like an act of aggression, was aimed against the Emperor in Constantinople, against the Frankish king, and against the people of Rome themselves, who were pressed into service for the ceremony by the Pope; they had to chant the ancient Roman acclamation, the ceremonial words of the old imperial liturgy, immediately after the coronation in order to make it legal and binding. The Roman citizens who collaborated with Leo in this act believed that it gave them the right to accept or reject the Pope's choice of Emperor—who might be a powerful ally in the still unresolved conflict of the Romans themselves with their popes. Pope Leo, however, intended their role to be merely one of helpers; the Franks, to their chagrin, were allotted the role of mere onlookers. They were allowed to do or say nothing at the ceremony.

Leo III would have liked to add a second ceremony to this coronation, the first time a Pope had ever crowned an Emperor. He had planned Charlemagne's betrothal to the Empress Irene at Constantinople—but she was deposed before the betrothal could be arranged. If he had succeeded in this, Leo would have achieved that world primacy as head of both Latin and Greek Christendom which the popes as leaders of Europe were to strive for at the time of the Crusades. Hadrian I, Leo's predecessor, had already declared that the Roman Church was *caput totius mundi*—the head of the whole world.

Why did Charlemagne accede to the Pope's plans? Why did he go to Rome at all? Why expose himself to the obvious risk that the Pope would take over the coronation and exploit it for his own ends? One must remember here that Charlemagne's chief aim was to be crowned as Emperor; but he intended

For the Germanic peoples who had been subjugated or won back by Charlemagne's "strong arm," his coronation was the divinely ordained confirmation of the great conqueror's role, since God had first made him "Emperor" on the battlefield.

It is certain that Charlemagne and his advisers did not consider the imperial coronation of A.D. 800 as a papal claim to spiritual and ecclesiastical authority over the rank and office of the Emperor. Charlemagne in any case wanted to avoid an act of provocation against the Emperor in Byzantium.

The Pope, who was the "second victor" of A.D. 800, had quite different intentions. Leo III, a problematical figure whose personality remains obscure, formed part of a great tradition which was to receive new impetus later in the ninth century and which led through Gregory VII to the powerful figures of the twelfth century, Innocent III and Innocent IV.

The popes and their assistants wove the strong web of ideology that later entangled and overthrew the power of the Western Emperors: from Constantine's day, the Pope was the real ruler of Rome; he always handed the imperial office on to *his* candidates, once the majesty of the Emperor

the coronation to take place on his own territory, after careful preparations by his political and religious advisers. On December 23 of A.D. 800, two days before the coronation, the Patriarch of Jerusalem's legates handed over to Charlemagne a key and a banner, to symbolize that they were handing over to him as master and protector of Christendom the sacred places in the Holy Land.

Charlemagne, as protector of Christendom, believed that the true Christendom was the ecclesiastical Latin Christendom of Rome led by the papacy. The Frankish church was firmly oriented toward Rome. The age-old Roman faith of the Franks was based on the sanctity of St. Peter and was centered on the papacy. Charlemagne was the father of the Latin West, of the traditions that have formed the basis of Western European culture and its schools and universities right up to the present day.

The Carolingian miniscule is the ancestor of modern European printing. It is true that in Charlemagne's Empire Latin, and to a certain extent also Greek, education were better and more productively represented by the English schoolmen than by the decadent, needy scholars of Rome. By Charlemagne's day, Rome had become a cultural and moral desert. It could not be compared in any way with southern Italy, where a rich culture based on ancient Greece still flourished, nor with the civilization of the Lombard kingdom in northern Italy.

The culture acquired by England from the time of Theodore of Tarsus and Bishop Benedict was available to the men of Charlemagne's Empire. The scholars from the Continent had free access to England's schools and libraries. Throughout the whole of the eighth century, England had sent the finest and most educated of her sons across the Channel as teachers and missionaries. From the time of St. Boniface to the time of Alcuin, the Church of the Frankish Empire depended very much on the wisdom and scholarship of British monks.

But these men also acknowledged Rome as their master. For Charlemagne, the laborious work of political and cultural unification of the varied peoples, races and territories of his great Empire could only be based on Roman (and this meant Latin and Christian) belief and culture. His title of *imperator Romanum gubernans imperium*, which he preferred to the less ambiguous *imperator Romanorum*, chiefly signified to him that he was Emperor of all Latin Christendom—the only divinely inspired Christendom, since the Greeks with their contentious discussions were always in danger of heresy.

It was in this context that Charlemagne needed the power of the Roman papacy against the Greeks. His aim was the coexistence of the two empires, and he strived for equality in rank and power with the Eastern Emperor, whose title he recognized as legitimate. He imitated his rival by calling his court "sacral" (*sacer*), following the custom of the Byzantines; and Greek elements were absorbed into the Carolingian civilization. The most obvious example of the imitation of Byzantium occurred in the adoration of Charlemagne by the Pope after the

coronation. Leo III stood to crown Charlemagne, when the latter rose after his prayers, and then threw himself down before Charlemagne in the Byzantine custom of homage and sacral recognition of the crowned Emperor. This seemed monstrous to subsequent popes and was never repeated, for in their conception St. Peter, that is, the Pope, "created" the Emperor.

The coronation of A.D. 800 must be considered from every point of view a decisive step in the development of the great conflict between East and West which has overshadowed Europe from late antiquity up to the present day. It is a conflict between Greeks and Latins, between the Greek and

Below St. Peter receiving the Keys of Heaven from Christ, a ninth-century fresco in Müstair church, demonstrating the belief which was the basis of papal claims to supremacy over Charlemagne's Empire.

Bottom The mosaic over the Imperial door in Hagia Sophia, Constantinople, shows the Byzantine Emperor doing homage before Christ in the attitude of humility which the Pope adopted towards Charlemagne at his coronation.

67

One of Charlemagne's achievements was the establishment of a stable currency. This silver denier bears the Emperor's head crowned with laurel and surrounded by a title in Roman letters, a style based entirely on imperial Roman tradition.

ꞁꞇ-ꞩꞺꞁꞺꞙꞼ

Late-seventh-century Anglo-Irish half-uncials.

uoſ faciaꞇ ımploꞃc

Eleventh-century English "Winchester School" writing, a variety of Carolingian miniscule.

ꞇꞡon epꞩꞋꞇanꞇꞇꞇ de be

Medieval "Gothic" writing still used in Germany well into the twentieth century.

ſꞻꞇꞇꞩ ꞇꞩoꞇꞇ ꞇꞇꞡꞺ

Fourth-century Roman cursive script, the origin of most forms of Western writing.

ꝺuꞇ꞊ꞯꞇꞇꞇꞇꞇuꞇ cꞯꞇꞇ

"Beneventan" script from Monte Cassino, the model for Carolingian miniscule.

ΠΡΟΤΟΥΔΕ

The fourth-century *Codex Sinaiticus* in "Cyrillic" script, developed from Greek writing for the transliteration of the Slav languages.

Early Medieval Writing

Acriꞇpediꞇ quaſto ꞇuliꞇ auꞃea coꞃnua cerui
Sꞇymphaliꝺaꞇ pepuliꞇ uoluerer diſcrimꞇꞇ ê quinꞇo
Threiciam ſexꞇo ſpoliauiꞇ amazona balꞇeo
Sepꞇima ꞇ augaeꞇſꞇabuliꞇ impenſ à labonꞇ
Oꞇꞇaua ꞇxpulſo numeꞇaꞇur aꝺoꞃea ꞇauꞃo
Inchomeꝺeꞇꞇ uꞇꞇoꞇꞇa non a quadꞇꞇꞡꞇꞇ
Ceꞇꞇone eꞇꞇꞇ ꞡoꝺecimà daꞇ hibeꞃꞇa palmꞇ
undecimo malaꞇ herpeꞇꞇ dum deꞇꞃꞇcꞇa ꞇꞇꞇumplo
Cerberuꞇ exꞇremꞇ ſupꞇema eſꞇ mꞇꞇꞇ labonꞇ

A BCD
EFGHI
KLMN

An example of Carolingian miniscules and capitals, a style of writing that developed under Charlemagne from Roman models.

Latin churches, Constantinople and Rome.

The synod of Frankfurt in A.D. 794 was the immediate prologue to the events of A.D. 800. It was an attempt to prove that the Greek Church had departed from the true Christian faith and gone over to the side of evil and the antichrist in its heretical worship of images. The "orthodox council" of Frankfurt represented an attempt to discredit the second synod of Nicaea (A.D. 787). It exploited the material that had been prepared in the *Libri Carolini* by a court theologian, probably Theodulf of Orléans. The Franks accused the Byzantine Church of setting up idols; the conflict over the right degree of worship to be accorded to the holy images in fact continued for centuries in Byzantium.

But the Frankfurt synod's real object of attack was the Eastern Roman emperors—the Byzantine rulers were accused of elevating themselves to the level of false gods in their claim to rule in conjunction with God, and to be themselves divine. It was said that in the evil city of Constantinople people even spoke of the "holy ears" of the ruler. The synod of Frankfurt maintained that far from being equal to the apostles (Constantine the Great was the first to describe himself as "equal to the apostles" and even "the thirteenth apostle"), these emperors were all-too-ordinary mortals in their pursuit of earthly, transient aims.

This attack on the part of the theologians coincided with the objectives of the Roman popes, who were attempting throughout the ninth century to undermine the sacral position of the Eastern emperors. The papacy assumed all the sacral title and claims of the Eastern emperors, and indeed went far beyond them; by the thirteenth and fourteenth centuries the ideologists of the curia were referring to the Pope as *papa-deus*, or "Pope-God."

This rivalry shown by the Carolingian theologians and men of politics with Constantinople was a symptom of the feelings of inferiority the Roman and Latin clerics and theologians experienced when confronted with the far finer civilization of the East. They were greatly inferior to the scholars of the Eastern Church intellectually, spiritually and ecclesiastically; in the fourth century, not a single theologian in the West could follow the subtle intellectual disputations in the Greek church on the question of the Trinity. And if, by the end of the eighth century, the West had caught up to a certain extent, chiefly through the work of the theologians of the British Isles and Spain, there was still no question of any equality between the Franks and the Byzantines in the field of culture and learning. Charlemagne's court theologians were all too aware of this, and knew that they would be considered barbarians in Constantinople.

The Frankfurt synod's goal was nothing less than a demonstration that, now, the Latin Church alone represented the true orthodoxy. The Greeks were denounced as false, heretical, unreliable, evil, gossiping and treacherous; right into the nineteenth century and beyond, such advocates of the Pope's infallibility as de Maistre have repeated this cliché.

This carved ivory book cover showing the Virgin and Child enthroned with St. John on the left and the high priest Zacharias on the right, is from Charlemagne's palace school *c.* 810, and clearly shows the influence of Byzantine craftsmen at Aachen.

The Utrecht Psalter is the outstanding example of the new mode of expression in Carolingian illumination developed from the fusion of Anglo-Saxon, Irish and Frankish techniques under the dominant influence of Byzantine painting. This illustration of uncolored pen drawings has a lively technique and depth of perspective.

If the "one true word of God" had gone over from the East to the West, surely the imperial crown should go as well. An unexpected event now came to the aid of the Carolingian politicians: in 797 the Emperor of Constantinople was deposed, and replaced by a woman. But, according to the masculine theology of the West, which denied equal birth rights to women from St. Augustine's day right up to the twentieth century, Irene was not entitled to rule. Once more Frankish goals coincided with the plans of the papacy. As the *Libri Carolini* expressed it, "the fragility of the [feminine] sex and the fickleness of the [feminine] heart do not permit [a woman] to assume the highest positions in matters of faith or rank, but force her to submit to masculine authority."

However, both "masculine authorities," Pope Leo III and the Emperor Charlemagne, knew that the reality of Byzantine rule could not be overcome with purely theological arguments. Once Charlemagne became Emperor he dropped the issue of

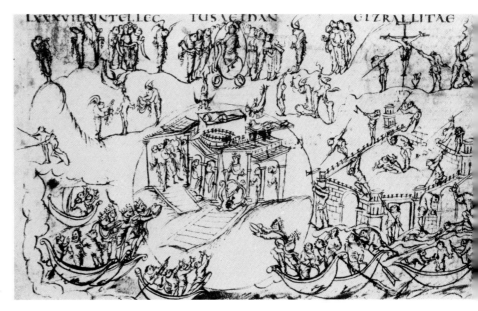

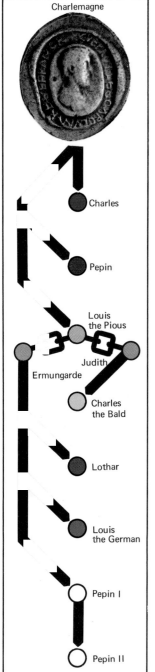

Charlemagne

- Charles
- Pepin
- Louis the Pious
- Judith
- Ermungarde
- Charles the Bald
- Lothar
- Louis the German
- Pepin I
- Pepin II

The Disintegration of Charlemagne's Empire

- Louis the Stammerer
- Louis II
- Louis III
- Louis of Saxony
- Carloman
- Boso
- Charles the Fat

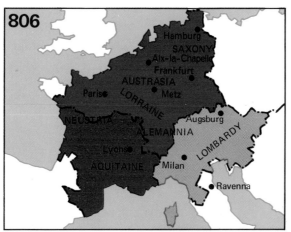

806

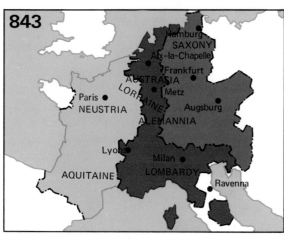

843

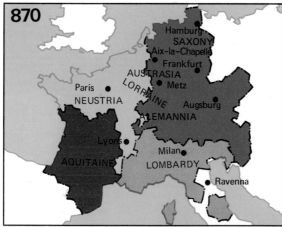

870

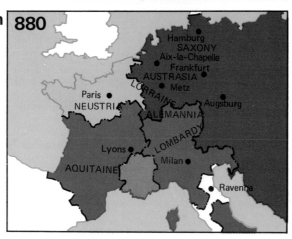

880

image-worship. As Emperor, he set out to establish friendly relations with the Byzantine court. We can safely assume today that an ambassador of Charlemagne's, accompanied by papal envoys, actually traveled to Constantinople to woo the Empress Irene, no longer in her first youth, as a bride for Charlemagne.

The Empress Irene was not unwilling to be Charlemagne's bride, but the powerful patricians of her Empire rebelled. Irene was banished to a remote convent and died a few months after this *coup d'état*, which took place before the eyes of the envoys from the West. Once again a man was Emperor in Constantinople: Nicephorus, formerly the Logothete, or minister of finance. However, the Frankish envoys returned with a Byzantine delegation which was to negotiate the recognition of Charlemagne as Emperor. Two years before his death, a settlement was finally reached: a new Byzantine delegation officially acclaimed Charlemagne as "Emperor"— though not as Roman Emperor. The Emperor of the Romans was to remain the Greek ruler, and he alone. According to Byzantine imperial law there could be any number of nominal emperors; later on, for example, an Emperor of the Bulgarians was recognized.

Charlemagne for his part gave up his claims to extend his dominion over the East. This was the more easily done as he was to be fully occupied until his death in trying to keep the peace among the different races and tribes of his enormous Empire.

The collapse of that Empire began after his death. The papacy at once made a bid to take over the dominant role, as the imperial coronation of Louis the Pious in Rome (A.D. 816) demonstrated. The Pope managed on this occasion to combine the anointing with the coronation for the first time. The Romans, who had been the Pope's adjuncts in A.D. 800, were now completely excluded and their approval disdained. The new, epoch-making liturgy of this imperial coronation made it clear that St. Peter created the Roman Emperor. Rome, the Rome of the papacy, became the focal point of the whole Christian world.

One final point needs to be made about the imperial coronation on Christmas Day, A.D. 800. In the thousand years that were to follow before the downfall of the old Europe, which received its first severe blow in the French Revolution and finally came to an end in World War I, this coronation was remembered by kings, emperors and princes of East and West, North and South alike. Right into the East, into Russia and beyond, and as far as Jerusalem and Baghdad, Charlemagne became the mystical definition of the great ruler, the Caesar and the Augustus, of the Christian world. Napoleon believed himself to be Charlemagne's reincarnation. After World War II, Western politicians spoke of the political and economic coalition of "Carolingian" western Europe which was to withstand the pressures from the East; and Soviet Russian diplomacy reproduced the subtle and devious methods of its "Byzantine ancestor." FRIEDRICH HEER

Eluuiuf quemheridanum dicunt hab& stellaf primo
flexu in secundo iii tertio vii quae dicuntur ora xiii
summa xiii huic sub est stella quae canopuf appellatur:

Piscif magnuf hab& stellaf xii in ordine positaf a capite
usque ad caudam

Ara siue sacrarium hab& stellaf iiii duaf in igne quiei
in positur ard&. & in basi duar.

Opposite page The *Divisio regni* of 806, Charlemagne's division of his Empire into roughly equal parts to be shared among his sons, avoided the issue of the imperial title. The seal, with the head of a Roman emperor, was used by Charlemagne.

Charlemagne's court at Aachen drew together the different strains of contemporary western culture. These manuscript pages show St. Matthew (*far left*) from the Ebbo Gospels, illuminated *c.* 835 in the Reims school; signs of the Zodiac (*left*) in an astrology text book from Metz, *c.* 840, typical of the survival of classical learning at the Carolingian court; and (*below*) the Anglo-Saxon strain exemplified by the opening pages of St. Matthew's gospel from the mid-eighth-century *Codex Aureus*.

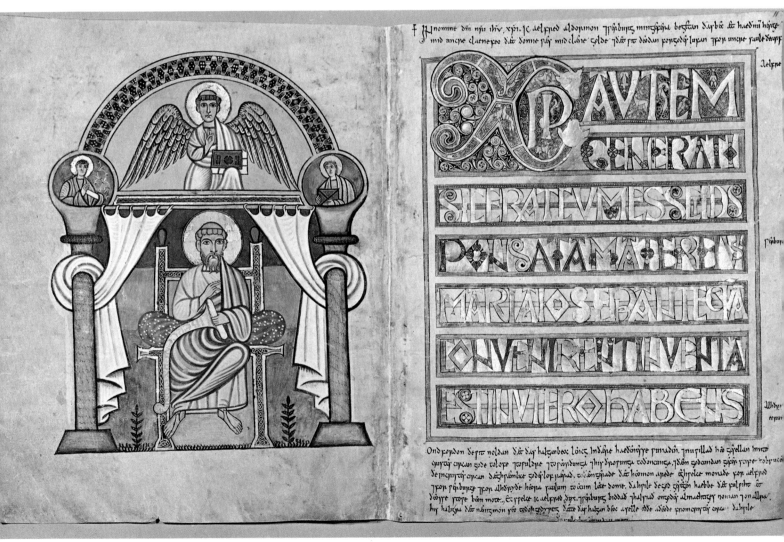

During the ninth century the Empire of Charlemagne dissolved and only the idea of "Europe" survived. And by the late tenth century the eastern and western parts of the Frankish kingdom had coalesced into the dim outlines of the future kingdoms of France and Germany. The Spanish March had disintegrated and been succeeded by the Basque kingdom of Navarre and the county of Barcelona. Italy, broken into a series of ineffectual kingdoms in the peninsula, owed a nominal allegiance to the Emperor (now the King of the east Franks) that was to become gradually less meaningful as the Middle Ages progressed.

After his death in 814, Charlemagne was succeeded by his son Louis I, called the Pious, an amiable

Louis the Pious, from a contemporary manuscript.

but often too compassionate man. Unable to command his unruly subjects or control his quarrelsome family, Louis compounded the faults of his virtues by his indulgence toward his second wife, Judith of Bavaria, and her son Charles. During his reign, Louis was constantly at war with his sons, who finally brought their conflicts to a conclusion with the treaty of Verdun in 843, three years after Louis' death. This treaty—one of the earliest records of the emerging vernacular languages, having both German and French texts—gave the imperial title and capital to the eldest son Lothair, who also received a huge tract of territory stretching from the Low Countries to the plains of central Italy. Louis, called the German, received the eastern lands; and the favorite, Charles the Bald, got the western lands. Verdun was the inevitable consequence of the Frankish prac-

tice of dividing a father's possessions; but in the years that followed the Carolingian house showed a lack of family loyalty and honest dealing that was remarkable even for the times. The settlement of Verdun was crucially revised at the treaty of Mersen in 870, when the

Cup of Tassilo, last great leader of the tribal Duchy of Bavaria.

artificial central kingdom of Lotharingia (present Lorraine) was divided between the western and eastern kingdoms—a division which, for a thousand years, was a fruitful source of conflict between the successor states of Germany and France.

The Empire begins to crumble

The factious rivalries of the Carolingians themselves were compounded by the growing power of the local princes, some of whom had received their lands as the feudal tenants of the royal houses, others of whom claimed the rights of the old pre-Carolingian duchies of Bavaria, Aquitaine and Burgundy, while still others had achieved power as the descendants of the appointed officials of Charlemagne.

The Carolingian Empire in the East came to an end with the reign of Louis the Child, who was succeeded as German king in 911 by Conrad, Duke of Franconia. The chronic divisions of his reign were made worse by the continuing depredations of the Magyars. Throughout the ninth century

Europe suffered constant incursions.

In the year 911 the strength of the Norse invaders was formally acknowledged by the Carolingian king, Charles III, known as Charles the Simple. He granted to their leader, Rollo, territories in the north that were to become the duchy of Normandy. The Carolingians in France had been hampered by the opposition of the mighty nobles; since the late ninth century, the chief contender had been the family of Robert the Strong, whose son Eudes was for a time king. Eudes' son, Hugh the Great, died in 956, virtual ruler of France. The final demise of the Carolingians came thirty years later, when Hugh the Great's son, Hugh Capet, was elected king.

A pattern of allegiance was imposed on the political divisions that emerged during the tenth century, whereby all but a very few of Europe's *de facto* rulers acknowledged their theoretical subordination to some other lord. For, during the ninth century, the socio-political structure of medieval Europe, known to later historians as the feudal system, had taken shape. The term is misleadingly precise since feudal Europe was a patchwork of conflicting allegiances, but generalizations can be made. First, power rested in the possession of land; second, the underlying assumption, whatever the practice, was that power and obligation were inseparable. The lord held his land from the king on the condition that he supply a specified number of armed soldiers to the royal army when called upon. Yet even the king himself—who was also entitled to certain monetary "aids"—was obligated in his turn to be a good lord to his great tenants, and this

contained the seeds of the pretexts for rebellion that were often advanced. In their turn, the great lords might "infeudate" lesser men with lands, subject to similar obligations; while at the lowest level, the peasants either voluntarily or through force of circumstances surrendered their holdings to a great lord in return for his protection both against the central authority and against raiders.

Feudalism was intimately bound up with a system of agriculture, loosely termed the manorial system, in which the land of a village was divided into two or three large open fields, cultivated in common by the villagers, for whom the cost of the increasingly common heavy plough and its valuable ox team was too great for a single family to support. Under this system each peasant household was allotted strips within the common fields and was in return required to do specified days of work on the lord's holding.

Thus by the tenth century, despite near political anarchy, Europe had evolved the base of a political, social and agricultural system that was to provide the framework of history for generations to come.

England before Alfred

Before the reign of Alfred the Great, England was a country of one religion but divided political loyalties.

The central kingdom of Mercia was ruled by the pagan king Penda, whose reign opened in 633 with the defeat of the Christian Edwin of Northumbria. Christianity was restored in the northern kingdom under the aegis of the king, St. Oswald, and the priest St. Aidan, but in 651 Penda again overthrew

Peasant ploughing, from the eighth-century "Utrecht Psalter".

Saxon Settlement

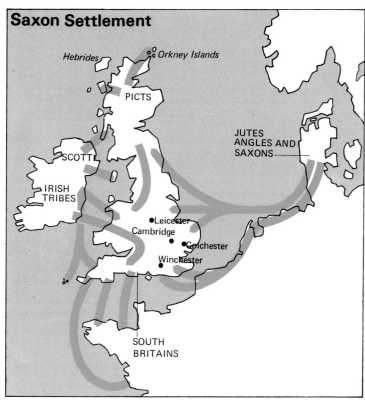

Map labels: Hebrides · Orkney Islands · PICTS · SCOTTI · IRISH TRIBES · JUTES ANGLES AND SAXONS · Leicester · Cambridge · Colchester · Winchester · SOUTH BRITAINS

Venerable Bede. Bede's great work, *An Ecclesiastical History of the English Nation*, can reasonably be considered the only true historical writing in the Middle Ages.

Almost contemporary with this brilliant northern culture, which far outshone anything in Europe and which, through Alcuin of York, was to contribute substantially to the revival of European civilization, the Church in the south of England made major contributions in the field of Church government. After the decision of Whitby, Rome sent a Greek monk, Theodore of Tarsus, to establish the basic structure of the ecclesiastical hierarchy of this new province of the Roman Church. By the time of his death in the early 690s Theodore had succeeded. Although political pressures in the next century were to cause modifications to his scheme, it retained its basic essentials.

Perhaps the most dramatic break in this pattern was the brief period which Lichfield enjoyed as an archiepiscopal see, to satisfy the demands of the powerful King Offa of Mercia. The defeat of Penda had by no means ended the might of the central kingdom. During the eighth century it dominated the political stage under its two great kings, Ethelbald and Offa, whose reigns spanned the eighty years from 715 to 796. Indeed, second only to Charlemagne, Offa was the greatest ruler in eighth-century Europe. He ruled by oppression, yet his code of laws was admired by Alfred; his gold coinage, modeled on that of the Caliphate of Damascus, was the first to be struck by an English king; and his European standing was confirmed by the commercial treaty he signed with Charlemagne.

Viking raids

Nevertheless it was with Wessex that the future was to lie. Under Egbert, who died in 839, the overlordship of Mercia was eventually challenged; the kings of Kent and Essex, for instance, acknowledged the overlordship of Wessex. Yet the kingdom exerted little effective influence to the north, and only bought the acquiescence of its own powerful vassals by extensive concessions to their ambitions. It was, in effect, the Viking raids that brought Wessex to the fore. Only under these attacks, predominantly from the north and east, did the West Country achieve any strategic

significance. And only through the historical chance that produced in Wessex the greatest of all the Anglo-Saxon rulers did that strategic position yield its greatest fruit.

The first raiders on the coast of Wessex landed near Portland in the year 800; taken by the port reeve to be traders, they were told to report to the nearest royal manor; instead, they killed the port reeve and his men. Such attacks soon became commonplace. In 835 a party of Danes landed at Sheppey; a year later Egbert of Wessex was defeated by an army of thirty-five shiploads of Danes. Two years later he defeated the Danes and their Cornish allies at Hingston Down.

Thirty years later the character of the attacks had changed. Instead of merely raiding, the Danes now intended to settle in England. In 865 a great host, led by Ivar the Boneless and Halfdan, sons of the great Viking Ragnar Lothbrok, appeared in East Anglia. In 867 they took York, and using it as their base, terrorized Northumbria

Coins of Offa of Mercia and the Viking invader, Halfdan.

and Mercia for two years. They then moved south, and in 870 established themselves at Reading. In that same year they suffered a great defeat at the battle of Ashdown at the hands of King Aethelred of Wessex and his twenty-year-old brother; but the Danes had recovered their position within a matter of months. Then, in mid-April, the young King Aethelred died. Even as the funeral was being celebrated, news came of another Wessex defeat. The new King Alfred began a reign that was to change the destiny of his nation.

his northern rival. Yet three years later the pagan king himself was overthrown and Christianity was finally established in Northumbria by King Oswy, brother of Oswald.

Northumbria's brittle political achievement was quite overshadowed by the cultural achievements of her churchmen. The aristocratic cleric, Benedict Biscop, made six visits to Rome, and by his foundations of the Benedictine houses at Wearmouth and Jarrow, provided the centers for the brilliant culture that was to follow. St.

Willibrord from Ripon (*d.* 739) was to be the first of a long line of English missionaries who worked for the conversion of the pagan lands to the east of the kingdom of the Franks. Willibrord's work was magnificently continued by a man from the southwest of England, St. Boniface, who was the first Archbishop of Mainz and was martyred by the pagan Frisians in 754. But the real flowering of Northumbrian Christianity was the work of the scholars and artists who stayed at home, the anonymous artists of the Lindisfarne Gospels and the Book of Kells, and above all the

Part of a Northumbrian manuscript, written for Ceolfrid, early eighth-century bishop of Wearmouth and Jarrow.

Evangelist symbol from the Echternach Gospels, a masterpiece of eighth-century Northumbrian art.

Earlier invaders of the British Isles had been assimilated, but the thin veneer of English civilization in the Dark Ages could not withstand the impact of Danish attacks at the end of the eighth century. The fragmented English kingdoms could not seem to unite against this new terror. Then a savior appeared—in the guise of the young prince of Wessex, Alfred. In the first few years after he came to the throne, Alfred fought many battles against the Danes—and lost most of them. Then the tide turned; in 886 Alfred took London. He had won a capital and he had also created a nation. More than just a soldier, Alfred was a scholar determined to foster learning among his people. He translated classical works into the vernacular and issued a new legal code based on the Golden Rule. For this combination of talents, Alfred—alone among English kings—has been awarded the title "The Great."

The Alfred Jewel made of rock crystal over *cloisonné* enamel, set in gold, is inscribed with the words *Aelfred mec heht Gewyrcan* (Alfred ordered me to be made). The base is in the shape of a boar's head with hollow snout. Found near Athelney, the supposed site of Alfred's fort, the jewel is commonly thought to have belonged to that King.

When King Alfred of Wessex captured London in 886, he did more than strike a heavy blow at the Danish invaders. In effect, he became the first King of England and established a new idea of nationhood. His action gave heart to Englishmen all over the land, made them feel that the Danes after all could be defeated, and kindled in them the sentiment of being English, of being members of a nation. Viewing Alfred as their sole overlord, they broke through the lesser loyalties to region and local leader. When Alfred died, he was King of all Englishmen free to give him their allegiance.

In the autumn of 865, a great host of Danes appeared in East Anglia, with many who claimed to be "god-descended" nobles among its ranks. Its leaders were Ivar the Boneless and Halfdan, sons of the great Viking Ragnar Lothbrok. Each autumn the host moved its headquarters; it seized a strong position, fortified it, then ravaged the countryside till the people there bought peace.

The Danes spent a year collecting the horses of East Anglia and forcing the folk to buy peace; then in 866 they moved as a mounted force on York, which they took on All Souls' Day and held unchallenged for four months. Northumbria was at this time embroiled in civil war and it was some time before the rival kings would cooperate. But on March 21, 867, they took the Danes by surprise and broke into York. Quickly driven out again, the two kings, with eight ealdormen, were killed. The Northumbrians bought peace, and the Danes wintered in Mercia, at Nottingham.

Inevitably, the Mercian king made haste to find allies. He was married to a Wessex princess and thus able to call on her kinsmen. He was fortunate; aid came from the King of Wessex, Aethelred, who with his youngest brother came at the head of an army. The Danes avoided battle and the Mercians were able to buy peace.

King Aethelred's young brother, Alfred, was twenty years old in 867. That same year he married

Ealhswith, the daughter of a Mercian ealdorman. At the wedding feast he was stricken with illness, and while he recovered from the attack, the same illness was to attack him intermittently for the rest of his life. (It was probably epilepsy, though this has never been verified.)

He rarely enjoyed peace of any kind; he was only married two years when a Danish army invaded his brother's kingdom and made camp at Reading. Aethelred and Alfred summoned their forces and marched on the camp, but their first attack was beaten back.

The host moved on to the great ridge of chalk (then called Ashdown) that runs east to west across Berkshire. The two brothers reformed their forces and followed. The Danes offered battle high up on the ridge in two divisions, one under their kings, the other under the earls. The English army was also ranged in two sections—Aethelred opposing the Danish kings; Alfred, the earls. The Danes fled back to Reading.

A fortnight after this initial success the two brothers, attacking from the marshy meadows of the Loddon, were beaten off by the Danes who fought on firm land. Two months later at Meratun (perhaps Marten, near Marlborough), another hard-fought battle ended with the Danes recovering their ground. Then in mid-April Aethelred died. Alfred was recognized as his successor without opposition.

His start as a king was unlucky. While he was at his brother's funeral at Wimborne, a Wessex force was scattered at Reading; then, a month later, he himself was defeated at Wilton. After a year's exhausting war, he had to buy peace. Ivar the Boneless seems to have disappeared from history at this point and Halfdan was left to command the Danes. In autumn 873 he led his men from Wessex, which had now had four years' peace, to winter in London.

A revolt of the Northumbrian English seems to have drawn them north in 872–73. However, they

Left The Fuller Brooch, a ninth-century Anglo-Saxon silver ornament with symbols of the five senses.

Below A coin minted during Alfred's reign. Alfred's court was an administrative center such as England had not known since the collapse of the Roman Empire.

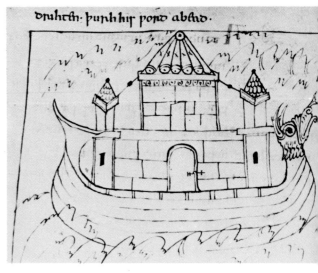

Above Two scenes from the Junius manuscript, a tenth-century document illustrating the book of Genesis by means of contemporary scenes: (*left*) The King mirrors Alfred's Court in many details; (*right*) Noah's Ark is a ship similar to those built for Alfred's navy.

A Viking sword of the tenth or eleventh century found in England and typical of the weapons used by the Danes in fierce hand-to-hand combat with the Anglo-Saxon forces.

wintered at Torksey in Lindsey, then moved to Repton in the heart of Mercia. Burhred, the Mercian king, was defeated; and he left England for Rome, leaving his kingdom at the Danes' mercy. They put a puppet king in Burhred's place, and then divided into two sections which never again united. Halfdan took one group of Danes north to the Tyne and for a year raided the Britons and Picts of Strathclyde. England, long devastated, was losing its value for loot or exactions, and the Danes began to consider permanent settlement. In 876 Halfdan carried out the first of three great partitions which gave over more than a third of eastern England to the Danes; in general, the occupied area was that now covered by the county of York—not till the tenth century was there any large Danish immigration north of the Tees or west of the Pennines. Halfdan left England at this time and was killed in 877, fighting in north Ireland.

Meanwhile, the second section of Danes, under three kings, had gone to Cambridge. They were considering a fresh attack on Wessex. An English force in the fens was keeping watch; but in autumn 875 the Danes slipped away on a dark night and spread across the country. The area around Wareham was laid waste. Alfred had a smaller body of Danes to meet this time; and though he was again obliged to buy peace, he was given hostages. The Danes swore to leave Wessex "on their holy armlet," a more solemn oath than they had so far deigned to swear to Englishmen. They had been a year at Wareham when, despite their oath, they moved off on a night march to Exeter. A storm off Swanage broke a reinforcing fleet; and in summer, they departed for Gloucester, the center of rich lands in Mercia. By the year's end they had cut Mercia in two; one half was held by a puppet-king, the other divided among the army. The area they took included the medieval shires of Nottingham, Derby and Leicester.

But settlement was a long way off—not all the Danish soldiers wanted to become farmers. Early in 878 a group moved south to Chippenham in Wessex, where Alfred often went to hunt. They were led by Guthrum, apparently the last survivor of the three Danish kings. Never before had a Danish army moved during winter, and their unexpected irruption forced much of Wessex to submit. Some West Saxons even went overseas, while Alfred retreated into the rough regions west of Selwood. East Mercia and Northumbria were lost; East Anglia, helpless. Luckily a Danish fleet from Dyfed foundered off Dorset, and Wessexmen won a minor victory at Countisbury Hill. But at Easter, his kingdom overrun and his army decimated, Alfred withdrew to the Isle of Athelney in the Somerset marshes, a thick alder forest with sparse clearings. The Danes held everything now—except the king's person. It seemed that soon Wessex too would be partitioned.

It was a critical time, and one that has passed into the legends of English history. It is only too believable that Alfred would have had the wit and the courage to visit the Danish camp as a bard, and listen to his enemy discussing the plans for attack. And Alfred *could* have done it—he loved music all his life and in that age it would have been essential for such a man to be able to play and sing himself. The famous episode in the peasant's hut probably took place at this period too, assuming that it actually happened. He was probably on the way back to his forest retreat after spying on his foes when, tired and hungry, he sought shelter and a morsel to eat at a humble dwelling. The good housewife, believing him to be an unknown wayfarer, set the bread to bake and promised him food and shelter, and asked him to watch the bread and see that it did not burn. Alfred, worn out with his exertions and preoccupied with the cares of his lost kingdom, of course forgot the bread. He sat there quietly while the poor woman, her batch of bread ruined, unknowingly scolded her king as a useless, idle fellow.

Alfred's courage and tactical skill saved the situation. He went on tackling Danish raiding-parties, and after seven weeks grew strong enough to think about the army itself. Leading the men of Somerset, Wiltshire and Hampshire (west of Southampton

·Water), he met the enemy at Edington and won a decisive victory.

For a fortnight the Danes resisted in Chippenham, then agreed to have their king baptized and leave Wessex. In the summer of 878, their still powerful host retired to Cirencester in Mercia for a year, then went back to make a final partition of East Anglia.

Wessex alone of the English kingdoms survived the Danish onslaught intact. In what had been Mercia, Northumbria and East Anglia, three large hosts of Danes had settled on the land. The next seventy years were to be taken up with the struggle to reimpose English rule (in the name of the West Saxons) on the lost areas; but nothing could wipe out the social effects of the settlements, all over the larger part of England, that came to be called the Danelaw.

In the autumn of 878, however, a new Danish host entered the Thames and wintered at Gulham. But Alfred had changed the whole situation. In November, 879, the Danes departed for the Low Countries. Guthrum no doubt had no wish to challenge Alfred again. The English were watchful; and when, in late 884, a part of the new host landed in Kent, Alfred drove them away. The Danes tried two more raids, aided by the Danes of East Anglia; and Alfred decided to teach the latter a lesson by sending a fleet into their waters. He managed to capture sixteen Viking ships off the mouth of the Stour, but before he could depart his fleet was beaten by a large Danish force.

It was at this time that Alfred took London, and while the details are scarce, it was an event of the first importance; it was after this victory that he assumed the supreme title. He showed that he meant to respect the traditions of each area coming under his overlordship; since London had been Mercian for some 150 years, he handed it over to Aethelred, ruler of English Mercia, who was henceforth his faithful ally and henchman. The settlement of the 886 war is preserved in a treaty between Alfred and all the counselors of the English people, and all the folk of East Anglia under Guthrum, the Danish king.

The treaty, as between two equal powers, laid down boundary lines. Alfred claimed no supremacy over Guthrum's area, but doubtless felt that the treaty gave him the chance of securing the interests of the English there. His power reached as far as the Humber River in the north.

Peace was not to be had for long. In 892 a great host, defeated in the Low Countries, assembled at Boulogne to invade England. The Danes of East Anglia aided the newcomers, and a protracted war resulted. Alfred realized that he must build a strong navy as well as reconstruct the land-defenses. The shire-levies were no longer adequate, so, by allowing half the peasants to stay at home while the other half campaigned, he was able to assemble a good army which could be held together much longer than before. He also saw to his defenses, and provided refuges for his menaced people; by the early tenth century every village in Sussex, Surrey and Wessex

east of the River Tamar was within twenty miles of a fortress. Thus a coherent system of national defense was built up. Though it was completed under Edward, his son, the scheme was Alfred's and he began its implementation. As for the navy, he ordered the making of warships that were swifter, steadier, and nearly twice as long as those of the Danes; he gave careful consideration to their design and they were constructed to his specifications.

His aim was to prevent the two companies in which the invaders sailed from joining forces; he took up a position between their camps at Appledore and Milton, near Sheppey. First he forced the smaller body at Milton to sign a treaty and leave for Essex; then in late spring 893, the militia under his son Edward met the larger force on land at Farnham and defeated them. The Danes took refuge on an island in the Thames. Meanwhile, Alfred, moving from the west, was held up by the news that a host from Northumbria and East Anglia was attacking Exeter. But Edward, reinforced from London, managed to hold the Danes on the island till they agreed to retire and join their allies in the east. It gave Alfred a respite, but a dangerously large number of Danes was thus concentrated in Essex.

The struggle that now ensued was the most exact-

The church at Bradford-on-Avon is one of the finest remaining examples of Anglo-Saxon architecture. The chancel is the narrowest in England, and the walls 2 ft. 6 in. thick. It is probably a seventh-century foundation with tenth-century additions.

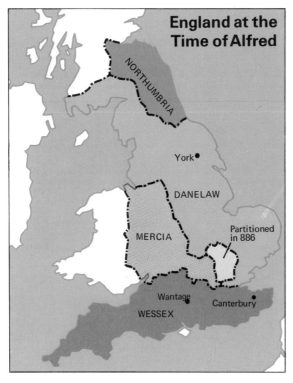

England at the Time of Alfred

NORTHUMBRIA

York

DANELAW

MERCIA

Partitioned in 886

Wantage

Canterbury

WESSEX

London. Alfred, not daring to take the smallest rest from the apparently endless fight, managed to dislodge them in the summer of 895—and achieved a resounding success. For the first time, the Danes seemed daunted by the courage and resolution of the English King. They sent their women home, and themselves made a forced march across the country to the Severn. Many of them left England; some made their way back to Danish East Anglia. Alfred could at least feel that a united and peaceful England was a real possibility.

This account of Danish movements is needed to bring out how shifting and varied a threat Alfred had to counter, and the flexible strength he showed in meeting the many threats. A navy had been inaugurated as a matter of settled policy. When he died on October 26, 899, the English were still on the defensive; but a solid basis had been built for checking the Danes and for ultimately unifying the Danish and English areas in a single kingdom.

His greatness appeared as much in his educational as in his military and administrative work. No other king of the Dark Ages had such a desire to master the available culture and hand it on to his people. A personal urgency drove him to explore the problems of fate and free will, to find out how a man came to knowledge and how the universe was ordered. His own long struggles, with their many setbacks and problems, aroused in him a need to grasp the thought of the past so that he could use it in shaping the future; he was stirred with a true reverence for human achievement. By initiating a series of translations from the Latin, he founded English prose literature. In the preface to the first of his own translations he described how low learning had fallen; very few of the clergy south of the Humber knew what their service meant in English or could turn a letter from English into Latin. By 894, when he wrote, there were once more learned bishops and a

"The Mump," the hill on the Isle of Athelney in Somerset where Alfred is thought to have built his fort in 878, at the most critical point in his lifelong wars against the Danes. Also associated with this site is the story of the burned cakes.

ing that Alfred, in a lifetime of war, was ever to face. His resources could not last forever, so he was forced to fall back on a desperate expedient. The Danes, a united host, seized the deserted Roman town of Chester, intending to use it as a base against English Mercia. But they found nothing to sustain them; Alfred had burned the corn and slaughtered the cattle. They had to withdraw from the scorched earth and turned to Wales, where they stayed until the summer of 894. Then they made their way eastward across England to Mersea, where they established a post some twenty miles north of

78

got information on the peoples of northern and central Europe; as a work of systematic geography the book is remarkable for its time. He then moved from the factual sphere to deeper matters, translating Boethius' *On the Consolation of Philosophy*, the work of a sixth-century statesman awaiting death after an abrupt turn of fortune. He was sympathetic to its creed that a man should rise above fate, convinced that Boethius gave a Christian value to Stoic ideas. Finally, he rendered the first book of Augustine's *Soliloquies* into English.

He thus did more than provide a primary basis for a system of secular knowledge and an outlook on life which, as expressed by Boethius, he felt did much to harmonize ancient thought with northern heroic tradition. He also carried out the difficult task of creating the instrument of English prose. Slowly, the language matured and became capable of expressing a wide range of thought. Moreover, near his reign's end, he issued a legal code into which he introduced the Golden Rule from *St. Matthew*. Though primarily transitional, his code included arrestingly new features for that age: provisions protecting the weaker members of society against oppression, limiting the blood feud, and stressing the bond of man and lord. It strongly aided the transformation of the tribal type of noble into the feudal type. The next two centuries were to see, all over Western Europe, the growth of conditions in which men sought lords and lords sought men: and Alfred's code facilitated this trend in the specific English form in which the national king played a key part. In the code, indeed, we see the unique qualities that marked the national monarchy which Alfred did so much to create. The code appeared at the end of a century in which no other English king had issued laws and the other kings of Western Europe were ceasing to exercise the legislative powers traditionally theirs. JACK LINDSAY

group of literate clerics, with whom he worked at a considered scheme of education for his people.

His biographer Asser, who had come from St. David's, tells how Alfred's curiosity had been awakened by two visits to Rome before he was seven, and how he set out to learn Latin between 887 and 893. Alfred's own translations began with a work by Pope Gregory the Great, *Pastoral Care*, on a bishop's duties; then came Orosius' history of the ancient world and Bede's *Ecclesiastical History*. In the Orosius, Alfred expanded many passages, drawing on his own experience and on that of travelers from whom he

England in the tenth century

As a soldier, Alfred, rightly called the Great, saved his nation; as a legislator, he established the concept of a nationwide law for all the English; as a patron, he not only launched an educational revival but himself translated Boethius' *On the Consolation of Philosophy* and sponsored the Anglo-Saxon *Chronicle*, a major historical source for another two centuries. Although he had consolidated the existence of an English nation, Alfred had been able only to contain the threat of the Danes. Vast territories in the north and east of England remained independent of the kings of Wessex and their client-kingdom of English Mercia.

Alfred's son, Edward the Elder, reigned conjointly with his sister Aethelflaed, the Lady of Mercia. At her death the kingdom was united. During this period the English, basing their defense on the series of fortified towns begun by Alfred, made headway against the incursions of the Scandinavian kingdoms that surrounded them. Even in the midst of a struggle for survival, Alfred had planned for the future. His fortified boroughs provided not only military bases but the foci of local administration and trade. Edward extended the military fortifications but an aggressive counterattack against England's enemies did not come until the reign of Athelstan (924–39).

Brother-in-law of the Carolingian Charles the Simple of France; of Hugh Capet, the greatest man in the French kingdom; and of the German Emperor Otto I, Athelstan mightily defended his position at home. He inflicted the crushing defeat of Brunanburh on the combined forces of the Scots, Irish, Norse and Welsh—a fight commemorated in one of the great epic poems of Old English. The glitter of the medieval English monarchy was at its most dazzling in the subsequent reign of Edgar; at his coronation in 973, eight client-kings are said to have paid homage.

English literature appears

It was in the tenth century that the potentialities of the Old English language, ancestor to that used by Chaucer and Malory, first became apparent. The triumphant song of Brunanburh is parallelled at the end

St. Dunstan kneeling in prayer.

of the century by the tragic and heroic poem on the defeat of the Earl Byrthnoth by the Danes at the Battle of Maldon in 991. Such verse was in the well-established heroic tradition of *Beowulf*, but in the tenth century, English found its primary power as a means of expression in prose. The Anglo-Saxon *Chronicle* itself was of course written in English, while the Church employed English prose not only in its preaching but also in magnificent homilies, lives of the saints, and translations of parts of the Bible.

Among these lives of the saints was one of St. Dunstan, Abbot of Glastonbury, Archbishop of Canterbury, close confidant of King Edgar and church reformer. It was through Dunstan that the great Continental movement in Church and monastic reform, launched by the founding of the Abbey of Cluny in 910, reached England. During a short stay in Flanders in the middle of the century, Dunstan had seen

King Canute and his wife dedicate a cross to Winchester Cathedral.

Moslem pilgrims on their way to Mecca, from a manuscript of the Baghdad School.

the work of the reformed Benedictines at first hand, and returned to England in order to transform the unregenerate Church there. But in the last twenty years of the century the renewed impetus of Danish invasions plunged the country once again into a dark night of disruption and despair. After the humiliating reign of Aethelred the Redeless—in which neither king nor people displayed the confidence of their ancestors—Britain was only to be saved by the enlightened rule of the great Danish king Canute early in the eleventh century.

The Arab world

Just as the armies of Islam had profited from the religious discontent of the great empires it conquered, so religion provided the pretext for the overthrow of the first Moslem dynasty. The population of eastern Persia, which had accepted the new faith, nevertheless felt aggrieved and discriminated against. The Persians claimed that they did not enjoy the full exemption from taxation that was their right as believers; more important, they resented the alien rule of the distant regime at Damascus. When the central

government ignored their protests, the local nobility of Khorasan, with the aid of discontented Arab colonists, rose against the Umayyads. Abu al Abbas, a descendant of Mohammed, was leader of this revolt. By 750 Abu al Abbas had founded his own dynasty, the Abbasids, and seen all but one of the Umayyad family perish in a sea of blood. Under the Abbasids, the Persian influence in Islam became increasingly marked; within a generation, the Caliphs had founded a new capital at Baghdad, on the banks of the Tigris, which was to become one of the greatest cities in the world.

It was at this time that the great collection of stories, now known as the *Arabian Nights*, first began to be assembled. Despite the Indian origin of many of the tales, they are a monument to the glories of the Arabic language and to the golden age of the Abbasid caliphate under the great Harun al Rashid or Aaron the Upright (*d.* 809) and his son Al Ma'mum (*d.* 833). During their reigns, the process of Persianization reached its highwater mark. In addition, under the impulse of Syrian Christian scholars, the Arabs began to discover the treasures of classical Greek philosophy and science, with incalculable consequences for the future of civilization.

Greek influence

Al Ma'mun founded a school at Baghdad for the translation of the classics of Greek philosophy and science. The impact was tremendous; not only was Arab scientific thought advanced, but the tool of Aristotelian dialectic was applied to all fields of thought, including theology. Some scholars aimed to reconcile Greek with Islamic thought, but a rival school opposed such liberalizing tendencies—a similar controversy was to arise in twelfth-century Europe. Greek theory also influenced music, and the scale used in Arab music shows remarkable similarities to that postulated in ancient Greek treatises. But here an equally important influence was that of Persia. Traditionalists opposed the seductions of the "romantic" Persian style on the gounds that it would corrupt the solemn and serene music prescribed by Mohammed; but despite opposition from famous musicians, the Persian style gained ground. Its music became one of the chief glories of Islamic civilization and the esteem in which it was held was reflected in the fame of the great musicians, which sometimes rivaled that of their princes.

The profound impact of the Arab conquests, from the frontiers of China's T'ang empire to Spain, is reflected in the spread of the religion of Islam today. During the Middle Ages the whole of this vast area was linked by a common religion, a common language, and common coinage. It was traversed by heavily frequented trade and pilgrim routes. Like the world of Christendom, it had many vital shared interests and beliefs. The political divisions that soon arose, while provoking more than their share of wars, did not seriously impede the flow of a common culture.

After the establishment of the Umayyad caliphates of Spain in 756, the unity of Islam was further broken. The Aghlabid emirs on the North African coast were plundering the Christian shipping of the western Mediterranean and sending raiding parties far up the rivers of mainland Europe. Farther west, in modern Morocco, a rival Shiite caliphate had arisen. And for the last half of the ninth century the emirs of Egypt, too, asserted their independence. The break-up of the vast Arab Empire was hastened by the fact that the Caliphs at Baghdad, unable to raise an army from the now settled populations of their flourishing empire, had to recruit Turkish mercenaries. After an attempt to weaken the influence of this Praetorian guard by establishing a new capital at Sammarra, the Caliphs were forced to return to Baghdad. As the tenth century progressed, their effective influence progressively waned. In Persia a new national dynasty, the Samanids, revived Persian culture; in Egypt the Fatimid caliphate founded a brilliant independent civilization which survived until the twelfth century; and in Spain the court of Cordova was legendary in Christendom as well as in Islam.

Spain—the legacy of the Visigoths

By the eighth century, the Spanish Visigoths had guaranteed the triumph of Catholicism over Arianism, given the Spanish monarchy a characteristic and continuing controlling interest in ecclesiastical affairs, and presided over the birth of a highly individual and brilliant culture. Spanish culture was eclectic in its inspiration, drawing on barbarian and classical motifs, on the art of Byzantium and, in the field of scholarship, on the tradition of the long-established, though persecuted, Jewish community. The very liturgy of the Church was a unique blend of Roman, Arian and Byzantine Eastern element.

Group of saints from a Spanish Apocalypse of the tenth century.

Brick minaret, *c.* 850, from the mosque at Sammarra, the largest in the world.

Archbishop Isidore of Seville, of mixed Spanish and Byzantine ancestry, was one of the most remarkable figures in the Europe of the Dark Ages. His writings continued to exert an immense influence through the Middle Ages. In jewelry, sculpture, book illumination and architecture, Visigothic Spain displayed a considerable and refined creative talent. One of the most interesting surviving monuments is the church of S. Juan de Banos, dedicated by the first Catholic king, Recceswinth.

The Visigoths left a lasting imprint on Christian Spain. The much-reduced kingdoms of Asturias and Galicia, on the northern coast, felt themselves the heirs of the Visigothic tradition. And the long-

delayed counterattack of the Christian kingdoms, conducted by the Visigoths' successors, Castile, Leon, Navarre and Aragon, was thought of by the Spaniards as the Reconquest.

Moslem rule in Spain began with the landing of a predominantly Berber army under the leadership of the Arab Tarik at Gibraltar in 711. The new rulers recognized the Caliph at Damascus; but in 756 the sole survivor of the Umayyad family, expelled from Damascus by the Abbasids, established himself at Cordova. His family, of whom the greatest ruler was Abd al-Rahman III (912–61), the man who brought Islamic civilization in the peninsula to its highest peak, ruled for another 250 years.

The Caliph of Cordova's Library

It was Europe's most glittering capital: a place where Moslems, Christians and Jews lived, worked, studied and thought. Tenth-century Cordova was as preoccupied with philosophy, poetry and medicine as Paris was to become in the eighteenth century. Spain's intellectual ferment was a product of the recently established Islamic society, but it was also concerned with the old, with preserving the ancient learning of Greece and Rome. Toward the end of the century, the Caliph Al-Hakam II gathered a library of 400,000 books and manuscripts—indisputably Europe's finest collection of writings on history, science and literature. The library was largely destroyed by a fanatical successor, and Cordova's days of greatness drew to an end.

Cordova, under its great caliphs of the tenth century, was the most splendid city of Western Europe. Ash-Shaquandi, the poet who sang the praises of his native al-Andalus (Andalusia) says that he rode for ten miles on end through its well-lit streets. A fine bridge spanned the river, which still bears its Moorish name of Guadalquivir, and on either side stretched the quarters of the dominant Moslem population—Arabs and Berbers from Africa, as well as descendants of Spain's indigenous inhabitants who had embraced Islam, and communities of Jews, Christians (*Mozárabes*) and slaves from Eastern Europe. One traveler counted 300 public baths; another, 600—a number perhaps not excessive for a population of over half a million, though it scandalized medieval Christians.

Cordova's other marvelous sights included innumerable workshops for the production of its famous leatherwork, carpets, ivory caskets and other handicrafts; more than four thousand markets; and many hundreds of mosques in addition to the Great Mosque. Although later converted into a Catholic cathedral, this remains one of the supreme glories of Moslem Spain. There were also the gracious residences of the rich, set amidst lovingly cultivated gardens; and the superb palaces of al-Madīna—az-Zāhira and Medinat az-Zahrā, the latter a great administrative and ceremonial headquarters for the Caliphate as well as a palace of unparalleled magnificence. In view of its subsequent history, however, the Caliph's library built up in the tenth century is of paramount importance.

Cordova was more than the seat of a powerful and prosperous empire. It was also, in the words of ash-Shaquandi, "the center of learning, the beacon of religion, the abode of nobility and leadership; its inhabitants had deep respect for the Law and set themselves the task of mastering this science, and kings humbled themselves before the doctors,

exalting their calling and acting in accordance with their opinions." During his long reign, first as Emir and then as Caliph, Abd-al-Rahman III (912–61) raised Cordova to its eminence. A great soldier and administrator, he was also a tireless builder and a munificent patron of learning and the arts.

His son Al-Hakam II was still more ardent in collecting manuscripts and attracting scholars to his court. His library was reputed to contain some 400,000 books and manuscripts—an incredible treasure, when one realizes that a few hundred volumes would then suffice to win fame for a Christian monastery as a great center of learning. Al-Hakam's patronage set the example for the nobles and merchants of Cordova, who vied with one another in building collections of their own. There was soon a flourishing book market, where rare and beautifully bound works fetched high prices. One Moslem bibliophile has left an amusing account of his pique on bidding in vain for a choice volume; the book was bought by a rich merchant who wanted it simply as an ornament to fill a gap on his shelves. A host of scribes labored to satisfy the literary appetite of the Cordovans, and are said to have produced between them some 70,000 copies of manuscripts every year.

So great was the power and prestige of Cordova that the rulers of the Christian kingdoms of northern Spain would humbly present themselves at the Caliph's court to solicit help in settling their political or personal problems. Sancho the Fat journeyed there to seek aid both in regaining his kingdom and curing his obesity. Both his petitions were crowned with success, the latter under the care of the Caliph's Jewish physician. Scholars from beyond the frontiers of Spain would come to imbibe knowledge from the learned men of Islam.

There were those among the Moslems, as well as among the Christians, who looked with suspicion

One of the main halls, possibly the throne room, in the Medina Azzahra, a pleasure palace decorated in typically complex and sumptuous style.

Opposite The door in the western façade of the mosque at Cordova, showing the detailed decoration in tile and bas-relief typical of the highpoint of artistic achievement under the Caliphate.

83

upon this passion for learning because it threatened to contaminate the purity of their revealed religion. After the death of al-Hakam in 975, power passed into the hands of a ruler of a very different stamp— Ibn Abī Āmir, known to his people as al-Mansūr, the Victorious, and to the Christians as the dreaded Almanzor. Starting as a chamberlain to al-Hakam's infant son, he rose to become the all-powerful minister and commander-in-chief of a puppet Caliph. Fanatically orthodox in his piety, he led his armies deep into Christian territory, sacking cities as far afield as Barcelona, Leon, and Santiago, yet finding time on his campaigns to transcribe a copy of the Koran with his own hand. As a usurper, he courted the support of the influential *faqihs* (religious mendicants) of the strict Malikite school, and it was to win the favor of those intolerant fanatics that he ordered a purge of al-Hakam's great library. The works of poetry, history and science lovingly collected by the Caliph were thrown out and des-

troyed; Ibn-Sa'īd of Toledo tells us that "some were burned and others cast into the palace wells and covered over with earth and stones." After the tyrant's death in 1002, there was further destruction. The great military and political machine of the Caliphate began to break up as Almanzor's sons and successors battled for power. Within seven years, Cordova was overrun by an army of Berbers and Castilians and its palaces sacked. The remaining treasures of al-Hakam's library and the many private collections were destroyed or dispersed.

But the eclipse of Cordova did not mean the end of Moslem civilization in Spain. Though fragmented into a mosaic of tiny principalities, each with its own "king," army, and court, the Moors attained a brittle but dazzling brilliance.

Of the many other scholars born in al-Andalus, or attracted to the cultured courts of its princes, three deserve special mention. All were admirers of Aristotle and sought to reconcile the wisdom of the

A Mozarabic patio, now the entrance to the convent of St. Clare Tordesillas. During the Caliphate's unique blend of religious beliefs and decorative styles, the Christians developed a style known as Mozarabic, chiefly characterized by the horseshoe arch, which was widely adopted by the Moors.

A chamber in the mosque at Cordova enclosed within foiled arches, reminiscent of the Mozarabic style, whose tilework carries Arabic inscriptions.

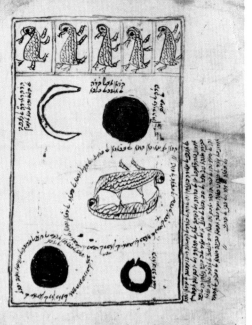

A manuscript in Hebrew on alchemy. Jews, Christians and Moslems collaborated under the Caliphate towards the pursuit of all learning and culture. Alchemy, the basis of modern science, was one of the major preoccupations of these remarkable scholars.

A page from a decorated Arabic treatise on poisons.

Andalusian Moslems as little better than the Christians.

The Christians were repulsed by the Africans and their puppet rulers were ousted, but the invaders themselves came under the civilizing but enervating influence of al-Andalus, until driven out in turn by a fresh wave of fanatics from beyond the Straits. In the process, most of the *Mozárabes*, or Christian minorities, who had been tolerated under the Caliphate but had been increasingly tempted into collusion with the advancing Christians, migrated northwards into Christian territory. So did many Jews, who had likewise lived peacefully with the Moslems but now feared persecution. The population of the expanding Christian kingdoms thus came to include strong elements, both Jewish and Mozarabic,

who were familiar with Moslem ways and impregnated with Islamic culture. This they transmitted to the Catholic communities in which they now lived and to the scholars who came from other parts of Christendom in quest of learning.

The natural center for this work was Toledo, the ancient Visigothic capital situated in the heart of the peninsula and recaptured by the Christians in 1085. Though no Christian kings, until the time of Alfonso the Learned (1221–84), could compare personally with the Moslem princes in intellectual sophistication, they could be tolerant monarchs and enlightened patrons. Alfonso VI, the conqueror of Toledo, prided himself on his title of "Emperor of the Two Religions," while King Ferdinand III, conqueror of Seville and eventually a canonized saint, added a reverence for Judaism and became "King of the Three Religions." At least one church in Toledo seems to have been used interchangeably by Jews, Christians and Moslems for the practice of their respective faiths. One Christian churchman, Archbishop Raymond of Toledo, was an admirer of Arabic learning and the chief promoter of what came to be known as the "School of Translators." This was not an institutionalized body, such as a university or school, but a tradition of practical scholarship in the translation of Arabic texts on all branches of philosophy and science into Latin and later into Spanish. It lasted for more than a century. Toledo was well chosen for such a task. Many of the surviving manuscripts from al-Hakam's great library had found their way there, and a body of scholars competent to translate them resided in the city. The usual method was for the Arabic text to be translated orally into Spanish by a Moslem, Jewish

one of the greatest of them. "Whichever way love's camels take, that is my religion and my faith." The way of the *sufi* sometimes proved remarkably close to that of the great Catholic saints such as St. Teresa.

The first Andalusian *sufi* of whom we hear was Ibn-Masarra, who lived near Cordova under the tolerant reign of the caliphs. His writings have not survived, but he seems to have been influenced by the Greek philosopher Empedocles. He taught doctrines, highly subversive in the eyes of the Maliki jurists, such as free will in place of Koranic predestination and the perfectability of the individual through ascetic practices. By the end of the twelfth century, *sufis* were to be found in all parts of Moslem Spain. Al-'Arabī has left us descriptions of 105, more than half of whom lived in al-Andalus, and were at one time or another Ibn-Masarra's spiritual masters. He himself died at Damascus after a lifetime spent in study, asceticism, and strange mystical experiences. Of the 400 or so books that his biographers tell us he composed, one has left a strong mark on our own Western culture. It furnished precedents for Dante's poetic fiction of a journey through the realms of the afterlife, with its geometrical topography, its glimpses of the bliss of the elect and its beatific vision of the divine splendor.

While the *sufis* were contemplating these mysteries and the Andalusian princelings were indulging their passion for literature, luxurious living and palace intrigue, the warlike Christians from the north were pressing in upon the little Moorish kingdoms. Their tactics were to force an "alliance" on a weaker Moslem prince, extort ever-larger amounts of tribute from him and demand the surrender first of key fortresses and eventually of the throne itself. The princes, no longer possessing the military strength to resist, turned for help to their co-religionists beyond the Straits of Gibraltar. It was a desperate choice, for Africa was an inexhaustible reservoir of fanaticism; the tribesmen who answered the call—first the Almoravides and then the Almohades or "Unitarians"—looked upon the sophisticated

An Arabic inscription in the Cordova mosque dating from the Caliphate.

The earliest part of the great Cordovan Mosque, the twelve naves built by Abd-al-Rahman I; the pillars are of jasper and other fine stones.

of one of his works), informs the thought of the greatest of the philosophers of Moslem Spain—Ibn-Rushd. Known to the West as Averroes, he was famous during the Middle Ages for his commentaries on Aristotle. Averroes held both philosophy and religion to be true and strove to reconcile the two in his writings. Because Averroes' works were denounced as impious by the *faqihs*, they found little echo in the rest of the Moslem world. Nevertheless, they came to be eagerly studied, debated, and ultimately condemned in the West as subversive of the Catholic faith, particularly in the great work of St. Thomas Aquinas. Thomas was also influenced by another thinker whose name may be added to those of the Moslem philosophers mentioned above—Maimonides, the Jewish scholar of Cordova who sought to synthesize faith and reason.

In the tenth century, new currents of spirituality from Egypt, Syria and other parts of the Islamic world brought the first *sufis* (pantheistic mystics) to Spain. "I follow the religion of love," wrote al-Arabī,

ancients with the truths of Islam. Ibn-Bājja (Avempace) is remembered chiefly as the author of *The Rule of the Solitary*, a critique of the materialism and worldliness of contemporary Moslem society. His ideas were further developed by Ibn-Tufayl, author of a remarkable allegorical novel, which became known to the West through translations into Latin and the vernaculars. Its hero—ancestor of Defoe's Robinson Crusoe, Rousseau's Emile and Kipling's Mowgli—is an infant castaway suckled by a gazelle. The child grows up to attain, through observation and reasoning, not only an understanding of the material world but, through mystical contemplation, an awareness of the Supreme Being. He eventually meets his Man Friday in the form of a Moslem hermit, from whom he realizes that the truths he had discovered by the light of reason were one and the same as those taught by revealed religion.

The same theme, the *Harmony of Religion and Philosophy* (to quote the title of a modern translation

This early-eleventh-century antiphonary designed for use during Christian worship is decorated with a fine Mozarabic horseshoe arch.

The fourteenth-century synagogue at Cordova carries Hebrew lettering on walls decorated in Moorish style. Under the religious tolerance of the Caliphate, the Jews made a highly significant contribution to the cultural life of the city.

or Mozarabic scholar, and then to be transcribed into Latin by a Spanish cleric.

The fame of Toledo soon attracted scholars from many parts of Europe. Daniel of Morley tells us that he left Paris in disgust at its obsession with law and the pretentious ignorance of its doctors and made his way to Toledo, where true learning was to be found. The Slav scholar, Hermann of Carinthia, made the same pilgrimage in order to study a manuscript of the *Almagest* by Ptolemy, the second-century astronomer whose theory of the movement of the sun and planets held the field in the Middle Ages until discarded in favor of the Copernican system. Hermann stayed on to study and translate many other works by Greek and Arabic scholars, as did Gerard of Cremona, another student of Ptolemy, who is credited with more than seventy translations on geometry, algebra, optics, astronomy and medicine. English scholars showed themselves particularly active in this field. Notable among them was Adelard of Bath, whose quest for knowledge took him as far afield as Africa and Asia Minor, and whose intellectual curiosity embraced the whole field of human interests from astrology to trigonometry, Platonic philosophy to falconry. Another Englishman, Robert of Chester, collaborated with Hermann of Carinthia and Spanish scholars in translating the Koran, and composed polemical tracts designed to demonstrate the superiority of Christianity to Islam. Michael Scot, who became an astrologer in the Arabicized court of Frederick II of Siciliy, probably acquired his Islamic learning in Toledo. Some Spanish scholars appear to have made the reverse journey to England. Pedro Alonso, a converted Jew from Aragon, played an important part in introducing Arabic astronomy into England and possibly served as physician to King Henry I.

Spain was not the only channel of cultural communication between the Islamic world and Western Europe—Sicily was another intermediary —but it was the most important. Writing in the middle of the twelfth century, John of Salisbury laments the prevailing neglect of mathematics, geometry and logic "except in the land of Spain and the borders of Africa." In the course of that and the following century, the flow of Greek philosophy and science—the metaphysics and natural science of Aristotle, the medical treatises of Hippocrates and Galen, the works of Ptolemy, Euclid and many other thinkers—enriched by the commentaries and original contributions of the Arabs, began to quicken the intellectual life of a Western Europe that had known them only in scraps or not at all.

The Moors had first been lured to Spain by its wealth and fertility; they stayed on to transmit to the West the riches they had inherited from Greece and the East. After nearly seven centuries they were driven from the peninsula. The Spanish *Reconquista* was a long and complex affair—a tide of Christian conquest ebbing and flowing over the land, but leaving islands where, for considerable periods, Moslems and Christians lived more or less tolerantly together and became influenced by each others' culture. But gradually fanaticism and intolerance were to gain the upper hand until, under the Catholics, Ferdinand and Isabella, at the end of the fifteenth century, religious conformity became the touchstone of national unity.

Granada, the last outpost of Moslem civilization in Spain, was captured in 1492, and there Cardinal Cisneros presided over bonfires of Islamic texts—as Almanzor had once presided over the purge of the Caliph's great library. But long before the spirit of tolerance and cultural interchange vanished in the smoke of the Granada holocaust, the scholars of Spain had fulfilled their mission as the industrious middlemen of culture, and transmitted to medieval Europe the forgotten learning of the ancient world.

STEPHEN CLISSOLD

Left An eleventh-century ivory casket intricately carved in the Spanish-Moorish style.

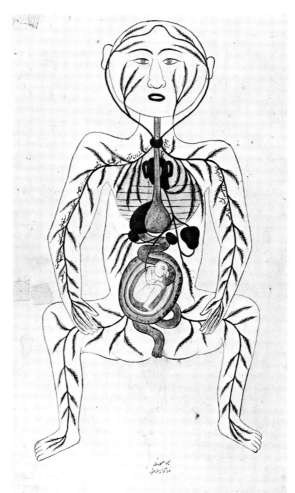

Above An Arabic medicine pot.

Left A diagram from a Persian copy of an eleventh-century Arabic medical text. The physicians of Cordova based their learning upon the discoveries of the ancient Greeks.

Cluny, the greatest Benedictine Abbey in

After the reign of the great Abd al-Rahmān III, Islamic Spain was increasingly subject to internal division, and the overthrow of the Cordovan Caliphate in 1013 allowed the Christians to capture the great city of Toledo. The Spanish Arabs now called on the newly converted and fanatical North African Berber tribes known as the Almoravides. By the beginning of the twelfth century, these allies, whose empire was based in Morocco, were in control of Islamic Spain. Within seventy years, they in their turn fell to the still more puritanical sect of the Almohades. In 1195 the Almohades inflicted a crushing defeat on the armies of Alfonso VIII of Castile, but this was more than reversed by the great victory of the united kingdoms of Castile, Leon, Navarre and Aragon on the field of Las Novas de Tolosa in 1212.

Islam fails

After that defeat, Islam never recovered its old power in Spain. Under the caliphate of Cordova, both the industry of the Moorish invaders and their religious toleration of the conquered Christians and the formerly persecuted Jews contributed essentially to the great cultural flowering of the period. The *Mozārabes*, Christians who retained their faith on the payment of annual dues, were allowed their own places of worship. And throughout the Islamic period—save for a few years before its recapture—the city of Toledo kept its cathedral, its archbishop and its liturgy. Despite the strict religious principles of the twelfth-century Moroccan rulers and the subsequent flight of numerous *Mozārabes* to the Christian kingdoms of the north, the cultural traditions of earlier ages was strong. It was the works of men like Avempace (*d.* 1138) who drew on the Aristotelian commentaries of the tenth-century Al Farabi of Damascus, and above all his great follower Averroes of Cordova (1126–98) who contributed so essentially to the intellectual ferment of twelfth-century Europe.

Church reform in Europe during the tenth century

The ninth century was a period of fierce rivalry for the control of central authority, of cynical and brutal struggle by lesser potentates for independence from that authority, and of invasions from outside Europe. Yet gradually, if only by force of custom, lay society was evolving commonly accepted principles of organization and legitimacy that were slowly to gain—during later generations—ever-growing effectiveness.

In terms of power, the ninth century was a secular period. The immense power that the Church was to exercise in European society was a thing of the future, and as the tenth century opened the Church, in all its organs, was at one of its lowest points. Many of Europe's greatest bishoprics were, in effect, the hereditary fiefs of the local great family. If the family did not actually occupy the see, it appointed its own nominees as a matter of course. In other sees, the appointments were made by the king. The bishops themselves shared the ambitions and morals of their turbulent class and were also expected to pay a considerable sum of money to their patrons on entering their office. In feudal terms this was construed as the "relief" that any heir paid his overlord on taking up his inheritance, to clear him of the outstanding obligations of his predecessor and as recognition that he held the fief from a higher power.

Sins of Simony

In ecclesiastical terms such payments amounted to the sin of "simony." The name was derived from the Samaritan sorcerer, Simon Magus, who, according to the account in the *Acts of the Apostles*, attempted to buy spiritual power from Christ's apostles. In practical terms, simony produced a chain reaction: the bishop, who had paid a heavy fee to enter his see, recouped his payment by charging for the rights of ordination to his inferiors, and they in their turn charged the faithful for the very benefits of religion. It is not hard to understand the outrage of ecclesiastical reformers. But to the kings and magnates of early medieval Europe it seemed totally reasonable that bishops, who after all were vast landowners, should accept the same obligations as their lay colleagues.

Not only were the bishops subject to the feudal ceremony for receiving their lands from their lord, but by the ninth century the king was also investing them with the ring and staff, the symbols of their spiritual power. Thus the regular offices of the Church had become almost indistinguishable from the great secular estates which they often equaled in wealth. The secularization of Church property extended to the lowest levels. The parish church was usually the personal property of the local landowner who disposed of it at will; often the priests—most of whom were married, clerical celibacy being a thing of the future—treated their parishes as hereditary holdings and might well enrich their own families by granting Church lands to laymen in return for payment.

Conditions of Monastic life

Conditions were little better in the monasteries which, springing from the great movement initiated by St. Benedict in the sixth century, were the heirs to a great tradition of piety and retreat from the world. During the course of the centuries, they had grown rich through large endowments which they had received from pious benefactors. In their turn, they became objects of the ambitions of the lay aristocracy. It was not uncommon for the richer monasteries to be controlled by absentee lay abbots who unscrupulously engrossed the revenue of the house to their own uses. In other cases the monks themselves might form themselves into a college of canons, forsaking their monastic vows and the ideals of the life of communal poverty in order to live off the income of the monastery in their own houses complete with wives and families.

When matters had reached this pass, the very nature of the Benedictine Rule contributed to increase rather than mitigate the decline. St. Benedict's Rule had been merely a rule of conduct not dependent on a central organization. In the past, the autonomy of each monastery in this cell-like structure had been an element of strength, and the monasteries' adherence to the Rule had been ensured by visitations from the local bishop. But in a world where the episcopate was itself in dire need of reform, European monasticism was without a guardian. There are many recorded instances from both the ninth and tenth centuries, and indeed later, of reforming abbots being maltreated and expelled by the inmates of the house they had come to purge.

The respect for the ideals that monasticism had proclaimed was not dead, and pious laymen and ecclesiastics were to be found. But the Church as an organization was desperately in need of leadership from outside to help in putting its own house in order. In the eleventh century, as we shall see, the very papacy itself was to require the strong hand of a pious emperor for its reform.

Monastic reform

In the early years of the tenth century, however, the movement for monastic reform, so important to the Church as a whole, owed its effective beginning to the initiative of a lay ruler. In 910, Duke William I of Aquitaine, called the Pious, founded a monastery at Cluny, in the French province of Burgundy. It is possible that this initiative might have produced few lasting results had it not been for the forceful personality of the second abbot, Odo. During his reign, from 927 to 942, Odo made Cluny the leader of

Manuscript from the monastery of Luxeuil, one of the earliest foundations of the Benedictines.

Europe, is founded in 910

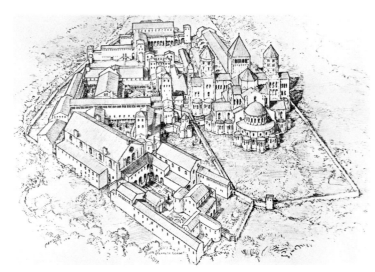

Reconstruction of the abbey buildings at Cluny when this was the greatest church in Christendom.

the movement of reform that was gathering strength everywhere in Europe. However, Duke William had given the new house one priceless advantage, which made Cluny a truly remarkable institution at the time of its foundation. The Duke surrendered, for himself and his heirs, all rights that he had as founder.

Thus from the outset Cluny was freed from the dangerous ties to the lay aristocracy that had brought disaster to so many monasteries in the past. Abbot Odo added to this another great guarantee of independence when he won exemption both for Cluny and her sister houses—both present and future— from episcopal visitation. On these bases, and on that of his own immense reputation, Odo was able to begin a process which, under the autocratic rule of a great line of abbots, was to produce what was in effect a new monastic order. Odo himself was summoned by Hugh the Great, the virtual ruler of France, to reform the house of Fleury on the Loire, and this was to become in its turn a major center of reform.

At the very end of the tenth century began the rule of Abbot Adilo (994–1048). Under him and his successor Hugh (1049–1109), Cluny reached the highwater mark of its influence and wealth. The strength of the reform rested not only on the qualities of these great abbots but, more important still, on the tight organization whereby Cluny itself retained control over all the houses that accepted its reforming agents or were founded under its auspices. Every year the priors of the Cluniac houses, of which there were some two hundred

by the late-eleventh century, met at Cluny under the presidency of the abbot. The effect of this annual convocation was carried through by a well-administered system of visitation, the houses of the order being divided into ten provinces.

Thus within two centuries the prestige of European monasticism, once so low, was immense, and its leaders were men of considerable influence both in the Church and in lay affairs. But it is perhaps not surprising that an organization as

The garden of Paradise ; Romanesque sculpture from the abbey of Cluny.

powerful as Cluny began, in its turn, to lose touch with the spirit of the reform. The abbey building of Cluny proclaimed its great wealth; the luxuriant carvings and gold and jeweled church ornaments might be regarded as celebrating the glory of God, but by the critics of Cluny they were looked upon as a betrayal of the monastic vows of poverty. Thus in the early eleventh century Cluny itself was to give birth to a movement devoted to another great reform of European monasticism.

The Saxon kings of Germany

As the body of the Church gained in vigor through the reform of monasticism, the greatest power in medieval Europe, the German empire, was also gathering its strength. Its true founder is generally recognized as being Henry I, known as Henry the Fowler, the Duke of Saxony, who was elected to succeed Conrad I in 919.

During his reign, Henry succeeded in recovering the duchy of Lotharingia, part of the old central kingdom, from its allegiance to France. Then, after having been forced for five years to pay tribute, Henry defeated the Magyars at the

Henry the Fowler, Duke of Saxony.

battle of Riade in 933. In addition, he extended the northern frontiers of Germany at the expense of the pagan Wends in Brandenburg, and he took measures to protect his frontiers with fortified strong points and by introducing reforms into the training of his Saxon army.

Internally he did nothing to hamper the great power of the old duchies, ruling what might almost be described as a federal state. Nevertheless, he secured the recognition of his son, Otto I, as his successor. In 936 Otto I became King of Germany. His position was, however, contested at first by his brother Duke Henry of Bavaria,

Duke Henry of Bavaria, known as the Wrangler.

while Eberhard of Franconia also rose in rebellion. The new king successfully met the challenge and survived another wave of rebellion in the 950s in which his son was involved. In 951 he assumed the title of King of Lombardy, and eleven years later he was to be crowned Emperor.

Otto is often regarded as the true founder of the medieval German Empire. The title had been in abeyance for fifty years when he revived it. Certainly the Ottonian empire was essentially different from its Carolingian predecessor. Geographically, it was virtually coterminous with the kingdom of Germany, though its rulers still retained ambitions in Italy and nourished even more wide-reaching claims.

The monarchy was now in theory elective, and that theory was eventually to have far-reaching consequences. By the second half of the tenth century, the power of the regional German landowners had become so entrenched as to be a permanent danger to the central power. Otto attempted to meet this situation by balancing the power of the lay magnates with that of the great prelates of the Church. Under what has sometimes been called the "Ottonian system," Otto relied increasingly on these ecclesiastical magnates for the chief officers of the administration of the empire. As we shall see in a later chapter, this close involvement of Church and State was to have historic consequences.

Battle at the Lechfeld

On a battlefield littered with corpses and discarded weapons, the victorious Otto I had his cheering troops proclaim him Emperor. Germany had been close to civil war, and rebellious nobles had allied themselves with the barbarian Magyars, who were intent on destroying what passed for civilization in tenth-century Germany. It was Otto's achievement to unite the Germans against both the rebels and the invading Magyars. His new "Roman" Empire differed from the old in its strongly Christian character. Otto was the protector of the Church and constantly encouraged missionary work among the Slavs. His territorial ambitions also lay in the East, but in these he was largely frustrated. Nevertheless, Otto's victory at the Lechfeld in 955 ensured that much of Central Europe would be safeguarded for Latin Christianity. And even the defeated Magyars, who settled in Hungary, became, under their great king St. Stephen, a Christian nation.

Part of the Chalice of St. Udalrich, Bishop of Augsburg loyal priest and military leader under Otto I, and hero of the battle of Lechfeld against the Magyars.

Opposite Otto II, his Empress Theophano and the future Emperor Otto III pay homage to Christ in Majesty by the traditional Byzantine proskynesis. To the left and right of Christ are St. Maurice and the Virgin.

The battle fought on the Lechfeld outside Augsburg on St. Lawrence's day, August 10, A.D. 955, was highly significant for the whole of Europe. The victory of King Otto I over the Magyars was directly connected with the foundation of his empire—and with the constitution of the German imperial Church as a leading political power—which was to survive till its destruction at Napoleon's hands. The other consequences of Otto's victory were the realignment of the eastern frontier of Bavaria with Austria; the foundation of the Hungarian kingdom with the coronation of Stephen as king; and the formation of Germany's eastern policy for the next 1000 years.

On August 8, 955, Udalrich or Ulrich, Bishop of Augsburg, stood at the eastern gate of the town—clad only in his stole and without shield, helmet, coat of mail or sword—while the attack on his beleaguered town was at is fiercest, and exhorted his people to stand firm. When the attack had been fended off, Udalrich spent the night in prayer. While the nuns walked in procession through the city streets praying and chanting, he lay prostrate in devotion on the cathdral floor, beseeching the Virgin Mary to protect his people and liberate the city. On the following morning, he celebrated communion with his people; the Magyars withdrew from the city as Berthold, the son of Arnul, the Count Palatine, brought them the news of Otto I's approach.

These strange and deadly enemies, the Magyars, had already made a deep impression on the peoples settled in the German territories by the time they confronted Otto I's army in 955. Contemporary chroniclers testify to the shock the inhabitants experienced on seeing them; they called the Magyars monsters, fiendish deformities of the human race. According to Widukind of Corvey, Otto I called them "the enemies of God and man" and "the enemies of Christ" before the battle. This gives some indication of the degree of terror aroused by the Magyars, with their Mongolian features, when they swept into western Europe on their raiding expeditions in the fifty years prior to the Battle of Lechfeld.

Who were the Hungarians or Magyars? They had been settled for centuries in the south Russian grasslands between the Don, Donets and Dnieper rivers until they were driven out in A.D. 889 by the Petchenegs from the region of Atelkuz. They invaded Bulgaria in 894 at the instigation of Byzantium, were repulsed by Simon, and crossed the Veretz Pass to settle on the plains on the other side. Under Arpad's leadership, seven Magyar tribes, and an eighth tribe of Khazars known as Kabars, settled on the banks of the River Tiza and the middle reaches of the Danube. The Hungarian plains served as a gathering ground for these nomads, from which they set out on their raids. After the death of Arnulf of Carinthia in 899, they penetrated into Frankish territory across the Danube and destroyed the empire of Great Moravia. Between 896 and 955 they mounted campaigns into central and western Europe. They made thirty-two raids into east Frankish territory; Bavaria was attacked in 907, Franconia in 918, Lotharingia in 920, and Saxony in 924. In 899, 921 and 947 they penetrated into Italy, burning Pavia and reaching as far as Spoleto. They plundered Burgundy, West Franconia and Swabia in 937 and 951, and reached Spain in 943.

The battle of Lechfeld threw the Magyars back towards Hungary, where they finally became settlers. The young Vajk, son of Arpad's great-grandson Gezá, married Gisela of Bavaria in 995 and was baptized with the name of Stephen, patron saint of Passau. His kingdom survived until Horthy, the imperial regent, gambled it away in World War II.

The Magyars, in fact, had had close acquaintance with Christendom since the sixth century, through their Alanic and Armenian neighbors, their contacts with Byzantium, and some of their countrymen who were Roman mercenaries. In fact in the background to the Battle of Lechfeld was the struggle

between Byzantium and Rome for the religious and political hegemony over central and eastern Europe, the same region that today is the battleground of the conflict between the western world and Russia. In the early part of the tenth century, the Bulgarians went to Rome for help in their fight against Byzantine imperialist designs, while the Moravians went for help to Byzantium out of fear of the Bavarian Latin Church and Carolingian imperialism.

It was a Bavarian nobleman, Berthold, who reported Otto's approach to the Hungarian forces outside Augsburg. The ties between the Bavarians and the Magyars formed the direct prelude to the Battle of Lechfeld, which occurred in the middle of civil war in the German lands, and was its peak and its turning point. In the years before 955, Otto was involved in quarrels with his brothers and then with his sons. In the year 954 the dukes who were in revolt against Otto, and the nobility of Swabia, Bavaria and Lotharingia, were in communication with the Magyars through the intermediary of the Count Palatine, Arnulf. Otto's traitorous son Ludolf provided Horka Bulcsu, the leader of the Magyars, with guides into Franconia and opened the way for him into the heart of his father's territory. In Bavaria, Duke Henry and Ludolf, brother and son of Otto, were fighting each other for power. Widukind wrote that "even the bishops showed themselves not a little irresolute, as they sent envoys to both parties."

Yet King Otto I's greatest victory was won before the battle: in the reaction against the Magyar forces that swept across large areas of Germany in 954, he was able to bring the civil war to an end and unite the Franks, Swabians, Bavarians and Bohemians under his command. The Magyars were surprised to find a powerful coalition ready to meet them since, till then, they had been able to exploit the civil strife dividing Germany. The Saxons took no part in the battle, for they were fighting the Slavs from the Elbe; neither did the Lotharingians, nor Henry of Bavaria, who was still suffering from a wound received in an earlier struggle against his brother, Otto; nor did Otto's son Ludolf, who had been rendered powerless.

Otto's victory at Lechfeld thus secured his kingdom, and according to Widukind's account, he made his troops proclaim him *Imperator*, Emperor, on the battlefield itself. In those days, victory in battle was seen as God's verdict and so Otto's claim was legitimized. His coronation on February 2, 962, in Rome marks the foundation of Germany: a precarious consolidation of the Germanic races who had fought each other for their independence ever since the collapse of the Carolingian Empire. This was the origin of the "Holy Roman Empire of the German Nation" which survived until 1806.

It is true that the adjunct "Roman" originated with Otto II; "Holy" was added in the twelfth century by Frederick Barbarossa; and "of the German Nation" did not come until modern times. Otto I and his successors did not lay claim to Charlemagne's position. As rulers over Germany and the greater part of Italy (and from 1033 over Burgundy too), these German emperors occupied a special position as protectors of the Church and the papacy. The Emperor had a degree of honorary precedence over other western kings (even this was frequently challenged) but no overlordship or power to command.

Once peace was secured in central Germany by the victory of 955, Otto was able to pursue his territorial gains in the south, in Italy, and in the northeast. Italy was still in the power sphere of his Byzantine opponent, who had been the unseen ally of the Magyar Horka Bulcsu on the Lechfeld. And there was still a chance that the Byzantine Church could gain ground in Hungary, Bohemia and Moravia, and in Poland, and thus indirectly gain political support for the Eastern Emperor.

Early in 955 Otto had driven the Slavs back to the Oder with his victory at Recknitz in Mecklenburg, and before the Lechfeld battle began he had sworn to found at Merseburg a missionary bishopric dedicated to St. Lawrence if he were the victor. It seems highly probable that Otto considered it his life's vocation to incorporate the northern and eastern Slavs into his empire. The victory at Lechfeld, which ensured the safety of the southeast, created the necessary military conditions, and Rome was

Left The Holy Lance, sacred symbol of the Ottonian Empire. It represented the Emperor's authority in military and political as well as religious spheres.

Below This illustration of an attack on a fortified town from an eighth-century manuscript reflects the style of battle of the Ottonian Empire.

to provide the spiritual impetus. The emperorship would confer a mandate as guardian of the Church and protector of Christendom, and the papacy would sanction this role.

The most important experiences of Otto's youth had had to do with the Slavs: he had already taken part in the Slav wars of 928–29, he spoke Slavonic, and a Slav princess bore him his son William, later Archbishop of Mainz. Conversion by the sword, the *deus teutonicus* or "German god," proved its worth by success in battle. The war against the Slavs was pursued with utter ruthlessness by the margraves Hermann and Gero, and by Otto himself, from 938 to 950. Widukind testifies to the Saxons' admiration for the enemy's bravery (many of the Saxon nobility were confederates of heathen Slav princes, or even related to them by marriage). The Slavs suffered terrible losses and those who survived defeat in battle were often hanged.

With Otto I began the German expansion towards the East, which penetrated as far as Riga and Reval in the twelfth and thirteenth centuries. In the tenth century, this expansion encountered formidable opposition. The Saxon nobility was opposed to German colonization east of the Elbe because it could not raise as high levies from the Christian German peasants as from the heathen Slavs. (Later on in the Middle Ages the Teutonic Order in Prussia reacted in a similar way.) In any case, Germany lacked the population and the economic power for such an undertaking. It was not until more than three hundred years later that settlers from Germany and the West penetrated into the regions that German swords had fought over in vain for so long.

Otto I himself saw his political expansion into Eastern Europe as a missionary obligation to propagate the faith of the Latin Church. In 955, probably immediately after the Battle of Lechfeld, Abbot Hadamar of Fulda was sent by Otto to lay his plan for Magdeburg before Pope Agapetus II. Agapetus entrusted the creation of new bishoprics to the king's judgment. Magdeburg was to become a "German Rome." At the Synod of Ravenna the new metropolitan see was allotted the suffragan bishoprics of Havelberg and Brandenburg, the new bishoprics of Merseburg, Zeitz and Meissen, and the newly founded Polish bishopric of Posnania. Otto even thought of adding Prague. Magdeburg was to rank first among all the churches to the east of the Rhine, and her establishment was to consist of twelve cardinal priests, twelve cardinal deacons, and twenty-four cardinal sub deacons, on the pattern of Rome.

This was a great plan and, if it had been realized, a huge area of Eastern Europe would have come under German domination. But it could never become reality: the German church had too little manpower or spiritual strength to carry the eastern mission through. In 959, Otto had the greatest difficulty even in finding a bishop and a priest for his proposed mission to Russia.

The strongest resistance to Otto's over-ambitious

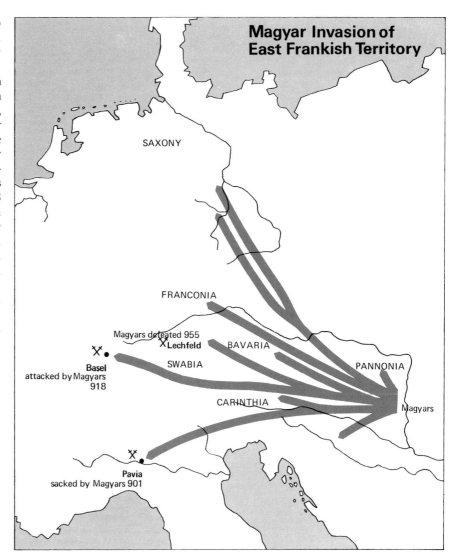

Magyar Invasion of East Frankish Territory

SAXONY

FRANCONIA

Magyars defeated 955

Lechfeld

BAVARIA

SWABIA

PANNONIA

Basel attacked by Magyars 918

CARINTHIA

Magyars

Pavia sacked by Magyars 901

mission to the East came from Mainz and Rome. William of Mainz, the first bishop of Germany and Otto's son by a Slav wife, entered his protest in a letter sent directly to the Pope. According to William, his father's explanation that he was extending the boundaries of Christendom by converting the Slavs to Christianity was simply a cover for his real motive: their political subjugation. The son's attack on the father must have startled the empire—but William maintained this allegation to his death. Then, in 968, Pope John XIII set the boundary of the archbishopric of Magdeburg at the River Oder. In this, the papacy sought to appear as protector and ally of the nations whose previous independence was now threatened by the might of Germany. The Pope, like the Holy Roman Emperor, certainly wanted a Latin Western Europe to oppose the heathen and the Greek Byzantine East; but he was not eager to see it take the form of an eastern German empire.

So the greatest of Otto's plans for the East failed. It was not until several hundred years later that Magdeburg exerted any influence in the eastern territories, and then through its municipal laws and its citizen's rights. The great Slav uprising of 983

A coin bearing the figure of the warrior-Emperor Otto the Great.

A tenth-century German ivory plaque showing Otto the Great bringing a model of Magdeburg Cathedral to Christ. Otto founded Magdeburg as a German Rome which would unite his Empire with Eastern Europe.

repulsed both Christendom and the German rule east of the Elbe. Contemporary witnesses such as Dietmar of Merseburg and Adam of Bremen thought the aggressive behavior of the German princes was the immediate provocation. Dietmar complained further that even Christians were rejoicing over the renewed power of paganism among the Slavs.

At that point, however, Otto the Great's grandson, the young Otto III, had the wisdom to rescue Otto's work and preserve his achievement from complete destruction. His conception of the new Europe gave the victory at Lechfeld and the German mission to the East a more lasting significance.

Otto III had the courage to reject the conception of the empire as a military alliance of a dozen German nobles and more than a dozen German prelates seeking to extend their rule eastwards. He tried to give the empire a reality as a federation of Latin-Christian peoples. Therefore, he named the Polish Duke Boleslaw "brother and colleague of the empire" (*frater et cooperator Imperii*). In the face of the strongest resistance both within Germany and

from the papacy, Otto III succeeded—with the aid of his Slav friends—in converting Poland and Hungary to Christianity, and thus won them for the West. In both countries he founded an independent church. Voytech-Adalbert, Otto III's great friend and the first Czech Bishop of Prague, became the great Western apostle to the Slavs, with support from both the Emperor and Pope. Adalbert founded the Benedictine monastery of Brewnow near Prague and settled it with Roman Benedictines, as a starting point for the conversion of Poland and Hungary.

Adalbert's pupil, Astrik-Anastasius, founded the great Hungarian abbeys of Martinsburg and Pecsvarad; Adalbert baptized King Stephen (who was later canonized); and Astrik became the first leader of the Hungarian Church. Adalbert died a martyr's death at the hands of the Prussians in 997, and his funeral at Gnesen was a moving demonstration of faith. He was buried by Duke Boleslaw in the presence of the Emperor, and his martyr's grave became a rallying point for the foundation of the Polish Church. Gnesen was created an archbishopric

96

in his honor. Otto III's friend, Bruno of Querfurt, set out from Hungary and traveled as a missionary into the Russian steppes as far as the Volga, coming into friendly contact with the new Christian state of St. Vladimir in Kiev.

As for Hungary, the foundation of the archbishopric of Gnesen as a see independent of the German Church gave King Stephen the legitimate hope that conversion to Christianity need not mean submission to Germany. Shortly after the creation of the see of Gnesen, Stephen married Gisela, sister of the Duke of Bavaria, and they carried through the conversion of Hungary to Christianity together.

Otto III wanted to complete the work begun at the Battle of Lechfeld by his grandfather Otto I, using new, more modern means. To mark the new European status of his Polish "brother and colleague" Boleslaw, Otto gave him a golden circlet and a duplicate of the holy lance (said to have pierced Christ's side on the Cross) which Otto I had borne in the Battle of Lechfeld. Otto III even traveled to Aix—as his grandfather, Otto the Great, had done before him—and descended into the tomb of Charlemagne, opened his grave, took the golden cross from his neck and some of his clothing, drew a tooth from his mouth and clipped his fingernails. In this way he hoped to transfer to himself some of Charlemagne's power and charisma. When he died prematurely in 1002, his successor Henry II buried Otto III's remains in Augsburg, in Udalrich's tomb chapel. The holy power of the bishop who had seen the Battle of Lechfeld, together with that of the dead Emperor, were to help Henry bear his heavy burden of office.

These, then, were the consequences of the Battle of Lechfeld. If the Magyars had won, the Byzantine East would have penetrated with them deep into the heart of central Europe. Otto I's victory made it possible to gain Hungary and Poland and to safeguard Bohemia and Moravia for the West and for its Latin Church. Byzantium gained Russia and came to a halt at the Balkans—where the Roman papacy and the central European powers came into conflict with Russia and the Orthodox Church in 1914.

FRIEDRICH HEER

Left The crypt of the church at Quedlinburg founded by Otto the Great on his eastern route.

Below left and right The four provinces of the Ottonian Empire, Sclavinia (Slavs), Germania, Gallia and Roma bringing tribute to Otto III in attitudes of total subjection. Otto is shown enthroned and crowned in Imperial majesty.

The birth of Hungary

The battle of the Lechfeld, so important to Western Europe, had an equally profound influence on events in Central and Eastern Europe. The almost total annihilation of their army compelled the Magyars to settle in their new home on the Hungarian plains, and within sixty years they had embraced

The Holy Crown of St. Stephen, King of Hungary.

Christianity. Under King Stephen I (997–1038), who was later canonized, they accepted Christianity from Rome, a process that had been begun by Stephen's father, Duke Geza. The new king accepted not only religion but also his royal title and crown from Pope Sylvester II. Although he had to face opposition from some of his pagan nobility, he was able to push through his religious programs and also to lay the basis of a royal administration closely modeled on that of the German empire. During the eleventh century the new kingdom, halted in its westward advance, also lost part of its territory in the southeast to the nomadic Patzinaks. But this loss was balanced for a time by the Hungarian conquest, which gave the new state an important seacoast on the Adriatic.

Thus in the early eleventh century the main contours of medieval Europe had emerged and the political position of the German emperors seemed assured.

Sung China

The empire of Otto and his Saxon successors was roughly contemporary with a renewed period of grandeur and prosperity in the world's largest empire, China. We have seen how in the late ninth century the glories of the T'ang dynasty were subject to internal divisions and attacks over the frontiers by Asian barbarians. After the deposition of the last T'ang emperor in 907, there followed the fifty-year period generally known as the age of the Five Dynasties. The largest single territory was that in the north, which was subject to the fluctuating rivalries of short-lived emperors—some remotely related to the T'ang, others of barbarian extraction. But in fact the true inheritors and preservers of the T'ang civilization were large states to the south—states that had already begun to assert their independence in the last years of the ninth century—for the most part well ordered and free of internal or external strife. In the north this period saw the surrender of a large stretch of territory between the Great Wall and Peking to the nomad tribes of the Kitans. This surrender was to be confirmed by the consolidating and peacefully intentioned Sung dynasty. The area was not recovered for another three centuries, when the whole of China came under the rule of the Mongols.

The Sung dynasty, regarded by some as the most enlightened age of Chinese history, was founded at a time when the Chinese were fully conscious of their national identity, one based on a common written language, an old tradition that the lands of the Middle Kingdom

Palace in a landscape; Sung dynasty painting by Chao Po-chü.

should be governed by no more than one head, and by an administration with a common training and a common devotion to the religious and philosophical teachings known as Confucianism. The turmoil of the Five Dynasties was generally felt to be an unwarranted disturbance of the natural and proper order of things. The Sung came to power through a *coup d'état*, but the first Sung emperor, Chao Kuang-yin, was a man of unusual stamp. Such was the force and moderation of his character that he was able to prevent the massacre of the deposed imperial family, and to free himself of the threat of a military coup by awarding large estates remote from the capital to the chief commanders of his own army who, in exchange, resigned their commands. He then set about restoring the civil administration. Thus began a period marked throughout by moderation and a remarkable concern on the part of a line of outstanding emperors for the arts of government. Within thirty years, the rulers of the southern states had accepted with comparatively little opposition the new dynasty. The eleventh century was to be one of the golden ages of Chinese history.

Buddhism

Ruled by an imperial house whose main concern was the maintenance of peace and the efficient administration of the empire's immense resources, China was free from the rebellions and threats of rebellion that had been all too common under the dynamic yet oppressive rule of the T'ang. The period was one of renewed study of the Chinese classics, and also of an attempt to integrate foreign systems, such as Indian Buddhism, into a single all-embracing universal system based on a radically rethought Confucianism. The advance of scholarship was greatly facilitated by the fact that, even under the Five Dynasties, the classics had been printed for the first time; their resulting diffusion and availability produced an intensity of commentary and study that may be reasonably compared with the impact of the printing of the Christian texts on the age of the sixteenth-century Reformation in Europe.

After an abortive attempt to expel the Kitans in the first years of the eleventh century, the third emperor of the Sung dynasty accepted the situation and agreed to

pay a large annual subsidy to those nomadic invaders. The outcome was a century of peace for the Chinese and a century of exposure to civilization for the Kitans themselves. In an age when the settled populations of the Far East were always liable to the depredations of more barbaric and aggressive neighbors, the Kitans were to suffer the fate of the Chinese themselves and fall to the armies of their former subjects, the hardy tribes of the Kin or Chin, the "golden people." Sung China failed to appreciate the gravity of this new threat, and as a result still larger territories to the north were lost.

A Golden Age

Yet despite its reduced state, China, thanks largely to the pacific policies of the Sung emperors, was able to boast a population far in excess of its predecessors and of course far larger than anything beyond its frontiers. It has been estimated, on the basis of the contemporary imperial census of families, that in 1124 the population of China was already at the 100,000,000 mark. The prosperity of the empire was due both

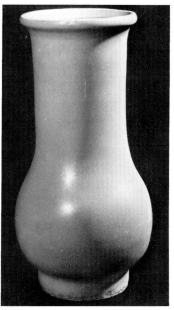

Fine example of a Sung vase.

to the long period of internal peace and also to the enlightened policies of its rulers.

Wang An-shih, the finance minister of the Emperor Shen Tsung (1068–85), believed that the wealth of the Chinese empire derived from the peasants; he aimed at lessening the tribute owed by the provinces to the capital, substituting money taxes for labor obligations and thus weakening the hold of the money lenders.

The "New Laws" were certainly not aimed at social justice but rather at introducing greater efficiency and flexibility into the administration of imperial finances. Wang An-shih belonged to the party of the Innovators; and the political struggles between them and their opponents, the Conservatives, contributed to the weakening of the empire and hastened its capitulation to the Kin. The eventual triumph of the Conservatives, who rested their policy on strict conformity to the precepts of Confucianism and the continuance of the practices of the past, was to color all aspects of Chinese civilization. It certainly mitigated against originality of expression in the established arts, such as bronzeworking. However in the relatively new art of porcelain, not discovered until the eighth century, artists enjoyed comparative freedom; and Sung porcelain is generally regarded not only as the first, but also as the finest produced in China.

The Viking World

The explorations of Eric the Red, remarkable as they were, are only a part of the story of Viking conquest and exploration. The raiders from the sea were a fearful and bloody terror to the sedentary populations of Europe, from Scotland to the Mediterranean. The predatory attacks of the Vikings seemed to threaten the new civilization rising from the Dark Ages with utter destruction. The sack of the Holy Island of Lindisfarne off the northeast coast of England in 793 presaged the storm. Adventurers from Denmark and Norway set up kingdoms in Ireland and Man, won control of most of the northern and eastern parts of England, established themselves in northern France, raided in the Mediterranean, and carved a kingdom for themselves in southern Italy.

For centuries, the Scandinavian peoples had been in trading contact with the Roman world, and one of the most important of their routes led down the rivers of European Russia to Byzantium. The famous Varangian Guard of the Eastern Emperors, in fact, was recruited from Norse adventurers. And in the ninth century, Swedish leaders set up a number of "Varangian"

Head of a Viking; carving from the Oseberg burial.

principalities, chief of which were Kiev and Novgorod. Under the semi-legendary Rurig of Novgorod and Igor of Kiev, the traffic in luxury goods going north and slaves and fur going south flourished, and the new states rapidly increased in wealth and power. By the end of the ninth century they had been united under the princes of Kiev and, with the defeat of the Magyars and the Patzinak Turks, the supremacy of the Varangian-Slav principality of Kiev was assured from the Black Sea to the Baltic.

Civilizing influence

Despite their well-earned reputation for brutality and vandalism abroad, the Scandinavians had developed a vigorous and confident tradition of their own. They produced, for instance, a unique and extremely beautiful style of animal carving and some of the world's finest masterpieces of the metal workers' art on their weapons and ships. The ship was central to Viking life; it was not only a mode of transport but also played an important part in the rituals of the dead and the beliefs about afterlife. But to a later age, it is the breathtaking beauty of the lines of these long, rakish yet supremely elegant vessels that catches the imagination. Perfectly adapted to their function of sea voyages followed by periods of river navi-

gation, the Viking ships are in themselves proof of the artistic and engineering skill of this wild, terrible but talented people.

The Scandinavian kingdoms

The Vikings were distinguished from the first wave of Germanic invaders of the fifth century by the rapidity with which they became assimilated with the conquered peoples. In Normandy, Norman England and Sicily the same pattern

Animal head, probably from a Viking ship.

is seen; and in vast areas of Slavic Russia, the adept and probably not very numerous conquerors had soon merged into their surroundings. Barely a century after the arrival of the first Varangian or Swedish princes, the Russian states accepted Christianity. Their leader, Grand Prince Vladimir of Kiev, was in effect a Slav.

Yet the heroic epic of exploration, rapine and conquest, in addition to peaceful trading, which even took the Vikings to the confines of Persia, should not blind us to the evolution of the Scandinavian kingdoms themselves. Under Harold Bluetooth (d. 985), Denmark was already a Christian kingdom. Although there was a short period when Denmark reverted to paganism under his son and successor, Sweyn, the great Canute not only restored the religion but also confirmed earlier conquests. He ruled over an empire that comprised England, Norway and Denmark itself.

The empire fell apart after Canute's death, but his successors were able to assert their independence from their great southern neighbor, the German empire. With the reign of Waldemar, Denmark achieved the frontiers she was to maintain for the rest of the Middle Ages, the southern provinces of Sweden and large tracts along the Baltic coast. Waldemar used the power of the Church to consolidate his rule, finding in Archbishop Absalom an able and willing right-hand man.

At about the same time, St. Eric IX of Sweden was using the pretext of holy war to conquer the territory of the pagan Finns on his eastern frontier. But the first of the Scandinavian countries to achieve a degree of unity was Norway, under Harold Fairhair (d. 933). His successful campaigns against the petty kings of the time led many to flee Norway for Iceland, but the history of the country after his time remained troubled. Many attempts were made to establish Christianity on a firm footing, but it was not until the eleventh century that solid progress was made.

In this period, too, Christianity became the dominant faith in Iceland, although the country had already been settled by Irish monks, themselves driven out by the ninth-century refugees from Harold I's Norway. In the year 930 the oldest surviving European parliament, the Icelandic Althing, was established at Thingvellir.

Voyagers West

A thousand years ago, the Norsemen or Vikings—Danes, Norwegians and Swedes—were terrorizing the greater part of Europe. Their earliest activities were chiefly limited to raiding and destroying, occupations for which their mastery of the sea admirably suited them. But in time they came to settle down—in the British Isles, in Iceland and in Greenland. It was this last, snow-covered and icebound land that was first colonized by Eric the Red—a man so named because of the color of his hair, his fiery temper and the murderous blood on his hands. Eric's son Leif, introduced Christianity to Greenland and in a voyage even farther west came upon a land, rich in grapes, that he named Vinland the Good. The Vikings did not stay long in Vinland and the colony in Greenland eventually expired. But five hundred years later, another voyager west, Christopher Columbus, rediscovered the "lost continent" and the world called it America.

To the eyes of a man born in Norway the western coast of Greenland had perhaps a homelike look. In the year 982, Eric the Red and his small band of Vikings rowed up a fjord—to this day called Ericsfjord—and found, hidden behind the barren cliffs, slopes and valleys where the grass grew lush in the long Arctic daylight.

Eric was not actually the first Norseman to visit Greenland. Some eighty years before, an Icelander named Gunbjorn had sailed along the glacial east coast of the island. Gunbjorn, however, had judged the land uninhabitable. Eric was now testing this verdict and disproving it. He sailed farther west than the boldest of earlier navigators, and spent three full years in systematic exploration.

Only after this long expedition was Eric able to return to Iceland, for his period of banishment was over. He had been called the Red, not for his red hair alone but also for the blood on his hands. Even among a people as quick as the Vikings to take up the sword or battle-axe, Eric and his family were noted for their feuding. When his father was exiled from Norway for a killing, the family emigrated to Iceland. After a couple of his serfs had offended a neighbor and been slain, Eric fought that neighbor and killed both him and another. For this offense he was driven out of the region.

Eric, however, had married a wealthy man's daughter, Thjodhilde, and he moved now to her lands in another and richer part of Iceland. While he was building his house of stone and sod, he entrusted to a neighbor his wooden beams—treasures in a land where wood was scarce. When he wanted them back, the neighbor refused to return them, and in the fight that followed, Eric killed two of his neighbor's sons. At the spring moot—the assembly of free men where cases at law were tried—Eric had the backing of his wife's family and other powerful friends. His punishment for the second double slaying was fairly light: three years in exile.

He used those years in a brilliant feat of explora-

tion. Perhaps even more brilliant was his calling the new island by so deceptive a name. For on his return to Iceland he invited his countrymen to join him in colonizing the fertile valleys of "Greenland," maintaining that "men would be much more eager to go there if the land had an attractive name." Eric was evidently a gifted promotor. He persuaded some five hundred persons to sail, with their cattle and equipment, over perilous seas to establish a colony in a land that they had never seen. Of twenty-five ships that sailed from Iceland that summer, only fourteen arrived. The others were either forced back or lost *en route*.

Yet the Viking ships were probably the finest in the world at that time. Viking craftsmen knew how to shape and fit the narrow planking of the hulls for speed, strength and water-tightness. Though the planking was only an inch thick, and thus light and flexible, it withstood the battering of the Atlantic waves. The shipwrights had iron and steel tools, but no iron was used to hold the vessel together; ribs and planks were joined with pineroot pegs. Wide and low amidships, with deep keels and even deeper side-rudders, these ships could resist the currents of the sea and sail almost directly into the wind. Prow and stern curved high out of the water, surmounted by the gleaming dragon's head and pronged wheel-like dragon's tail that were meant to frighten both human foes and evil spirits.

Members of the colony proceeded in various traditional ways to the "land taking." Some consulted fate by throwing their wooden beams overboard and settling wherever these drifted ashore. Eric, however, made his home on the most fertile spot in the whole country, which suggests that he was a man who left little to chance. He called his farm Brattahlid (Steep Slope), and it became at once a kind of headquarters for the colony.

It was Eric's son Leif who brought Christianity to the Greenland colony. On a voyage to Norway, he drifted off course to the Hebrides, where he stayed a

A gilt-bronze winged dragon, 11 in. long, from the front of a seventh-century Viking shield; part of the treasure found in a buried Viking royal ship at Sutton Hoo in East Anglia.

Opposite A half-excavated Viking boat burial in Denmark, showing the graduation towards the stark prow of the ship tomb. Stones were often used in the symbolic shape of a boat, probably when a real boat could not be spared.

winter, fell in love, and perhaps was converted. When he finally reached Norway he was officially baptized at the court of King Olaf Tryggvason, himself a recent convert. Olaf gave Leif a priest to accompany him to Greenland.

Christianity eventually overthrew the Norse gods, but for a long time the old beliefs and the forms of Norse society persisted with little change. The people continued to practice magic, divination and witchcraft. Men seem sometimes to have combined the old beliefs with the new, for tombstones have been found in the shape of the Christian cross, inscribed with prayers asking that the dead warrior may enter Valhalla. In remote Greenland, unconsecrated laymen collected the tithes and even administered the sacraments. Yet, when a man had to be buried without a priest to officiate, "a stake would be set up from the breast of the dead, and in due course, when

clerks came that way, the stakes would be pulled up and holy water poured into the place, and a service sung over them."

During its first century as a Christian colony, Greenland was part of the remote German diocese of Hamburg-Bremen. It was not until 1126 that Greenland received a bishop of its own who could consecrate priests there. This first resident bishop, Arnald, taught the Greenlanders how to make sacramental wine (which could also be used for other purposes) from the crowberries that grew plentifully on the high heaths. Arnald built a cathedral at Gardar—and the Greenland colony eventually had no less than sixteen parishes, with many churches, a monastery, and a convent. The churches were built of huge blocks of stone in a Cyclopean style of masonry quite unknown in Norway or Iceland. Apparently the Greenlanders borrowed the technique from the Scots.

Clearly, the colony prospered and achieved virtual self-sufficiency. The people ordinarily lived on fish and on milk and meat from their scrawny livestock, and on such vegetables as they could raise in the short growing season—mainly brassicas, leeks, and radishes. They had great difficulty in cultivating any sort of grain, so they had to do without beer and bread until a trading ship came in from Iceland, England, Norway or Ireland. What attracted traders to them was their walrus ivory and furs and the sturdy frieze cloth woven from the wool of their great flocks of sheep. They took advantage, too, of the one commodity they had in surplus—time; they carved utilitarian objects out of soapstone and wood. They also made miniature walruses and boats, chess pieces, draughtsmen and other playthings.

Trade and communication with the outside world became so vigorous during the twelfth and thirteenth centuries that the colony seems to have grown to two or three thousand people. A population of this size

Top The Oseberg cart, a ceremonial object found among the grave goods at Oseberg, is covered with elaborate carving representing scenes from myth and legend.

Above A runic inscription carved on stone, thought by the Germanic peoples to contain occult powers and used for magic and for monuments.

Right The ninth-century pictorial stones on Gotland represent scenes from myth and legend with mounted ships and warriors predominating. This is an unusual piece of carving showing a domestic scene.

paid thirteen danegelds or tributes. Seven of these payments are known to have amounted to 39,700 pounds of silver. The regular levies of danegeld in England were patterned on the Frankish example. In order to pay off the invaders, the Anglo-Saxon kings imposed on their subjects the first regular tax in English history.

Yet the Vikings could not always be bought off, because often tribute only whetted their appetite. Their kings and chieftains had little control over the young warriors who organized marauding expeditions. Such expeditions formed part of the usual education of the young Scandinavian aristocrat—and often the basis of his further fortunes. Later sagas explain the Viking conquests of England and Ireland as the work of vassals rebelling against the feudal authority of kings at home. But such explanations spring from an age in which feudal ties were more binding. The original movement, in fact, was chaotic and diverse. Norsemen were attracted by the political weakness of the Carolingian empire. In one instance, two of Charlemagne's sons invited them to fight the third. Usually, however, they did not wait for invitations, nor did they obey when their kings commanded peace. In general, the invasions appear to have been the response of a multitude of local aristocrats to land hunger and the pressure of overpopulation. The Viking expansion was a kind of *Völkerwanderung* by sea.

By 875 the Norsemen seemed to have surrounded Europe. They attacked it from every quarter and seemed on the point of conquering the entire continent. The century of raids was followed by a second century during which the invaders settled into the society that they had conquered. In the West they became lords of Frisia, Flanders, Normandy, and most of England and Ireland. In the East they introduced political unity to Russia by distributing cities among the brothers of a ruling house. They followed the odd practice of rotating the seats of power among the rulers whenever one of the princes died. The Vikings also assimilated the language and much of the culture of the Slavic milieu. By the year 1000, Byzantine missionary work had converted the Norse princes and the Russian populace to Christianity.

In Western Europe, effective resistance to the invasions followed the establishment of centralized governments. New kingdoms were organized independent of the decaying structure of Carolingian authority, and the Norsemen were contained. By driving the Danes back to the Humber, Alfred of Wessex became the only king in English history to receive the epithet of "the Great." Reconquest of much of the Danelaw by Alfred's sons and grandsons permitted the development of an English monarchy that ruled over a mixture of Anglo-Saxon and Christianized Danish subjects. Similarly, in France, Count Oddo of Paris in 887 drove a besieging force of Vikings back to Burgundy. This sort of resistance paved the way for the famous treaty between Rollo the Norman and Charles the Simple in 911. Rollo received all the region of the lower looted and left to their lamentations. Another expedition about the same time plundered Lisbon and Cadiz. Twice the same band of Vikings rowed up the Guadalquivir and sacked Seville. Finally they were driven off with the loss of many ships and men, but the survivors managed to regroup in France and to carry some Moorish captives, "blue men," into Ireland. Meanwhile, the Swedes exploded eastward, to conquer and rule the "land of the cities" that they found flourishing in western Russia along the Neva and Dnieper rivers. "We called them in to settle our quarrels and rule over us," a later Slavic chronicle explains. And it is true that the conquerors' rule first unified this land. In 865 these Swedish princes, known as the "Ros," organized a fleet that sailed down the Dnieper and across the Black Sea to besiege Constantinople. Only a storm, attributed by the inhabitants to the intercession of the Virgin, saved the Eastern capital of Christendom.

The Vikings sometimes agreed to forego pillage in return for regular tribute. As early as 810, Gottfrid of Denmark invaded Frisia with a fleet of two hundred ships and broke down the defenses organized by Charlemagne. He extorted from the local lords a tribute of one hundred pounds of silver. In subsequent raids on the Frankish lands, staggering sums were collected. By 926 the Frankish kingdom had

Left Buddha-like figure of Hiberno-Saxon origin on the handle of a bucket found in the Oseberg ship burial.

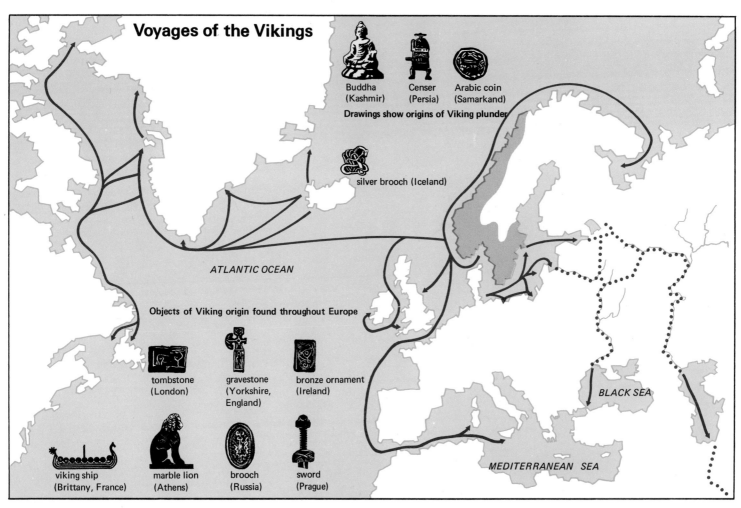

Voyages of the Vikings

Buddha (Kashmir) Censer (Persia) Arabic coin (Samarkand)

Drawings show origins of Viking plunder

silver brooch (Iceland)

ATLANTIC OCEAN

Objects of Viking origin found throughout Europe

tombstone (London) gravestone (Yorkshire, England) bronze ornament (Ireland)

viking ship (Brittany, France) marble lion (Athens) brooch (Russia) sword (Prague)

BLACK SEA

MEDITERRANEAN SEA

been curious dead ends. Hundreds of colonists were willing to forsake Iceland for more remote and inhospitable Greenland; it was only a short step to the far more abundant land of Vinland. And yet no permanent colony was ever established there. Our sources are so sparse that the reasons for this cannot be deduced. Certainly the Vikings usually showed no fear of long sea voyages or of hostile populations. Their chief historic role, after all, was that of the last great invaders of Europe.

Some say blandly that "Scandinavia had nothing to contribute to European civilization," and comment on the Vikings' taste for sacking monasteries, which were indeed the richest treasure houses they could find. They were, in their time, as dreadful as the earlier Germanic invaders in theirs. Others have seen the Vikings as shrewd traders, craftsmen technologically in advance of the Christian world; as men who, though illiterate, expressed in their art and epic an ample and creative spirit.

Norwegians began their first incursions into northern England in 787. Thereafter, they or their Danish cousins returned repeatedly. At first the raids came in summer; then the Norsemen built strongholds so that they could winter in the land. Later they took possession of whole districts of England. Other Vikings drove the Celtic hermits out of the far northern and western islands and likewise overran most of Ireland. Dublin and Limerick fell to them, and for a few short years—from 834 to 841—Norsemen ruled a unified Ireland. Central government did not survive, but for a long time the Norwegians kept firm regional control of the country. After 845, the chronicler says "there came great sea-cast floods of foreigners" to Ireland.

In 842, meanwhile, the Danes sacked London and Rochester. They expanded the "Danelaw"— the countries in which Danish law prevailed—until it embraced all England. At the same time other Danes were transforming Frisia and the Netherlands into bridgeheads for deeper incursions into the Holy Roman Empire and into France. They sacked

Utrecht, Nantes, Bordeaux and Paris, to name only some of the major towns. In the 860s, Paris fell again: "The number of ships grows," a chronicler wrote. "The endless stream of Vikings never ceases to increase. Everywhere the Christians are victims of massacres, burnings, and plunderings." The Vikings looted the city, established themselves on an island in the Seine, and were only driven away by other Vikings who had been bribed by French lords. Then in 886, came another siege of Paris: "The town trembles, and horns resound, the walls are bathed in floods of tears, the whole region laments, from the river are heard the horn blasts."

While Vikings thus pushed up the rivers of France from both the North Sea and the Atlantic, laying waste the land and especially the towns, other Norsemen sailed past Gibraltar into the Mediterranean. In 860, Pisa and Lucca fell to them, were

must have spread out to every pocket of land usable for pasture or tillage. In the twelfth and thirteenth centuries, walrus ivory was a highly valued product. Papal agents traveled all the way from Lucca to Greenland to collect it in lieu of a monetary tithe. By the fourteenth century, however, African ivory as well as English and Flemish cloth were displacing the exports of Greenland. With shrinking demand, trade diminished sharply and communication with the outside world became more and more infrequent. Bishops continued to be appointed to the see of Greenland, but seldom resided there. A papal letter of 1492 said that they had been reduced to venerating the altar cloth, as they had no priest.

That pathetic note is the last mention of the Greenland colony in the archives of Western Europe. What had happened to this community, seemingly so solidly established for five hundred years, to bring about its total extinction? Legends, both of Iceland and of the Eskimoes, tell us of battles with the nomadic hunters of the far north whom the Greenlanders called "Skraelingen." These attacked and destroyed the eastern part of the colony in 1360. According to their own story, the Eskimoes eventually destroyed the western settlement also. The last group of Greenlanders, they say, were burned down in their church.

What had happened and decimated the settlers before this, however, and reduced them gradually to helplessness, was the growing severity of their climate. These last settlers still had some contact with Europe, for fifteenth-century graves reveal that their clothes were in the current European middle-class fashion—long gown, short cloak and hood. Their bones, however, show that their bodies were stunted by malnutrition and scurvy. The glacier, moving into their fjords, had shut them in from marine hunting; the ice rising to a higher permanent level in their soil had destroyed their crops. Nature thus reduced all who did not join the Skraelings in their nomadic life or, as some surely did, emigrate back to Iceland or Norway. In 1540, an Icelander curiously named John Greenlander found on the site of the west coast settlement only the dead body of a man wearing hood and frieze clothes. "By him lay his iron knife, bent and almost worn away." In establishing a colony in Greenland, European man had apparently arrived at his natural limits.

It is one of the ironies of history that in 1492, the very year all communication between Greenland and Western Europe ceased, a Western European rediscovered America. For, as we know, a Greenlander had found the American continent five hundred years earlier. It was Eric the Red's son, Leif, who sailed far to the west and south of Greenland and, about the year 1000, discovered a place rich in grapes, which he called Vinland.

Vinland the Good, the sagas call it. Authorities debate the bearings indicated in the saga, but there is no doubt that Leif had happened upon North America. The first to follow up his exploration was his brother, Thorstein, who reached America three to six years later. Then another chief, Karlsevne,

A carved pictorial stone, one of a series on the island of Gotland c. 900, showing a Viking ship probably carrying the dead to the Other World.

took a colony to winter in Vinland. For a Greenlander, the new country was closer than Norway. Karlsevne encountered many Skraelings—the Greenlanders seem to have made no distinction between Indians and Eskimos—and traded bright red cloth for their furs. But eventually the colonists and the natives clashed. The Indians descended in a "great multitude of boats," and although the attack was beaten off, the Vikings realized that they were too few in number to conquer a hostile country. They sailed back to Greenland. There is no record of any later settlement, but for some time the Greenlanders continued to visit America for purposes of trade. Perhaps they were mainly seeking wood—some of their coffins were made of larch, which is thought to have come from the American coast.

Both Eric the Red's settlement of Greenland and Leif Ericson's discovery of America seem to have

The manuscript recording the discovery of Vinland by Leif Ericson, son of Eric the Red in A.D. 1000. The country he found full of vines is now known as North America.

Seine—henceforth known as Normandy—on condition that his men defend the land, receive baptism and do homage to Charles as their overlord.

The treaty tacitly assumed that the Norsemen would continue their raids on Brittany; the Bretons had to establish a line of defense themselves. The Normans soon acquired the language as well as the religion of their subjects and their nominal overlords. They also acquired outstanding skill as horsemen and as builders of forts and siege machinery. Firmly bound by feudal ties of allegiance, they became in the eleventh century the conquerors of England. In the same period, they sent an expedition into Sicily which, with the blessing of the Pope, seized the island from the Moors and founded a new south Italian kingdom. As in other places, the Vikings' native talent for war and government remained in evidence long after they were fully absorbed by the language, the economic system and the culture of their new land. A similar pattern of resistance and assimilation may be seen in Ireland, where in 1014 Brian of Munster defeated the Norse kings of Dublin; after this, the Norsemen became part of the complex tribal society of Ireland and dominated some of its cities, but their role of alien masters had ended.

At this very time, the Danes invaded England once more and almost gave a *pax normana* to England. From 1013 to 1042, King Canute and his sons undid the work of Alfred the Great. They tried to unite what remained of the Danelaw, Anglo-Saxon England, Scotland and Denmark under a single Scandinavian king's rule. Quite different from the old-style Viking raids, this was a unifying operation by a strong monarchy, no longer pagan, but Christian. "Merry sang the monks at Ely as Cnut the king rowed by."

In history, the Vikings remain an experience on the poetic fringe of the European memory. Perhaps because they were the last incursion of an unlettered and pagan people upon the Europeans, they left the impression of a primal tribe of brothers: rapacious, lusty, loyal to their chiefs and to each other, but given also to rebellion and fratricide. Yet they were skillful craftsmen and energetic traders who eventually governed thriving cities. In war they were subject to the madness they considered divine, the "going berserk" that doubles a man's strength and makes him immune to pain.

In the names of our Wednesday, Thursday, and Friday we still do honor to their three chief deities: Odin, Thor, and Frey. Odin: the subtlety and craft that built their ships, guided their merchants, taught their sailors the use of arms and horses and forts. Thor: the thunder god of violence. Frey: the god of fertility who made men rich in kinsfolk and ever poor in land. All are implicit in the three symbols sacred to Thor: the hammer, the battle-axe, and the sacred ring. These gods symbolize forces that drove the Vikings to exploration and conquest, forces not unrelated to the European "restlessness" that ultimately drove men to navigate and conquer most of the globe.   RENÉE WATKINS

Left A bronze die from Öland, showing a Norse hunter and two attacking bears. These dies were used to make bronze metal plates for helmets and other pieces of armor.

Detail of an animal headpost from the Oseberg ship burial; these headposts, intricately carved with zoomorphic designs, were probably meant to protect the dead.

An ornamental Danish axe-head of iron inlaid with silver.

During the eleventh century, a view of world history is dominated by the splendors of the Sung empire in China. Founded in the last decades of the previous century, it reached a peak during the eleventh century that entitles it to be regarded as one of the most brilliant epochs in the history of civilization. The European stage is commanded by the prestige and apparent power of the German empire founded by Otto I and ruled over by his descendants. But both the ambitions of the emperors and the ever-growing power of the great vassals contributed, with other causes, to a decline which even the reign of the great twelfth-century emperor Frederick Barbarossa did not reverse. By 1200, power in Europe was slipping from the hands of the German emperors and was taken up by the central kingdom of France.

The emergence of France as the dominant power in European affairs during the high Middle Ages was by no means a foregone conclusion. To observers of the coronation of Hugh Capet as king in 987 it must have seemed a very unlikely event. It is worth remembering how slow this rise was. Not for another two and a half centuries —centuries of constant struggle— was the French ascendancy to become obvious.

The French monarchy from Hugh Capet to Louis VI

At the time of his coronation Hugh Capet was perhaps the most important man in France. His family, founded over a century before by Robert the Strong, had already provided two kings during the troubled years of the later Carolingians. His lands, grouped around the important towns of Paris and Orléans, were strategically well-placed; among his feudatories were some of the most powerful men in the kingdom; and he himself enjoyed the support of the Church, to which in large measure he owed his election. But there were many houses with more extensive possessions, and at the opening of the eleventh century the map of France dramatically reveals the considerable threat of the provincial powers with which the Capetians had to contend.

In the south, the duchy of Gascony and the county of Toulouse were remote; to the north of them stretched the great duchy of Aquitaine, controlled by the house of Poitou; to the northwest, Brittany, never subdued by Charlemagne, maintained its ancient independence; and still farther north was the powerful duchy of Normandy, which was soon to be transformed into the strongest province of France by the efforts of Duke William. These were the main territories; but as the century advanced, the lands between Normandy and Aquitaine were gradually mastered by the small but dynamic county of Anjou.

Throughout France, the great lords who pressed upon the king were in their turn continually struggling to contain the ambitions of a mass of lesser vassals. Nowhere else in Europe did the full effects of feudal land tenure make themselves felt so rapidly as in France. Amid this multitude of magnates, each already striving to maintain his position within his duchy (the dukes of Burgundy, for example, failed and themselves became little better than bandits), each aimed to strengthen his position at the expense of his neighbors. The kings of the Capetian dynasty were in territorial terms one of the weaker groups in the kingdom. Their advantages were nebulous but, as it turned out, important. The change of dynasty from Carolingian to Capetian did not weaken the respect in which the kingship itself was held. Well aware that their hold on their own vassals was often little stronger than the ties of feudal obligation, the great feudatories were eager to acknowledge the theoretical supremacy of the king from whom their own authority ultimately derived.

The king, then, was the suzerain of all and beholden to none save God. Second, the monarchy enjoyed and cultivated the support of the Church, an element to be of increasing importance as the century went by. Third, the dynasty, by a remarkable demographic feat, was able to provide an unbroken line of male descendants for three and a half centuries. Each Capetian was careful to have his son crowned king before his own death. The ancient principle of election, never forgotten in Germany, was gradually, if only by force of custom, displaced by that of hereditary kingship.

Finally, the Capetians, unlike their Carolingian predecessors, were never greatly tempted to assert the full theoretical power of their office. They were content to devote their energies to making themselves absolute masters in their own domains and vassals.

The kings had to tread warily. In the middle of the century, Henry I—attempting to preserve his position in the dangerous wars between his two great vassals, William of Normandy and Geoffrey of Anjou—shifted alliances between them and suffered two humiliating defeats at the hands of William. His son and successor, Philip I (1060–1108), showed more circumspection and wiliness in seizing his

King Philip I of France.

advantage at the most opportune moment. He managed to extend the royal domain with small but significant accessions and to draw some advantage for himself from the civil wars which raged in Normandy between the sons of William the Conqueror.

The tide turns

It was during the reign of Louis VI that the tide finally turned. After a century of acceptance, the Capetian dynasty, whatever its weaknesses, had become the focus of what may be regarded as a nascent national feeling. Louis VI, tireless in his efforts to put down the petty baronage within the royal domain itself and active in asserting his rights as king in France abroad, left to his son a country more firmly governed than ever before. More important still, by marrying the young prince to Eleanor, heiress of the vast lands of Aquitaine, he seemed to have supplied the French

Illustration of the move to hereditary kingship: the eldest son is associated with the king in power.

Eleanor of Aquitaine.

monarchy with a firm base from which to assert its control of the whole country. It is one of the tragedies of French history that the weak and monkish Louis VII was unable to satisfy his passionate wife.

England before the Conquest

The empire of Canute the Great, King of Denmark, Norway and England, fell apart after his death

Page of an Anglo-Saxon royal Bible with an image of St. Ethelreda.

in 1035. For England his reign had been a period of peace and prosperity, but his sons were unable to continue the tradition of their father. In 1042, when the last of them died, the English recalled the senior surviving member of the house of Wessex from exile in Normandy. The son of Aethelred and his Norman wife, Emma, Edward was forty years old when he came to the throne. He had grown to manhood in a foreign land, and he now found himself in a country

where the great families, well-entrenched in the years after Canute, had little interest in a return to a powerful kingship.

Chief among these families was that of Earl Godwin, who was able to force the king to contract marriage with his daughter Edith. The marriage was merely a formality, for Edward seems to have taken a vow of celibacy on religious grounds. Despite a period of exile and disgrace during which the king was able to consolidate the position of his many Norman friends and ministers at court, the house of Godwin returned in irresistible strength in 1052. That same year, Edward made an immensely unpopular move by promising the throne to his cousin, William of Normandy, a promise he did not have the power to enforce. Godwin, who died the following year, and then his sons, soon gained control of the apparatus of government. Thanks to Edward's celibate life within marriage, there was no natural heir to the throne, and all but one of the remaining branches of the ancient royal house of Wessex had died out.

When King Edward himself died in January, 1066, he was succeeded by Harold Godwinson, elected by the Witan with the approval—so it was claimed—of the dying king. Revered during his own lifetime for his saintly character and in a later age beatified and canonized by the Church, Edward the Confessor has as his enduring monument the Abbey of Westminster, which was his foundation and to which he devoted most of the last years of his life.

It is easy perhaps to write Edward

Seal of Edward the Confessor.

off as a weak and ineffectual king, and indeed the facts of his reign reveal him as lacking the wily and aggressive ruthlessness required of a successful monarch during the eleventh century. But we should not forget the powerful position that the English earls had already built up by the time when the new king arrived from overseas to take up a taxing kingship, nor that Edward was then already past his prime. More important, it was Edward, who, by his choice, gave William of Normandy his strongest claim to the throne. Despite the immense power and prestige of the hated Godwin family during the last ten years of his life, Edward never went back on that choice. In fact, he did all in his power to ensure its acceptance by his English earls, to whom the choice was so unpopular. Although it was undoubtedly colored by hatred of the Godwin clan, Edward's decision on the succession was a wise one for England. He chose as his heir one of the most effective rulers in a Europe crowded with overmighty vassals and ineffective kings.

The Danegeld

One of the most remarkable powers of the English monarchy was that of levying a universal tax—called the "Danegeld"—on the population at large; and this was to provide a valuable source of revenue for the first Norman kings. Compared with any other state in contemporary Europe, except possibly the Empire, the England of Edward the Confessor boasted an administrative system and a monarchic potential second to none. It was a tool that the autocratic and gifted William of Normandy knew well how to use. When we add to these advantages the fact that by the very act of conquest William was able to rapidly eliminate the powerful territorial interests of the earls and replace them with chosen men who owed their very position in England to him, we can see that the strength of the Norman English monarchy—so important a factor in medieval English history—was by no means fortuitous.

It was soon demonstrated that, despite the inevitable humiliations and brutalities attendant on conquest, the saintly Edward had chosen his heir with considerable shrewdness. Finally, it is worth noting that Harold, Edward's successor, owed his kingship to election. Without the Norman conquest, England might well have found herself saddled with the divisive effects of an elective monarchy which, in the long run, was to destroy even the power of the mighty German emperors.

Edward the Confessor enthroned at Westminster.

109

William the Conqueror

The disputed succession following the death of King Edward the Confessor brought new invasions and new wars to England. Then, two great battles fought in the fall of 1066 decided the country's future. At Stamford Bridge, Harold, King of England, defeated his cousin and namesake Harold of Norway. His joy was short-lived ; immediately after the battle, King Harold learned that another cousin and claimant to the throne, William of Normandy, had crossed the Channel from France and had landed only one hundred miles away. Overconfident after his recent victory, Harold rushed south with but half his army, and was soundly defeated by William at Hastings. Although undertaken with the blessings of the Pope, William's invasion was in a sense the last great Norse conquest, and ironically it brought England more closely into the orbit of continental Europe.

The first seal of William the Conqueror, showing the Norman king enthroned.

Opposite top The coronation of King Harold at Westminster Abbey ; the Bayeux Tapestry c. 1100. This tapestry, about 231 ft. long and 20 in. wide, depicts the entire story of the Norman invasion of England and its historical circumstances.

Opposite bottom Norman soldiers pillage the English countryside. Here a woman her child are shown fleeing from a house set alight by soldiers, with the buildings of Hastings close by ; Bayeux Tapestry.

At about nine o'clock on the morning of October 14, 1066, two armies of approximately equal size faced each other across the valley between Telham Hill and a nameless rise marked by the presence of a "hoary apple tree," close to the modern town of Battle. William, Duke of Normandy, commanded a motley host of Norman retainers, Breton allies and Flemish mercenaries—the majority of them adventurers whom he had persuaded to cross the Narrow Sea for loot and land. William's army has been estimated at somewhere between six and seven thousand men; it was probably nearer the lower figure. Perhaps 1,200 of these were mounted knights who had brought their horses with them in the boats. The rest were infantry, and included an unusually large number of archers. The knights wore heavy hauberks of leather plated with rings of metal, reaching to the knees, and their legs were protected by high leather boots. In battle they used swords and lances. But the ecclesiastics among them, such as William's half-brother Odo, Bishop of Bayeux, wielded maces. A mace could crush a man's skull *sine effusione sanguinis*—without that shedding of blood which the Church forbade to clerics.

Harold of Wessex, King Harold II of England, had perhaps a thousand more men than the Duke, drawn up in tight formation around his two standards: the Dragon of Wessex and his personal banner, the Fighting Man. The nucleus of this force consisted of professional soldiers: Harold's housecarls, who were armored like the Normans. There had been much Norman influence in England since the accession of Edward the Confessor, who had grown up in Normandy—and the armorers of England had learned from their fellows across the Channel. But Harold had ordered his professionals to dismount, in order to stiffen with their shield-wall the levies of inexperienced men hastily assembled from London and the vicinity. The latter were armed with whatever they had: slings, axes, javelins, even hammers and scythes. The housecarls relied on their Danish pole-axes—fearsome weapons—and on spears used either for throwing as javelins, or as lances to turn charging horses and unseat knights.

Harold's men were tired. They had marched the sixty-odd miles from London in two days and had taken up their positions only the previous night. Harold himself and the housecarls were even wearier than the levies; in the course of the past month they had covered nearly four hundred miles from London to York and back again, and had fought a great battle. For 1066, the "year of the comet," had seen other invasions besides Duke William's expedition.

According to medieval belief, "the star with hair" portended the death of a king or the destruction of a kingdom. Certainly Halley's comet, which shone in the skies over England at the end of April, 1066, justified all such fears. King Edward the Confessor had died at the beginning of January, and Harold Godwinson had been crowned as Edward's successor on the day of his funeral. (Whether you thought this right or wrong depended on whose partisan you were.) There were at least three other strong candidates for the throne. Closest in descent from the English royal line as well as the line of Norman dukes was Edgar the Atheling, but he was still a boy. Another candidate was Harold Hardraada, King of Norway, who had formed an alliance with Harold Godwinson's brother Tostig. Tostig had recently been deposed from his earldom of Northumbria; he seems to have been of a treacherous and vicious disposition and had roused the whole countryside against him. The strongest claimant of all was William the Bastard of Normandy, who was also descended from English kings and who was convinced that King Edward had promised him the succession.

During the last years of Edward's life, however, Harold had been the effective ruler of England. That was why he had been able to seize the throne so quickly; and in the nine months and nine days of his

HAROLDO: REGIS hIC RE SIDET:HAROLD REX:AN GLORVM: STIGANT ARChIEPS

VN TIATVM EST: LM DEHAROLD hIC DOMVS:IN CENDITVR: hIC:M

HIC WILLELM:DVX ALLOQVITVR SVIS

William, Duke of Normandy, at the head of his army, dressed for battle in chain mail and armor, and exhorting his men to fight with courage; Bayeux Tapestry c. 1100.

reign, he succeeded in consolidating his popularity. To quote one of his supporters, he "abolished unjust laws and made good ones, patronized churches and monasteries, and showed himself pious, humble and affable to all men."

He also proved to be a remarkably good soldier and a foresighted organizer. When—soon after the appearance of the comet—his brother Tostig raided the Isle of Wight and harried the southern coast of England, Harold rushed down to Sandwich from London and drove him away. Then, hearing that William of Normandy was gathering forces to make good his claim to the throne, Harold posted ships and men all along the coast and kept them there through the summer. But few generals or kings in those days could master the logistics of large standing armies. By early September, provisions had run out. Moreover, the danger seemed past; spring and summer was the time when "kings go forth to war." Harold allowed the men of the *fyrd*, the national levy of Anglo-Saxon England, to disband on September 8. He himself returned with his ships to London— disastrously losing many of them in the same storms that were keeping William of Normandy from crossing the Channel.

The dissolution of the army came at the worst possible moment. Barely back in London, Harold learned that his Norwegian namesake, Harold Hardraada, had invaded the north. Tostig had joined forces with him, and in a fierce battle at Fulford the English traitor, the Norwegian king, and a mixed force of Norwegians and Flemish mercenaries had crushed the defending English led by the earls of Mercia and Northumbria. Southern England seemed to be wide open to invasion.

Harold at once set out for the north with his house-carls. He must have gathered up the dispersing *fyrd* as he went, for by the time he reached York he is said to have had an army of "many thousand well-armed fighting men." He covered more than two hundred miles at such speed that he caught the Norsemen and their allies by surprise. On September 25, 1066, the armies met at Stamford Bridge. The Norsemen, though weakened by Fulford, which had been a costly battle for both sides, fought ferociously. But Harold achieved complete victory; both Tostig and King Harold Hardraada were killed and the bulk of the invading force destroyed. The comet had truly foretold the death of kings. But its influence had evidently not yet waned. Harold had also lost many of his best men, and in the midst of his triumph he learned that the Duke of Normandy had landed at Pevensey. With his mounted house-carls, Harold returned to London at top speed, leaving the rest of his army to follow at slower pace.

William of Normandy was at this time approaching his fortieth year. Brutal, avaricious, ruthless, consumed by ambition, he was also a courageous and resourceful leader, a magnificent administrator, a pious Christian, and a good ruler who used tyranny to achieve the ends of stern justice. He had overcome the handicaps of bastardy and a frightful boyhood under savage tutelage and had clawed his way to unchallenged power in a duchy racked by dissension and treachery. Two years before, he had tricked or forced Harold Godwinson into swearing to support his claim to the English throne. As soon as Harold seized the crown, William initiated a skillful propaganda campaign in all the courts of Europe, accusing the new king of perjury. He secured papal

† LEVVINE· ET·GYRD·FRATRE[S·HA

blessing for his expedition to punish the "oath-breaker," and at once began gathering men and building ships for the invasion of England. Unlike Harold, he succeeded in holding his forces together for six dreary weeks, while he waited for contrary winds to change so that he could cross the Channel with his host. His big, heavy ships, built to carry horses and ponderous equipment, were propelled only by sails, not by oars.

Although he did not know it, the delay was providential. Had he embarked when he was ready, he would have encountered an intact English navy and coastal guard and might never have succeeded in landing. As it was, when the wind finally shifted to the south and the Normans disembarked at Pevensey, they met no opposition. By the time Harold, with fatal impetuousness, reached the Sussex Downs with his available men—half his army had not yet come up, one chronicler asserts—William was fully ready for him. Nevertheless, the Normans had the disadvantage of terrain; they would be attacking uphill against the English. And William could not take the risk of avoiding battle, for Harold's army was blocking the road to London. It was clear that the English would only grow stronger with each passing day, for they had vastly greater resources. Good sense could only have urged Harold, for his part, to wait, retreat, draw the Normans deeper into a hostile countryside. But he chose to fight, perhaps from overconfidence after his recent victory, perhaps to save his lands from further pillage.

The story goes—and it is a pretty one, though it may not be true—that the first blow on the Norman side was struck by the minstrel Taillefer, who rode in the van performing juggling feats with his sword

The battle is joined at Hastings between the Anglo-Saxon forces of King Harold and the Norman invaders led by Duke William, a scene of ferocious slaughter vigorously depicted; Bayeux Tapestry.

Left Twelfth-century stone statue of a Norman warrior in chain mail and armor in the church of St. Martial, Limoges.

The nave of Romsey Abbey in Hampshire illustrates the round arches characteristic of the Norman architectural style, which was preferred by William's newly appointed, high-ranking priests.

Right St. Stephen's Church at Caen from which Duke William set out to invade England, and where he was buried, displays the Norman Romanesque style, which William's victory introduced into England.

and "singing of Charlemagne and all his men." (Perhaps he sang an early version of *The Song of Roland*.) The mounted Norman knights formed the center, just as the English had the housecarls in the center of their line. On William's left were the Bretons; on his right, Robert of Beaumont—one of the heroes of the day—with a mixed force of Flemings and French. The infantry advanced first, sending a rain of arrows into the English shield-wall, and receiving all kinds of missiles in return. Then the Norman cavalry attacked. But they were toiling uphill against superior numbers, and the English line stood firm. The terrible slaughter, the ferocity of the hand-to-hand combat, the slain being stripped of their armor in the midst of the carnage—all this is vividly depicted in the Bayeux Tapestry.

After suffering heavy losses, William's forces broke and retreated in confusion. William himself had his horse killed under him (he lost three in the course of the day), and the rumor spread that he was dead. Harold's undisciplined levies broke formation to pursue the fleeing enemy. In this crisis, William snatched off his helmet to show himself to his men. "You are throwing away the victory!" he shouted— and together with his brother Odo, he succeeded in rallying the knights. The mounted Normans, with their superior mobility, quickly surrounded the isolated detachments of Englishmen and cut them down. The incident had given William the key to the battle. Now he ordered his men to feign flight, and twice the ruse succeeded. Then the Norman army resumed its struggle against the thinned English ranks. In the final assault, William commanded his archers to shoot high, so that the arrows flew over the protecting wall of the housecarls' shields. Simultaneously, his cavalry charged. Still the English fought on until Harold himself was killed, perhaps in the melée, perhaps by a fortuitous arrow that struck him in the eye. His two brothers had already fallen, and with their leaders dead the English soldiers lost heart. At nightfall they began to flee in disorder. The battle that decided the fate of England was over.

The Battle of Hastings did not spell the end of English resistance, but it definitely transformed the Duke of Normandy into William the Conqueror. William proceeded to encircle London, cutting the capital off from the rest of the country until the city had no choice but to surrender. By the end of the year, he had entered London. And on Christmas Day (in conscious imitation of Charlemagne's coronation as Emperor on Christmas Day, A.D. 800), he was crowned by the Archbishop of York.

After his victory and coronation, William swiftly consolidated his rule. He rewarded the Norman barons who had fought beside him by parceling out among them the lands formerly held by Englishmen who had died in battle, or who afterwards rebelled against him. As the *Anglo-Saxon Chronicle* bitterly commented: "He gave away every man's land." Within twenty years of the Conquest, nine-tenths of the land of England had changed masters. By scattering the holdings of his new magnates all over the English countryside, he gave the lords wealth but retained the essential power in his own hands. Thus by adroit policy, he established the strongest and most stable monarchy in Europe.

The Conqueror's system of land tenure was strictly feudal. The king himself remained the overlord and landlord of all England, so that even the greatest nobles were his tenants. Starting afresh in a new country, William was able to organize the feudal hierarchy on more logical principles than existed in Normandy, where the land tenure and political and social organization had resulted from haphazard growth. England had been moving toward the development of a feudal society before the Conquest; the general principle of "no man without his lord" was well-established. But the full development of feudalism with all it implied awaited the arrival of the Conqueror and his redistribution of land.

One ironic incidental effect of William's victory was the "return" to England of the Bretons, descendants of families that had been driven across the Channel by the Anglo-Saxon invasion five hundred years before. There had been many Bretons in the Norman army, and they were appropriately rewarded. Men like Alan the Red, Ralph of Gael, and Judhael of Totnes received vast estates, especially in southwest England, where Gaelic was still spoken.

It is curious to find, at a later date, Bretons and Saxons uniting in rebelling against the Normans. For there were rebellions, especially among the Danes of northern England. William suppressed them with an iron hand; in his "harrying of the north" he almost wiped out the population in the Vale of York. Twenty years later, when he ordered virtually every cottage and hide of land in the country to be counted, so that the king could know—and tax—what he owned, the Vale of York was still deserted. That first great medieval survey, incidentally, was so thorough that it was compared to the Day of Judgment; the record came to be known as the Domesday (i.e. Doomsday) Book. The census caused much discontent and local revolts. But William and his successors nevertheless succeeded in winning the confidence of their subjects—so much so that William's son, William Rufus, found he could depend on English levies to defend him against his own Norman barons.

William had come into England with the papal blessing, carrying a papal banner and wearing around his neck at Hastings the holy relics on which Harold had allegedly sworn fealty to him. Once in control of England, he proceeded to introduce into the English Church the principles of Gregorian reform. He attempted to improve the education of the clergy and to enforce the celibacy of priests. Guided by the great churchman Lanfranc, whom he appointed Archbishop of Canterbury, he furthered the internationalization of the English Church, replacing English bishops and abbots by learned Frenchmen and Italians. He separated secular and ecclesiastical courts in order to assure the immunity of the clergy from secular interference—a step that was to have far-reaching and often unpleasant consequences for his successors. William agreed to the payment of "Peter's Pence" to the papacy. But at the same time he strongly rebuffed the efforts of Gregory VII to assert feudal authority over the Crown of England, and he saw to it that control of the English Church remained firmly vested in him alone. Appeals to Rome, or the entry of papal

St. John at Palermo, erected in the early twelfth century in Roger II's Sicilian kingdom, illustrates the way that the Normans preserved the Oriental stylistic traditions of the earlier Arab rulers.

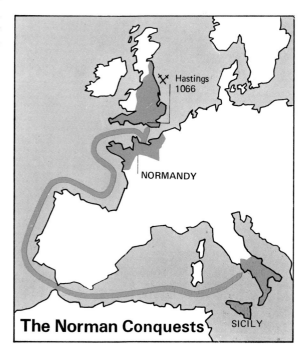

The Norman Conquests

115

Above St. Albans Cathedral, one of the powerful ecclesiastical seats built under King William in the Romanesque style, near the ancient Roman town of Verulamium.

legates into England, were forbidden without his consent; and he resisted all the Pope's efforts to interfere with his prerogative of appointing high prelates of the Church. His firmness gave England a privileged position which his successors maintained. Because of his policy the full fury of the Investiture conflict that racked Central Europe never burst upon England. A life-and-death struggle between the English Church and the monarchy was delayed for a century. When it came at last, it culminated in the shocking murder of Archbishop Thomas Becket; but the monarchy emerged from that contest with its hold over the English Church basically strong.

In one sense, the Norman Conquest can be considered the crowning accomplishment of that great wave of expansion which carried the sea-rovers of the Scandinavian world to Iceland, Greenland and even the shores of America, and enabled them to found the Russian monarchy and guard the gates of Constantinople for the emperors. For Normandy had, after all, been a Scandinavian settlement, and in the boyhood of William the Conqueror Old Norse was still spoken at Bayeux. But the majority of the Northmen settlers in Normandy had adopted the language and the Latin civilization of their surroundings. What they brought to England, as well as to their far-flung settlements in Sicily and the Holy Land, was French speech and Roman traditions in government, law and church affairs, along with Viking energy and a new organizational talent that seems to have sprung from the amalgam. These descendants of Viking pirates actually put an end to what may be called the Scandinavian period in English history. Until 1042, a Dane had been King

Below Domesday Book, a survey that William's officers drew up after the conquest of England, listing all the land and buildings of his new domain.

of England; after 1066, England became too strongly centralized a monarchy for further incursions from the north to be possible. Moreover, the union of Normandy and England under one monarch, although it was not destined to last, brought England fully into the orbit of the European world. English history remained, after the Norman Conquest, a process of alternating approach to and withdrawal from the Continent—a process that has continued to the present day. While Scandinavia withdrew for centuries from the main arena of European politics, the English played their part, at first through their Continental possessions, later through Continental dynastic and political alliances.

In the first century after the Conquest, language remained one of the strongest links. Although the Norman nobility rapidly learned the Anglo-Saxon language—which, after all, closely resembled the language spoken by their own grandfathers—they continued using French at court. Literature, which was always directed toward the literate leisure class, ceased to be written in Anglo-Saxon. The *Anglo-Saxon Chronicle* continued to be kept for ninety years after the Conquest, but it ceased with the accession of Henry II.

On the other hand, there was a remarkable outburst of literary creativity in the twelfth century, the consequence of growing wealth and a stabler society. In architecture, too, there was an enormous outburst of vitality; Canterbury, Lincoln, Wells and Salisbury cathedrals, to name just a few, remain witnesses to the Norman style. The generosity of William and his successors also resulted in the building of many monasteries throughout England, and led to a revival of monasticism. The monks reclaimed and cultivated many of the fens and forests of England, thereby adding materially to the wealth of the country. They contributed to the reform of religious life, and often brought from their motherhouses in France the learning of the Continent.

Altogether it can be stated—at the hazard of all such generalizations—that the Norman Conquest, though it caused much suffering, also brought fresh air and an infusion of new energy into a somewhat stagnant society. It reorientated England into the mainstream of European history. As it turned out, William the Conqueror's successors enlarged his Continental domains so greatly that they nearly succeeded in swallowing all of France. The struggle of the kings of France to right the balance of power influenced much of the subsequent history of Western Europe. RICHARD WINSTON

The Tower of London. The White Tower, built by William to consolidate London's position as the administrative capital of England.

The sheer white cliffs of the English coast, where William the Conqueror is thought to have landed with his army.

The successors of William I

William had ruled both in England and Normandy, but at his death the inheritance was divided. The ancestral duchy on the Continent went to his eldest but feckless son, Robert, and the newly conquered island kingdom to his second son, William Rufus, or William II. For England, despite the subsequent notoriety of William II, the arrangements were beneficial. Whatever his faults as a man and his harshness as a king, William Rufus maintained the royal authority unimpaired, suppressing the baronial revolts which followed the Conqueror's death and holding the northern

Galilee Chapel in Durham Cathedral. Durham was the greatest of the Norman ecclesiastical border fortresses in the north of England.

frontier with Scotland. In comparison with even the strongest of Continental kingdoms, England enjoyed a priceless advantage in the incontestable position of the central monarchy. In twenty years, William I had made this ever more sure, and his son was strong and intelligent enough to capitalize on it. However, his means to this end and the oppressiveness of his ministers provoked the discontent both of the baronage and the people at large. Yet his position was further strengthened in 1096 when he won control of Normandy when his indigent brother Robert pledged the duchy to the king to finance his participation in the crusades.

William Rufus had no more bitter enemy than the Church, which objected not only to his personal morals but, more vehemently, to his refusal to fill vacant sees while channeling their revenues into the royal exchequer. Indeed, much of William's ill repute with posterity stems from the bad press he got from the ecclesiastical chroniclers. William had made Anselm Archbishop of Canterbury during an illness that terrified him with the fear of death. His father had forbade the English clergy to appeal to Rome without royal permission, and his brother who succeeded him was to fight hard—and largely successfully—to maintain the royal claim to invest bishops. William Rufus, by his unyielding opposition to Anselm and the papacy, sturdily upheld the rights of the Crown.

William Rufus was killed while hunting in the New Forest on August 2, 1100, by an arrow fired by one of his companions; the speed which his younger brother showed in taking advantage of this turn of events has led to speculation that Henry may have been prepared for what happened. Whatever the circumstances of his succession, however, there can be no doubt that the reign of Henry I was of lasting advantage for England. It is a remarkable and crucial fact that for the first seventy years of its existence the Norman kingdom of England was ruled by three strong-willed and efficient kings whose principal enemies were the Church and the discontented elements of their own Norman baronage. Such English resistance as there was, was effectively contained, but for the most

Duke Robert of Normandy.

part the conquered nation seems to have accepted royal oppression as preferable to the dangers of an uncontrolled baronage. Not only did the young Henry succeed in usurping the claims of his older brother, Robert, to the kingdom, but in 1106, with an army in which the Anglo-Saxon infantry was a vital element, he won final control of the duchy of Normandy at the victory of Tinchebrai. Even so, during the rest of his reign, Henry had to face threats to his position in Normandy.

Growth of central government

In England, with the help of such great ministers as Roger, bishop of Salisbury, Henry introduced a system of financial and judicial administration that was to leave the mark of its reforms on English life for centuries to come. The exchequer, founded under Henry I, exercised a more effective control over the officers and finances of the English king than that enjoyed by any other European sovereign, while the quality of royal justice was such that even members of the nobility were prepared to pay handsomely for it. Once the system of traveling royal judges, "the justices in eyre," was launched, the power of the king's court came to be felt throughout the land.

Yet for all the efficiency and strength of Henry's monarchy, he did not seek to eliminate either the baronage or the Church—the two great mainstays of a feudal monarchy. The quality of medieval government depended on the quality of the king, and when Henry died at the end of 1135, an era of strong government had come to a close. Henry had planned for his daughter Matilda, wife of the former Emperor Henry V, to succeed

him, and had compelled his leading subjects to swear allegiance to her. But Matilda's claim was contended immediately after Henry's death by her cousin Stephen of Blois, a powerful man in England, thanks to lands received from Henry himself. A decisive body of the English baronage, affronted by the prospect of petticoat rule, offended by the imperious and haughty nature of the ex-Empress and no doubt well aware of the pliant good nature of Stephen, renounced their oaths of allegiance to Matilda. In 1136, after he had granted a charter of liberties to the Church far in excess of anything conceded by his predecessors, Stephen was recognized by Pope Innocent II. But Matilda did not abandon her claim, and there followed a decade of civil war which left an indelible mark on the memory of England. Stephen's own weakness and chivalry were delightedly traded upon; and the nobility of England could hardly believe their luck in having on their hands a fully fledged civil war in which the rival claimants were only too eager to bid for their support.

Undoubtedly the gloom of the period is heightened by the paucity and bias of our sources. Nevertheless, it was undoubtedly a difficult period, which only ended in 1147 when Matilda retired to Normandy, which had been taken over by her second husband, Geoffrey of Anjou. In 1153 their twenty-year-old son, Henry, Duke of Normandy, Anjou and Maine, and also of Aquitaine by virtue of his marriage to its duchess, Eleanor, went to England, where he found many supporters. King Stephen, broken by the death

Interior of Canterbury Cathedral built by Anselm, who succeeded Lanfranc as Archbishop.

Geoffrey Plantagenet.

of his own eldest son, acknowledged Henry as heir to his throne. When he died the following year, the crown passed without dispute to a young man who was to prove himself one of England's greatest rulers.

Emperors and Popes before Canossa

Thanks to the hard policy of William I and his successors, England maintained a firm stand against the claims of the reformed papacy, and in 1106 Henry I won a compromise settlement much to his advantage. In the Empire the struggle was both longer and much more bitter, if only because the principles at stake affected the plenitude of papal power in the most obvious way. It was one of the ironical aspects of the events leading up to Canossa that the papacy, which inflicted such dramatic humiliation on the Emperor. Henry IV, had been saved from its own incompetence and corruption only a brief thirty years before by his father, Henry III. The scandalous

corruption of the monastic arm of the Church had been slowly cauterized during the tenth century by the great reform movement launched by the founding of Cluny. But despite this, and despite the rising tide of popular piety throughout Europe, the papacy remained in a parlous state. For the first forty years of the eleventh century, it was virtually the dynastic toy of Roman families. And the sin of simony was not unknown at papal elections.

Lay intervention was essential if reform was to be successful in the body of the secular Church, where bishops and clergy were so closely involved in the secular world itself. The Emperor Henry II, fully aware of his power in church and state, had sponsored a series of synods to spur the Church to reform itself. The movement was interrupted by the reign of the Emperor Conrad II, but under his son, Henry III (1039–56), the problems of the papacy were solved. Henry succeeded in ensuring the election of his cousin who, known to later ages as St. Leo IX, was to be a chief architect of the reformed Church which was soon to challenge the pretensions of the Emperor himself.

The Normans in Sicily

Six years before William Duke of Normandy embarked for his momentous invasion of the Christian island of England, with the papal blessing on his banners, two members of a family of the petty Norman nobility had begun their conquest

of the Moslem island of Sicily, also with papal blessing. Despite their humble origins, Robert and Roger de Hauteville were the founders of a Mediterranean power which throughout the twelfth century was to hold at bay the forces of the Pope and Emperor of the West and prove dangerous enemies to the Emperor of the East.

The Norman presence in southern Italy began in the 1010s when a group of Norman pilgrims were recruited as mercenaries in the perpetual struggle among the last outposts of the Byzantine Empire, the Lombard principalities and the independent cities of which Naples was the leader. By 1030 their leader had received the fief of Aversa from the Duke of Naples. In the 1040s, Robert Guiscard ("The Cunning") of the family of Hauteville appeared in Calabria to begin a career of merciless but brilliant brigandage that by 1059 had forced a reluctant papacy to recognize his position in the treaty of Melfi. Leaving his brother Roger to complete the conquest of Sicily, Guiscard set out in the 1080s on a conquest of the Byzantine Empire itself, but died before his plans could materialize. After his death, his state in southern Italy soon fell apart.

Roger, however, who died in 1101, was able to leave a well-ordered and powerful kingdom in Sicily. This kingdom reached the height of its power and prestige under the rule of his second son, Roger II (1105–54). A true Hauteville in his ambition and in his

ruthlessness, Roger nevertheless recognized the realities of power in his island kingdom, in which a small group of conquerors found themselves ruling a motley population in which Catholics from France and Italy rubbed shoulders with Orthodox Byzantine Christians and Islamic Saracens. Throughout their history, the rulers of Norman Sicily, who soon brought the mainland territories into their kingdom, exercised a degree of religious toleration remarkable in Europe. Displaying to the full the Norman

Queen Constance with her child, the future Emperor Henry VI.

talent for assimilation, Roger II not only instituted a harem, but also provided himself with a first-class fleet, which enabled him and his successors to pursue an imperial policy. In the 1130s, exploiting a papal schism, Roger was able to have himself recognized as king—a title which, though it was granted by an anti-pope, he vindicated and later had confirmed by the true Pope.

At his death, Roger II left a seemingly powerful kingdom, one whose eclectic culture was to make a notable contribution to the twelfth-century "renaissance."

Through the silk industry of Palermo, founded by workers captured by raids on Byzantine territories, he brought the secret of silk to Europe. His sensual successor, William I, was swift to put down rebellion, and left the kingdom intact.

William II (1166–89), called the Good because of the degree of internal peace that he maintained, followed the traditional policy of his house against the Byzantine Empire. To further it he married his daughter Constance to the future Emperor Henry VI. William's ambitious policy eventually failed, however, and after his death the kingdom passed to the Empire. The marriage he had arranged was to have fateful consequences for the future of southern Europe.

The Norman King Roger II of Sicily, depicted on a Byzantine-style mosaic.

REX ROGAT ABBATEM / MAThILDIM SUPPLICAT ATQ;

Humiliation at Canossa 1077

For three days in January, 1077, Emperor Henry IV stood barefoot in the snow outside Canossa castle, waiting to see Pope Gregory VII and to beg him to lift the dread sentence of excommunication. Henry's action was the culmination of a conflict between Church and State that had been brewing for centuries. Medieval rulers had come to regard their bishops merely as feudal nobles who were expected to fill their proper roles in the functioning of their kingdoms. But some of the clergy wished to emphasize the religious office of bishops by removing them from the responsibilities, and the privileges, of civil government. The Pope's victory in forcing Henry to humiliate himself at Canossa did not resolve the conflict, but it did help play down the sacred character of kingship and thus paved the way for the creation of modern secular states.

In January of 1077, Pope Gregory VII was residing at Canossa, a castle on the northern slopes of the Appenines owned by the Countess Matilda of Tuscany. On the 25th day of that month, the Emperor Henry IV appeared in front of the castle as ordered, "and since the castle was surrounded by three rings of walls, he was allowed inside the second ring. His entourage had to wait outside. He stood divested of his royal garments, without the insignia of his dignity, without ornaments of any kind. He was barefoot and fasted from morning to the evening in expectation of the sentence of the Roman Pope. He had to do this for a second and a third day. On the fourth day he was allowed to appear before the Pope and was told that the excommunication would be repealed under certain conditions."

The chronicler to whom we owe this moving description, Lambert of Hersfeld, then tells of the conditions. The Emperor was to submit himself to a thorough judicial examination to determine whether he was to keep his domains; he was to sever his personal relations with certain evil men whose advice had led him to the point at which, a year before, the Pope had excommunicated him. At this, the Pope said Mass, and during the office he declared that in order to prove his innocence of countercharges that had been leveled against *him* (they ranged from murder and adultery to heresy and simony) he would eat one half of the Lord's body and hoped he would be struck down dead if he were not innocent. Having done so, Gregory invited the Emperor to do likewise. But Henry was obviously uncertain either of his own innocence or of the effectiveness of the test—it is impossible to say which. Caught unawares, we are told, he blanched and stammered and sought excuses and eventually begged the Pope not to insist, pleading that since the men who had accused him were not present the test could not possibly be significant. Gregory was won over, the tense moment passed and then the Pope invited the Emperor to share his breakfast. Henry must have sighed with

relief. But when the news of his reconciliation with the Pope was announced to the Italian bishops assembled outside the castle, there was a violent commotion. These men had supported Henry because they were jealous of the Bishop of Rome. They now felt let down and threatened to depose Henry and lead his son, who was still a minor, to Rome and there unseat the Pope. Only with the greatest diplomacy was this outburst of indignation suppressed. In the end, they all agreed to wait for the assembly at which Henry was to place his case before the magnates of the Empire and wait upon their decision.

The day of Canossa appeared to be a great triumph for the papacy and, as such, has become almost proverbial. In fact, the Emperor got the better of the Pope. By doing penance, Henry obliged Pope Gregory VII to lift the excommunication and thus removed the one great obstacle that had stood in his way. Henry could now rally his supporters, and by 1081 he was able to march an army into Italy, appear before Rome and, after lengthy battles, install there a Pope of his own choice, Clement III, the Archbishop of Ravenna.

Pope Gregory held out inside the castle of Sant' Angelo; but Henry was crowned Emperor in Rome on March 31, 1084 by his own Pope. Eventually the Normans from Sicily under their king, Guiscard, came to Gregory's rescue. The fighting in Rome was severe and the city suffered grievously. But no decision was reached and eventually the Normans withdrew, taking Gregory south with them in semi-captivity. He died in Salerno on May 25 of the following year, breathing his last with a somewhat ironical variant of verse 8 from Psalm XIV: "I have loved righteousness and hated iniquity; therefore I die in exile."

The clash between the Emperor Henry IV and Pope Gregory VII was the culmination of a long development that, but for the fiery intolerance of the Pope and the youthful temper of Henry IV, might have had a completely different ending.

Henry IV with his son Henry (the future Henry V) and two clerics. The combined opposition of Church and family pursued Henry to his tragic destiny.

Opposite Henry IV in St. Nicholas' chapel at Canossa asks Matilda of Tuscany to intercede for him with the Pope so that his excommunication (1076) might be revoked. He is supported by Hugh, Abbot of Cluny, in this cunning though bitter gesture of political ignominy.

Right Speyer Cathedral, the religious center of the Salian dynasty and their ambitions.

The iron crown and cross from the tomb of Henry IV in Speyer Cathedral.

The conflict between Church and State had been developing for centuries. One of the most far-reaching effects of the barbarian invasions of the Roman Empire in the fifth and sixth centuries A.D. was the blow to the Christian churches. The invaders were all Christians, but conversion to the new religion had been for them a mass movement; they followed their king. It had not been associated with spiritual regeneration, nor had it been an answer to a spiritual need. The barbarians needed a new communal ritual to replace the one they had lost when they had left their homesteads. Furthermore, the economic decline of the Roman Empire, which had in fact preceded the invasions but which was further hastened by them, had essentially meant a decline of urban life and culture.

With the advancing ruralization of the imperial territories, there disappeared also the economic and administrative basis of the churches. The urban Christian communities and their bishops declined in number and importance. By the seventh century, bishops were no longer churchmen; they were the owners of large landed estates. They came to share the customs and outlook of the landed magnates, and as such they were soon rendering military service to kings. All this was not so much an expression of declining piety as it was the result of the economic and social changes that took place during the early Middle Ages. With the centers of religious organization dispersed, educational opportunities—essential to a religion based on the knowledge of the Bible and a complex liturgy—declined sharply. Christian pastors of these centuries, in their simple-minded dislike of the pre-Christian, pagan cultures of Rome and Greece, lent an active, if unwitting, hand to that decline by decrying education—for to them education usually meant the study of pagan literature.

The short-lived idealism of Charlemagne (768–814) had no real lasting effect. But in the course of the tenth century, man's innate yearning for transcendence, for spiritual edification, for ascetic morals and ethical guidance began to reassert itself. There emerged, at first in the central parts of the old Carolingian Empire, in the so-called Middle Kingdom comprising the present-day Netherlands, Lorraine and Burgundy, a new monastic movement led by the monks of Cluny. This newly reformed branch of the old monastic order propagated the idea that the religious life was one of seclusion, dedicated wholly to prayer. The influence of Cluny's example was enormous. A vast number of daughter houses were established in Central Europe, and hundreds of new recruits for religion were enlisted. The reform movement also led to the reorganization of old religious houses. By the early eleventh century, a wave of revived religious activity was sweeping across Europe.

One of the innovations introduced by Cluny was the regulation that a reformed monastery should be exempt, no matter where it was situated, from the control of the local bishop. Bishops being potentates, this was an essential factor in the success of the reform movement. By the eleventh century, abbots of both reformed and not so reformed houses, such as Suger of St. Denis, Poppo of Stablo and Odilo of Cluny, tended to replace bishops as the trusted advisers and scribes of kings and emperors. The reason was that kings soon discovered they could benefit from this new movement. If the inhabitants of their kingdoms could be imbued with religious fervor, the kingdoms would receive a spiritual substance as a result.

The first monarch to recognize this was Henry III of Germany (1039–56). Henry's relations with the magnates of his kingdom were unhappy. In 1047 he was almost assassinated while visiting Adalbert, the Archbishop of Bremen and Hamburg. Adalbert was a very able administrator and had sought to turn his archdiocese into a territorial state. The Saxon nobility was highly suspicious of such nonfeudal behavior, and when they discovered that Adalbert had Henry's full support, they conspired against Henry— hence the attempted assassination. Similarly,

Emperor Henry IV; from the shrine of Charlemagne at Aachen Cathedral.

The twelfth-century chronicle of Otto of Freising shows how, after Pope Gregory VII had made peace with him, Henry IV betrayed him by appointing an anti-pope Clement III and expelling Gregory by force from Rome. The death of Gregory (*below*) at Salerno was embittered by his exile.

Conrad, Duke of Bavaria, angered by Henry's close association with the episcopate of Bavaria, rose against him. The rebellion was suppressed, but Conrad escaped and in 1055 organized a major conspiracy to assassinate Henry. Another long-standing rebel was Godfrey, Duke of Lorraine, whom Henry prevented from taking over the whole of his father's inheritance. Godfrey was not content with half and eventually married an Italian heiress in order to compensate himself for his loss of power. The Italian threat which thus emerged was considerable.

Faced with such threats to his authority, Henry turned to the Church for support of his throne. He decided not only to throw his weight behind the reform movement of the Church, but also to provide it with the administrative framework and centralized direction it would need in order to become truly universal. A shrewd statesman, Henry decided to introduce reform into the see of Rome, the bishopric which was the first see of Christendom.

Dictatus papae.

1 Quod Romana ecclesia a solo domino sit fundata.

II Quod solus Romanus pontifex iure dicatur universalis.

III Quod ille solus possit deponere episcopos vel reconciliare.

IIII Quod legatus eius omnibus episcopis praesit in concilio etiam inferioris gradus. & adversus eos sententiam depositionis possit dare.

V Quod absentes papa possit deponere.

VI Quod cum excommunicatis ab illo inter cetera nec in eadem domo debemus manere.

VII Quod illi soli licet pro temporis necessitate novas leges condere. novas plebes congregare. de canonica abbatiam facere. & e contra. divitem episcopatum dividere. & inopes unire.

VIII Quod solus possit uti imperialibus insigniis.

VIIII Quod solius papae pedes omnes principes deosculentur.

X Quod illius solius nomen in ecclesiis recitetur.

Left The opening page of the *Dictatus Papae,* twenty-seven propositions drawn up by Pope Gregory VII in 1075, setting out the superior authority of Pope over secular states, including the right to depose emperors.

Right The Virgin Mary receiving a book from Emperor Henry III and blessing the Empress Agnes. A scene commemorative of the height of power of the Salian Empire.

The bishops of Rome, during the century and a half preceding the reign of Henry III, had had neither desire nor opportunity for exercising the functions of the papacy. The office, the leading governmental institution in the city, had become the coveted prize of the aristocratic clans in and around Rome. These parties had fought over the papacy and had removed successful candidates by murder or blackmail. The incumbents who were willing to play along were always scions of these families, their minds and ambitions more on local power than on the welfare of the Church—of which most of them knew only by hearsay and which interested them little if at all.

In 1046, Henry III decided to intervene. He held a synod at Sutri, deposed the reigning Pope Gregory VI, declared several other claimants to the see also deposed and caused, in quick succession, a whole series of "foreign" popes to be installed in Rome. All those who took office under imperial patronage were ardent reformers and came from abroad. Thus the spirit of the reform movement captured the city of Rome, for with the new popes there also appeared a large number of foreign clergy, who supported the reform movement.

With this action, however, Henry III also introduced the possibility of conflict between Empire and Church. His objection to the deposed popes was based on the principle that simony was an evil practice. No man should be allowed to assume a spiritual office in return for material considerations such as money payments or promises of political influence. The reform party was only too happy to seize this opportunity, to capture Rome and to spread their ideas and practices from the central see of Christendom. At the same time, the fact that they owed their position to the Emperor raised an irksome question. It was becoming more and more clearly the object of the reform movement to make the Church independent of laymen and to see to it that in the Church none but canon law prevailed. But insofar as the reform party owed its capture of Rome to the Emperor, the Church could hardly be said to be independent.

Nevertheless, this was an issue which, given time and thought, could have been settled amicably. After all, the Emperor (and, for that matter, many a king) was not exactly a "lay" person. He was elevated to the throne by unction and wore garments of religious significance—not the least significant, his splendid crown. True, the crown was perhaps only a special kind of helmet, but its splendor of gold and precious stones made it into a symbol of the sun. An anointed ruler was another David and had divine sanction. His ascendancy in the Church and his protection of religion need not therefore necessarily be construed as an act of lay interference.

Under Pope Leo IX (1049–54), the reform movement made rapid progress. He brought a large number of his friends and associates to Rome and spent much time traveling. He used his authority to remove simoniacal bishops and abbots, and granted the vacant sees to adherents of the reform movement. The presence of his supporters in Rome created an institutional background to the reform movement by surrounding the papacy with a suitable clergy who would be likely to elect a suitable successor. A few years later, Pope Nicholas I formally created the College of Cardinals to ensure an orderly election by the presence of an advisory body. Both the prestige and the influence of the papacy rose enormously during this decade, and is reflected in the publication of the new collection of canon law, the so-called *Collection in Seventy-Four Titles*, which gave great prominence to the legal prerogatives of the see of St. Peter.

The death of Henry III in 1056 was a blow to the movement. He was succeeded by his son, Henry IV, a minor. During the necessary regency, Henry became so frustrated and depressed by the unpleasant forms of tutelage exercised over him that he failed to develop a prudent and balanced outlook. But a prudent and mature assessment of the situation was required. The close cooperation between Henry III

and the reforming party was based on mutual esteem. But, as we have seen, it had led of necessity to the strong assertion of the primacy of the see of Rome. To assert such primacy in regard to the Church was one thing; a personal clash, and a rivalry between Pope and Emperor could easily turn the question of primacy into one of who was master, Emperor or Pope. Although there were several ambiguous pronouncements on this question, the matter had never been settled. There had been occasions of conflict that in turn had given rise to further ambiguous pronouncements like the famous statements about the two swords—one wielded by the Pope, the other by the Emperor—or like the statement that Church stood to State like soul to body. But there had never yet been a confrontation, and everyone had probably preferred a merciful vagueness to any definite answer.

Henry IV came of age in 1065 and spent the first ten years of his reign subduing the rebellious Saxon nobility. In 1075 he thought he was at last firmly established. In that year there was a dispute over the succession to the archbishopric of Milan. Henry and Pope Gregory VII supported rival claimants. When Henry refused to drop his candidate, he received, on New Year's Day, 1076, a letter from Gregory in which he was tactlessly reminded that he owed obedience to the Pope. Henry, aware of Gregory's somewhat tenuous hold over the city and people of Rome, and made confident by his recent triumph over the Saxon nobility, was determined, after years of frustration, to use the full force of his authority. He wrote back to Gregory, charging him with all sorts of crimes and ordering him to relinquish the papacy. He also invited the people of Rome to rid themselves of their bishop. Gregory replied by excommunicating and deposing Henry.

This situation had been brought about by the temper of the two protagonists. There was some precedent for Henry's deposition of an unworthy Pope. There was none for Gregory's deposition of an unworthy monarch—he was, clearly, behaving in a revolutionary manner. But it needed little stretching of the major points of the reform movement to include among the prerogatives of the Holy See the right to depose kings. And Gregory had fortified himself in advance by adding a formal statement of his rights, the *Dictatus Papae*, to his register. The gist of this manifesto was that the Roman bishop alone, not the Emperor, had universal power. The kings of Christendom, with the exception of William the Conqueror, naturally became wary of Gregory. But needless to say, the nobility of Germany seized the opportunity of the Emperor's difficulties and rebelled against him. Formally excommunicated, Henry could do nothing. And so he humbled himself at Canossa.

Canossa by itself did not become a turning point: Gregory, as we have seen, died in exile; Henry never quite managed to restore peace in his empire. The disputed issue of the primacy of Pope or Emperor was never resolved. But as a result of the long war unleashed by Gregory's invitation to rebellion in Germany, the monarchy became weaker and weaker over the next half century.

For the papacy, the consequences of Gregory VII's actions were more far-reaching and in the long run, equally fatal. Since no subsequent Pope could disavow the reform movement and since the spirit, if not the letter, of the *Dictatus Papae* had become built into the reform movement as a result of the clash between Henry and Gregory, the papacy was launched on a course in which superiority over temporal powers was explicitly claimed from time to time.

Probably the nascent states of late medieval Europe, as well as the princedoms which sprang up within the confines of the old Empire, were indirectly the ultimate beneficiaries. For even if papal superiority over secular rulers could not be clearly vindicated, the status of kingship and of the Empire came to be desacramentalized. The unction became less and less of a sacrament; kings became less and less new Davids. And when the number of sacraments was officially defined as seven, at the Lateran Council in the early thirteenth century, the royal or imperial coronation was not one of them. Cut down to size as secular magistrates, and less and less frequently thought of as quasi-priestly rulers and divinely appointed kings, the new monarchs of Christendom settled down to the task of pragmatic government and utilitarian administration. As such, they all learned to treat their clergy, high and low, as their subjects. They mastered the techniques of taxing them and making the Church in their lands into departments of state. For good or ill, the modern secular state could not have evolved had the popes not taken the initiative towards making kingship less of a sacred office.

PETER MUNZ

Left Henry IV investing his son, the future Henry V, with the royal insignia at Aachen in 1099.

Right Henry V receives the imperial insignia at his coronation in Rome by Pope Paschal in 1111. The struggle for supremacy of the Empire between secular and ecclesiastical authority appears to end in victory for the Pope.

A triumph for orthodoxy

The events at Canossa and the condemnation of Peter Abelard under the auspices of St. Bernard of Clairvaux were signal triumphs for the papacy and the orthodox doctrines of Western Christianity. The capture of Jerusalem by the First Crusade, on the other hand, was an exhilarating achievement for European Christendom as a whole. Yet during these sixty-three years new forces emerged, forces that led to questions about the spiritual status of the ecclesiastical hierarchy, and even about the fundamental doctrines of the faith. Meanwhile, the successes of the crusaders diminished and the Latin states that they had established in the Levant fell into a decline in which even Bernard himself was implicated.

Within ten years of the humiliation of Emperor Henry IV, Pope Gregory VII ended his days in exile from Rome, supported only by the Norman army of adventurers that he had called to his aid. Although his great rival was to end his reign opposed by a papist party supported by his own son, that son, Henry v, soon demanded in his turn the rights of clerical investiture

Signature of Pope Calixtus II on the Concordat of Worms.

claimed by his father. The conflict was not resolved until the compromise of the Concordat of Worms in 1122. Its terms approximated the terms won by the Emperor's father-in-law, Henry I of England, some fifteen years earlier. In return for surrendering the right to invest bishops with the spiritual symbols of their office, the rulers won papal recognition of their right to have an effective voice in the election of bishops. But discord between the Church and the secular authorities was to remain potentially explosive for generations to come. Indeed, there were many people in Europe who deplored what they regarded as the worldliness of the Church.

Papal influence in Europe: 1198-1216

○ Papal States
○ Dependants of the Holy See
○ Holy Roman Empire

Arnold of Brescia

During the eleventh century, a movement had sprung up in Lombardy devoted to an ascetic and "primitive" Christianity and known as the *Humiliati*. But the opposition among the public at large to the growing secularization of the Church was most dramatically embodied in the career of Arnold of Brescia.

Probably a pupil of Abelard, and condemned with him at Sens, Arnold preached that only the lay power should own and administer property. In the last years of his life—before his execution at the order of the Pope—Arnold led a republican government in the city of Rome itself. Arnold's ideas, though politically subversive, were not as serious a challenge to the authority of the Church as was the intellectual unrest abroad during the twelfth century, an unrest

Albi, center of the Albigensian heresy; the cathedral.

symbolized by the career of Abelard. Arnold, indeed, had not been killed as a heretic; nor were the *Humiliati*, who after all claimed only to be returning to the teachings of poverty of Christ himself, at first open to charges of heresy. But the case was quite different with the sect known as the Cathari, whose successors were the Albigensians of southern France. The doctrine of the Cathari was less of a heresy within the Christian Church than it was a rival religion. It must therefore be regarded as one of the most serious manifestations of the new ideas abroad in Europe during the twelfth century. The Cathari had originated in the Bulgarian lands of the Byzantine Empire, and their beliefs show the strong influence of Eastern thought, as found in the teachings of the Persian Mani. They saw the world as the battleground of two equally powerful forces of good and evil, and regarded the physical creation of the world as the work of the evil one. Thus rejecting God's role in the creation, they overthrew one of the fundamental doctrines of Christianity. The speculations of an Abelard and the humble aims of the *Humiliati* in no way tended to the extreme anti-Christian position of the Cathari. Yet their searching questions into the substance of orthodoxy could only be regarded as menacing by the ecclesiastical establishment. The Church was in habitual political dispute with the lay power and was constantly on guard against the subversion of heresy.

The threat of Islam

In the twelfth century, religious speculation, as St. Bernard feared and foresaw, was not to be easily stopped. A substantial contributory factor to such speculation was Islamic civilization. It is true that in Spain Islamic culture had flourished on European soil for centuries. But it was only in the newly confident and outward-looking society of the twelfth century that all the conditions were right for Europeans to profit from the rich store of Greco-Arabic learning that had been on their doorstep for centuries. The movement had been gathering momentum throughout the previous century, and now the Arab influence was readily accepted.

The monk Gerbert, who became Pope as Sylvester II, had been the first Westerner to use the "Arabic" numerals, and it was probably he who introduced the astrolabe for astronomical experiments into Europe. At Salerno and then at Monte Cassino, thanks to the writings of men such as Constantine the African, the principles of Greco-Arabic medicine were being studied in Europe. Islamic thought, with its bases in the works of Aristotle and Plato and the science of India, was immensely influential in the early twelfth century at the great school of Chartres. And direct contact with the Greek texts of the ancient philosophers was possible for such Western scholars as James of Venice, who studied at Constantinople. But the main impetus was from Islam and above all from the cosmopolitan courts of newly Christian Spain. There, Arabs, Christians and Jews combined to initiate a revolution in mathematics that was to culminate at the end of the century in the career of Leonardo of Pisa. The much-traveled English scholar, Adelard of Bath, spent many years in Syria and Spain. His numerous important translations include the first Latin version of Euclid. Adelard, in fact, was one of those who introduced

Page from an early Byzantine herbal with later Arabic inscription.

the new Arabic writings on the study of alchemy from which European chemistry was to spring. Europe's contacts with the East and the Arab World were probably also crucial to the development of the Gothic style in architecture.

It is interesting that the impact of Arabic culture on European thought seems to have been at its greatest during the period when the Christian kingdoms of Spain were enjoying their greatest success in the long process of reconquest. Toledo, the ancient Visigothic capital, was recaptured in 1085, and by 1100 the combined kingdoms of Castile and Leon had pushed their frontiers well to the south of the Ebro River. Their advance was slowed during the twelfth century when the Moorish emirates in Spain were united under the Murabit dynasty.

Spain reconquered

The Spanish victories were important, but they were no compensation for the massive blow suffered by the Christian cause in the East at the Battle of Manzikert in 1071. Here the Byzantine Emperor Romanus IV was defeated by the armies of the Seljuk Turks, and the whole of Anatolia, the vital hinterland of Constantinople and Christendom's eastern bulwark, was suddenly put in jeopardy. The defeat in part had been due to treachery, as civil war compounded the troubles of the Empire. Now numbered among her external enemies was a new force, the Norman principality of southern Italy.

The domestic conflict of the Eastern Empire ended with the accession of Alexius I Comnenus in 1081. He was able to foil the Normans by a diplomacy that included an alliance with, and important trading concessions to, the growing power of Venice. But Constantinople itself was threatened by the depredations of nomadic tribes from the Asian steppes. Nevertheless, by the early 1090s, thanks to the Herculean efforts of Alexius, the Empire, although much reduced by the events of the previous twenty years, seemed to have weathered the storm. But a new problem now appeared.

Earlier in his reign, in his search for allies, Alexius had appealed to the West for mercenaries. With the arrival of the crusaders in the European provinces of the Empire in 1095, Alexius found himself with a force that threatened to overwhelm rather than support his realm. Instead of mercenaries, of the kind Byzantium had used for centuries, came a host of landless barons and footloose adventurers inspired with hatred of the Infidel, hope of eternal salvation and little respect for the "schismatic" Christian Emperor of the East. This vast and fervent body of men was under the command of a group of ambitious princes who included Alexius' old enemy, Bohemond the Norman. Nevertheless, the Emperor succeeded in transporting the crusader army away from his capital to Palestine. In addition, he exacted from most of the leaders an oath of homage for any lands that they might recover.

Among those to swear was Bohemond; but his subsequent attempt to hold Antioch as an independent principality led him at one point to call for a "crusade" against the Christian Emperor of the East himself. Such corruption of the spiritual ideals of the crusade was to be a dull thread throughout its history. But even from the outset, the motives and motivations of the crusaders had been mixed. What was the nature of the newly confident and aggressive Europe from which they came?

The Crusaders

Undoubtedly the religious impulse was strong. The crusade was launched by the stirring call to liberate the Holy Places made by Pope Urban II at the Council of Clermont in 1095. While Jerusalem had been controlled by the Arab Fatimid dynasty, access to the city had been comparatively easy for

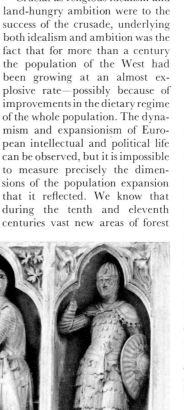
A crusader receives Holy Communion; sculpture from Reims Cathedral.

the growing flood of Western pilgrims, who were inspired by the new mood of piety abroad in Europe following the monastic reforms of St. Bernard. But with the conquest of Palestine by the fanatical Seljuks, advancing in the wake of their victory at Manzikert, the pilgrim routes were cut. Although the religious intentions of Urban II need not be questioned, he must have been aware of the massive increase in the prestige of the papacy already high after Canossa, that would follow from the recovery of Jerusalem under his aegis. Urban's call rang throughout Europe and was taken up by itinerant preachers such as Peter the Hermit. Indeed, Peter led a vast but disorderly band of common people to the crusade and, despite his own obscure and humble origins, he enjoyed some prestige with the army. Although the later crusades were to be led by kings and emperors, the first was undeniably a popular movement, even though most of its aristocratic leaders may have had ulterior political ends of one kind or another.

Crucial as religious idealism and land-hungry ambition were to the success of the crusade, underlying both idealism and ambition was the fact that for more than a century the population of the West had been growing at an almost explosive rate—possibly because of improvements in the dietary regime of the whole population. The dynamism and expansionism of European intellectual and political life can be observed, but it is impossible to measure precisely the dimensions of the population expansion that it reflected. We know that during the tenth and eleventh centuries vast new areas of forest

Dedication of the abbey of Citeaux to the Virgin by its early saintly abbots.

and marsh had been reclaimed for agriculture within the traditional frontiers of Christendom, and that the vast movement of colonization of the lands to the east of the German empire had begun.

The growth and increasing physical vigor of the peasant population that these facts indicate were caused, at least in part, by a revolution in agricultural machinery and techniques. In this revolution there were three vital elements that gradually merged: the development of a new plough, more capable of turning over the heavy and fertile soils of the northern European plain than its predecessor; the introduction of a new system for the rotation of crops, which made for a more efficient use of land and also made possible the introduction of new crops with higher protein content; and the gradual adoption of the horse as a draught animal, in place of the more slow-moving oxen of previous generations. The combination of these three factors created a new situation in northern European agriculture, which has been viewed as the basis of the cultural ascendancy of the north, above all of France, throughout the Middle Ages. There can be no doubt that the new agriculture played an important part in European life of this period.

But in saying this we do not forget that it was the new spirit of inquiry abroad in Europe that enabled the splendidly vigorous society of the twelfth century to adopt the new learning and evolve for itself a new intellectual orientation.

Abelard in Paris

Through the early Middle Ages, such teaching and studying as existed in Europe was centered on monasteries and cathedral schools, and theology was the "queen of sciences." The new universities that sprang up across Europe in the twelfth and thirteenth centuries made it possible for other branches of learning to flourish and develop. Groups of questing students gathered around such renowned teachers as Peter Abelard at Paris to form the nucleus for these universities. The dialectical methods introduced by Abelard were to have a profound influence on the thinking of his day and brought him into conflict with the Church—just as his celebrated romance with the lovely Héloïse earned for him the fury and the terrible retribution of her offended family.

The seal of Clare College, Cambridge. The foundation of the Universities of Cambridge and of Oxford was largely caused by the emigration of dissident students from the University of Paris.

Opposite Scenes from student life from the illuminated statute book of the College of Hubant at the University of Paris.

The road from Orleans to Paris was crowded with groups of pilgrims singing psalms, merchants driving pack-animals laden with bundles, horsemen with fine trappings and all sorts of riff-raff. The young student who had been making his way along it for several days saw in the distant hollow of the river, in the glow of the sunset, the bell-towers and roofs of the Ile de la Cité. He urged on his mount: "Paris at last!"

This emotion that Peter Abelard experienced on arriving in Paris was to appear later in his autobiography. Thanks to this work, which Abelard entitled *Letter to A Friend, or the History of My Misfortunes*, we are familiar not only with the quite exceptional restlessness that characterized his life but also with his course of studies and with the intellectual framework of the times.

The reader might well be surprised at the strength of Abelard's emotion upon reaching Paris, considering the city's condition in the year 1100. It was a small town, crammed between the banks of the Ile de la Cité, with houses rising in tiers even on to the bridges—the Petit-Pont on the left bank and the Grand-Pont on the right. It hardly extended any farther than the island; only a few small market towns had grown up in the vicinity of the abbeys of Saint-Germain-des-Prés, Saint-Marcel and Sainte-Geneviève. No one could have suspected that one day Paris would become the capital city. The King resided there only occasionally, and the Bishop of Paris was only one of a number of suffragan bishops under the Archbishop of Sens. And knowledge, like power, had yet to reach any degree of centralization; seats of learning were spread over a wide area like the châteaux of the lords of the manor, and like the towns that came into being and took shape at the same period. The monastic schools of Bec or Saint-Benoît-sur-Loire, and the episcopal schools of Chartres or Reims, were already much better known than the schools of Paris.

But Paris attracted Peter Abelard because of his enthusiasm for the subjects of dialectics. He had learned the elements of it in the various schools he had attended in his native Brittany—where his

father was lord of the manor of Pallet, near Nantes—and also at Loches where he profited from the lessons of the celebrated teacher Roscelin. But Guillaume de Champeau, the authority on dialectics, taught in Paris. Thus Abelard decided—when he was about twenty—to go to Paris to hear Guillaume lecture, and through him to perfect himself in the art.

The study of dialectics was pursued with enormous enthusiasm in the student world of the twelfth century, and it is important to know why. It is accepted that traditionally the subjects of learning were divided into seven branches, which we know as the seven liberal arts. Whereas the useful arts encompassed the manual crafts—carpentry, metalwork, etc.—the liberal arts were concerned both with the physical sphere—arithmetic, geometry, music and astronomy (the quadrivium)—and the sphere of the spirit—grammar, rhetoric and dialectics (the trivium). Every student would normally be expected to study these various subjects and to complete the whole cycle. The more gifted ones would then grapple with the "sacred science," to which Abelard later gave the name of theology. Grammar was the field we call letters—literature and the study of ancient and modern authors. Rhetoric, the art of expressing oneself, held then a position of great importance, for the whole of medieval culture was based on the spoken word and gesture. These were to be succeeded at the time of the Renaissance by a civilization based on writing and printing. Finally, dialectics was the art of reasoning; it was, as Rabin Maur wrote as early as the ninth century "the discipline of disciplines . . . it is dialectics that teaches us how to teach and teaches us how to learn: in dialectics reason discovers and shows what it is, what it seeks, and what it sees."

Dialectics, then, aroused great enthusiasm in scholastic circles. Its sphere can be compared to that of logic: it showed how to make use of reason in the search for truth. But it also presupposed an exchange of views, a discussion, which was called the "disputation;" logic does not necessarily entail this for it can be carried on by a thinker in the privacy of his own room. The "disputation" took a predominant

: yr pauet dire que il se conberoit eius eglise dyffidis wedo re
t chacris vna a oro de son saunt a saute a qui il seine e leu he
ue maria te a sair michel o grabel yer top paust au yele

Michaen pour .vi. esteneles apotas e a chaiaue
escenele trops pieces de pain:

Ie chaen ay a la feste de com saunt saint pieres de
eslieus neuy: Setem faculte loiment soliet que il puissent

Héloïse and Abelard; this sculpture is on a capital at the Salle des Gardes de la Conciergerie in Paris.

place among scholastic exercises. At the beginning of each study, there was a reading from a text, the "lectio." "Reading" was the equivalent of teaching; when later at the University of Paris it was forbidden to "read" Aristotle, this meant that it was forbidden to make use of certain of his works as a basis of instruction.

Whenever a teacher embarked upon the study of a work, he first gave a general introduction. He then made a commentary upon it which was called the "exposition" and was divided into three parts: the "letter," that is to say the grammatical explanation; the "sense," or comprehension of the text; and finally what is called the "meaning," that is the deeper meaning or doctrinal content. The "littera," "sensus," and the "sententia" (meaning) constitute the glossary. There are a great number of manuscripts from this period that reveal this method of teaching, even in their actual layout. Each page comprises one or two central columns of text, while the glossary surrounds the text and fills the top, bottom and sides of the page. A similar layout was to survive in printed books even to the end of the fifteenth century.

When it came to a question of the "sententia" or doctrinal content, a host of questions could be raised that had to be resolved, and it was this that constituted the disputation or "disputatio" which formed such a distinctive part of scholastic exercises. In the following century, there were a great number of works, in particular several parts of the *Summa* of St. Thomas Aquinas, which are given the name of *Questiones Disputate*, that bear witness to the conditions under which they were worked out, i.e. in the course of those disputations in which both teacher

and pupils took part. The disputations that are so much in demand by present-day university students were accepted quite naturally in feudal times and survived until modern times.

In fact, they were so readily accepted that an exceptionally gifted pupil like Abelard found it tempting to take advantage of the fact. He had originally been well received by Guillaume de Champeau, that indefatigable disputant, but in spite of his youth he did not hesitate to attack his teacher's propositions, even to the point of forcing him on two occasions to modify them. This success brought him considerable renown but it also aroused fierce jealousies, as much on the part of his fellow students as of Guillaume himself. Abelard responded to their attacks by opening a school of his own, first at Melun and then at Corbeil; but he had also set his sights on the chair of dialectics in Paris itself, at the school of Notre-Dame. He succeeded in his ambition, and later taught at Mont Sainte-Geneviève just outside the city. His reputation was a powerful magnet to the students of Paris—among them some from the provinces and some from abroad.

The story of his love for Héloïse, the niece of Canon Fulbert of Notre-Dame, is famous, as is the story of Fulbert's fury when he believed that Abelard was about to desert her. The emasculation that Fulbert's hired ruffians inflicted on Abelard in 1118 brought to an end, for the time being, his activities as a teacher. He became a monk and retired to the cloisters of Saint-Denis, where he stayed until 1120.

But the excitement that Abelard had aroused in no way abated. In 1127 the canons of Notre-Dame, finding that the student body had become far too boisterous, decided to expel them from the cloister which they occupied. The teachers and scholars found hospitality on the slopes of Mont Sainte-Geneviève, under the aegis of the abbey of the same name. Abelard himself taught there, at least from 1133 onwards; and the Englishman, John of Salisbury, has borne witness to the enthusiasm that he aroused. The originality of his teaching was embodied in his use of the resources of dialectics to prove the truth of certain articles of faith. It was a rash position to adopt; he drew upon Aristotle—as yet little known in the West—when making a commentary on certain fundamental dogmas of Christianity, such as the Trinity. This was to arouse distrust and to scandalize certain defenders of the faith, such as St. Bernard of Clairvaux, to such an extent that Abelard was to find his propositions condemned at the Council of Sens in 1140. He appealed to the Pope, who upheld the Council, and Abelard decided to submit to their decision.

The philosopher's life was to reach a peaceful conclusion in 1142 in the shade of the abbey church of Cluny.

Meanwhile, the "student explosion" had determined the physical layout of Paris. The left bank became the home of the intellectuals, and was soon filled with schools which little by little replaced the vineyards; while the right bank, which afforded easy access for river traffic, became the home of commerce. Paris became honored as the "fountain of knowledge" and the "paradise of pleasure" for students all over Europe. In the following century, Alexander Neckham was to write, "it is there that the arts flourish, it is there that divine works are the rule."

Even so, there was still no such institution as a university. When Abelard died in 1142, the methods of teaching had not yet appeared in texts, and there was no organization in this effervescent student life. Teachers and pupils found themselves in the houses that from this time on formed compact rows on the slopes of Mont Sainte-Geneviève and on the approaches of the Petit-Pont. The Rue du Fouarre, in what is now the Latin Quarter, is a reminder of the bales of straw (*feurre, fourre*) that normally served as seats, and the Rue de la Parcheminerie recalls the material which was after all the medium for the transmission of thought: the humble lambskin, cleaned and degreased to provide a surface for writing. Each of the folio volumes of those times, so reverently preserved in our libraries today, represents a whole flock of sheep.

In general, the teachers lived in a very hand-to-mouth fashion and the question of their salaries was one that gave rise to fierce debate. Was it permissible to disseminate knowledge for financial reward? Peter Abelard openly declared that his pupils owed him both material rewards and honor, but preachers like St. Bernard of Clairvaux argued violently against those who used teaching for their own profit. No problem existed for those who were assigned a benefice by a cathedral church or abbey, and this applied in the case of Abelard, who

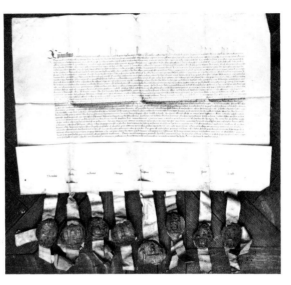

Left The seals of the faculties of the University of Paris.

Below The act of foundation of the College of Robert de Sorbon, soon to became the faculty of theology.

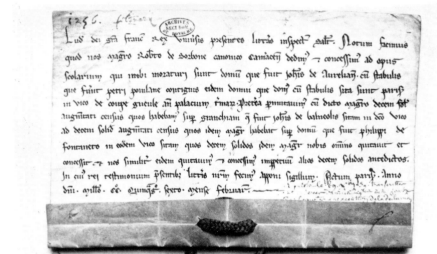

The seal of the University of Paris.

enjoyed the office of prebendary canon, although this did not mean that he was a priest; nor for those members of the mendicant orders, notably the preaching friars who at the beginning of the thirteenth century had a special duty to teach and were maintained by their orders—despite the opposition of the secular clergy.

The bond that linked this sphere of activity to the bishop upon whom in principle it depended was somewhat tenuous. It was the bishop who in the person of his chancellor granted throughout his diocese the *licentia docendi*, the permission to teach from which arose the term "licenciate" that is still in use. The abbot of Sainte-Geneviève, however, claimed the right to do this throughout the area under the jurisdiction of his abbey.

We learn from a bull of Pope Innocent III, dating from the end of 1208 or the beginning of 1209, that a number of disputes arose about the year 1200. Teachers and pupils of Paris then united in a single association and nominated a commission of eight members from among themselves whose responsibility it was to draw up statutes by which they would be governed. Thus there came into being the *Universitas Magistrorum et Scolarium Parisiensium*, the University, that is to say the association in a united body of the teachers and scholars of Paris. The Pope ratified its autonomy and denied the bishop and his chancellor the right to refuse a licence to whomsoever the teachers nominated as qualified to teach. In 1215 the papal legate Robert de Courçon confirmed the rights of the University by approving the statutes that freed both teachers and students from the tutelage of the bishop. At the same period (to be exact the year 1200) the King of France had of his own accord freed the University from the jurisdiction of the royal courts, and it was now answerable only to the ecclesiastical courts. Judicial autonomy was thus added to administrative autonomy; the world of thought and knowledge became the epitome of freedom.

In the thirteenth century, the University of Paris was to earn a great reputation, with teachers like Albert le Grand from Germany, Thomas Aquinas from Italy and Roger Bacon from England. But for all that, its existence was marked by unruliness and agitation. The strike of 1229–31 was triggered off by a brawl which had broken out between some students and innkeepers of the Faubourg Saint-Marcel one Shrove Monday. But the royal troops put down the disturbance rather too rigorously. And there was the well-known struggle waged by the secular teachers against the friars of the mendicant orders whom they wanted to ban from teaching in their universities.

From this time onward poor students found board and lodging in colleges. The first of these was founded in Paris in 1180 by a middle-class Londoner named Josse. Similar foundations were to spring up: the college of Saint-Thomas du Louvre in 1186 and the college of Bons-Enfants in 1280. But all those were to be eclipsed in the future by the one established in 1257 by Robert de Sorbon, the chaplain to Louis

A teacher of grammar above the figure of the grammarian Donatus, an allegorical representation, in the masonry of Chartres Cathedral, of the studies pursued at a university.

Top right Plato and Socrates depicted in a book of astronomical tables and prognostications, from St. Albans.

Bottom right A bastion in the city wall at Oxford, the scene of many fierce disputes between representatives of the opposing factions of "town and gown," which were characteristic of university towns in the medieval period.

the Pious. He founded a college in a house that the King had given him, situated in the Rue Coupe-Guele, which is now the Rue de la Sorbonne. In fact, although the colleges started off as hostels for poor students, they became in time centers of teaching; for example, the College of Robert de Sorbon was the headquarters of the Faculty of Theology of the University.

Although Paris remained famous for its teaching of the liberal arts, as in Abelard's time, the curriculum was nevertheless distinguished by the inclusion of medicine and theology. From the end of the twelfth century, the students at Paris formed various distinct groups according to their place of origin, in other words, "nations." There were four nations represented at the University of Paris: French—that is to say, natives of the Ile-de-France—Normans, Picards and English. At the end of the Middle Ages, because of the wars between France and England, the English nation was replaced by the German. Each one had its own statutes. One could discern in these spontaneous groups of students a foreshadowing of the nations that were born in the course of the wars of the fifteenth century.

It was in this period, however, that the University of Paris went into a complete decline. The scholastic methods founded upon Aristotelian logic, which had been introduced to the West through the Arab thinkers, particularly Avicenna and Averroes, became set from the beginning of the fourteenth century onwards in formulae which were to offer an easy butt for the skits of François Villon. Under Philippe-le-Bel and then under Philippe de Valois, the University had begun to adopt a political role, and its power in the state seemed to grow in proportion to the decline in the quality of its studies. And it was no longer the only university; its organ-

ization had inspired various other foundations during the thirteenth century.

University foundations were to multiply in the fourteenth and fifteenth centuries, but it was a period of the spread of learning rather than any advance or renewal of intellectual or technical research. The only progress in this period was seen in the science of armament and military equipment, with the introduction of gunpowder.

But at this period, the University of Paris was discredited because at the time of the wars between France and England it took sides with the invader. The Sorbonne, the Faculty of Theology, succeeded in maintaining its reputation under the *ancien régime*, even when the University as a whole went into decline. The brilliance and freshness of Abelard, and his enormous influence, had played a decisive part in establishing this reputation. Through his lectures, even more than his writings, Abelard brought reason to the traditional mystery surrounding faith and an independent intellect to the elaborated system of logic. In no small measure he laid the foundations for the advent of humanism.

REGINE PERNOUD

Students at Paris are shown carrying books and in other activities pertaining to the life of the University in the illuminated statute book of the College of Hubant.

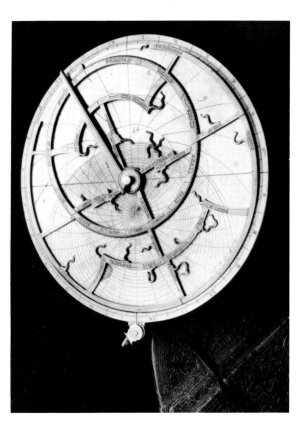

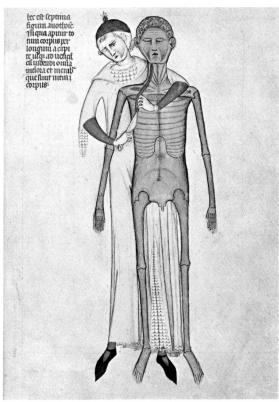

Left Fourteenth-century astrolabe, an instrument for astronomical measurement, and one of the many mathematical instruments that medieval European scholarship took from earlier Arab examples.

Right A mid-fourteenth-century medical manuscript of Guy of Pavia. Some of the greatest medical centers of medieval Europe were in France and Italy, their learning based directly on Arab sources.

The cult of courtly love takes root and

The glory of Chartres

In the glories of its new cathedral, the town of Chartres provided the fullest single expression of vigor and inspiration of twelfth-century Europe. The school of Chartres itself had been in the forefront of the revival of Neoplatonist philosophy that marked the intellectual ferment of that glorious century. Like other important centers, it had been receptive to the intellectual stimulus provided by that century's full discovery of Greco-Arab learning. Chartres also symbolized the cultural and political hegemony that northern France was to exercise throughout Europe during the thirteenth century and after. This hegemony was prepared for in the work of the great Abbot Suger, churchman, statesman and inspired patron of the arts, whose church of the Abbey of St. Denis provided both a fitting shrine for the French monarchy and the seminal building of the Gothic Age. Paris, as the home both of the kings of France who were to come into their own during the thirteenth century, and of the great new university, was to dominate Europe in the coming generations. Yet during the twelfth century itself, national leadership was located in the south, the home of the rich Provençal culture. Before turning to Provence, let us first look at the other strangely "un-European" society which had sprung up in Outremer, the lands "over the sea," in the Holy Land.

Outremer, heir to the Crusades

The fruits of the First Crusade had been the city of Jerusalem itself and several Christian principalities, representing roughly the modern states of Israel, Lebanon and parts of modern Turkey and Syria. Despite the mixed motives behind the crusading movement, popular religious sentiment had been strong. Throughout the first half of the twelfth century, the newly founded Frankish kingdoms in Outremer and the crusading orders of knights, the Templars and the Hospitalers, received occasional reinforcements in the shape of militant pilgrims from Europe anxious to defend the gains of Christendom in the Holy Land. But the recapture of the inland northern county of Edessa by the sultan Zangi in 1144 sounded the death knell of the

Christ in Majesty, from Vézelay, where Bernard of Clairvaux stirred Conrad III and the French King to embark on the Second Crusade.

Christian states in the Middle East. By the end of the century, they had been reduced to a thin coastal strip. Thanks to the stirring oratory of St. Bernard, two mighty armies under the command of the aging German king Conrad III and the pious but inexperienced Louis VII of France set out on the ill-fated Second Crusade of 1147.

From the outset the venture was weakened by divided councils, while animosity and distrust soon developed between the Westerners and the Byzantines. For Byzantine survival, and thus ultimately for the survival of the Christian cause in the East, Moslem disunity was crucial. Yet few things could be better calculated to unify Islam than the concerted attack of powerful Christian armies. The situation grew still worse when, as was the case, the objectives were ill-defined and ill-coordinated. Reluctant to assist his Christian allies for such reasons, the Emperor Manuel was dismayed at the ease with which the unruly crusading armies pillaged the Byzantine lands through which they passed. When the Germans finally met the Infidel, however, they were easily defeated and dispersed. When King Louis of France, with his beautiful and headstrong wife Eleanor, arrived at Antioch, he was urged to strike at Aleppo, the seat of power of the sultan Nur ed Din. The plan was sound, but Louis was suspicious of the very close liaison between Eleanor and her uncle, the Count

Raymond, who had suggested the strategy to him. Anxious to visit Jerusalem, Louis instead left Antioch for the Holy City. From Jerusalem the Christians attacked Damascus, a potential ally against their main enemy, Nur ed Din. In fact, the army was forced to abandon the siege and the crusade did nothing but demonstrate the vulnerability of the western crusading effort.

To the Provençal ladies of Queen Eleanor's train, the semi-Oriental court of Antioch must have been a magical world, and the soldiers were often reluctant to quit the ease and comfort of these rich cities for the battlefield. But still they could not accept the ease with which their cousins had adapted themselves to the mores of the East. The astonished northerners found themselves in a supposedly Christian and crusading society—yet one where even the pleasures of the harem were not unknown, and where princes often conducted diplomatic negotiations in Arabic. For their part, of course, the second-generation crusaders were living in a political environment that made the simple equation of Christian versus Infidel an impossible recipe for continued survival. Inevitably, as the rival civilizations of Islam and Christianity came to know one another at first hand, they discovered that the religious-political tags that made them enemies could not obscure the fact that they were all men. We have touched on the eagerness of

Christian scholars in Spain to learn from Islam, but in the Norman kingdom of southern Italy an even greater degree of cultural miscegenation made itself apparent. In Outremer the fusion was complete; they were, of course, potential enemies, as the kings of France and England were enemies, and both sides found it advantageous when calling up help from outside to emphasize the element of the religious war. But if Outremer shocked the northern crusaders, the vibrant and revolutionary principles of the culture of southern France threatened them—and it was closer to home.

The culture of Provence

The political rivalry between the kings at Paris and their many powerful vassals was of long-standing, and the most serious threat was posed by the virtually autonomous dukes of Aquitaine and the counts of Toulouse. Southern France was also a separate area

Carving of a troubadour.

flourishes in southern France

Miniature of lovers, and a majestic head of the Virgin, which exemplify the the eleventh-century cult of woman.

linguistically, and it was culturally separate, with a virtually unbroken tradition stretching back to Roman Provence. Moreover, there was close contact with the Arab World, and, as the twelfth century progressed, the separatism of the south was reinforced by the rapid spread of the Albigensian religious heresy.

The heralds and agents of this new civilization were the troubadours. Their verses, probably influenced by Arabic models, survive from the eleventh century; the earliest troubadour known to us by name is Duke William of Aquitaine (1071–1126). The most distinctive features of Provençal culture, when compared with that of other European regions, are the active participation of a cultured aristocracy and the development of a specifically court culture as opposed to a Church culture. Vernacular lyric poetry may be said to have been born in Provence during this period; forms that were invented by the Provençal poets continued to be used down to the Renaissance and indeed beyond. More important, however, than the forms was the subject matter.

Until then the main subject of court poetry had been the heroic deeds of great emperors and warriors—of Charlemagne and Roland

St. Dominic, who led the crusade against heresy in the eleventh century.

or, in the far north, the mythological hero, Beowulf. The poetry of the troubadours instead dealt with love between man and woman, and a unique and revolutionary love at that. Suddenly woman became an object of respect in the male society of the Middle Ages. The cult of courtly love was the cult of woman, which in religious terms was paralleled by the equally sudden appearance of the cult of the Virgin during the twelfth century; Chartres itself was the first great church to be dedicated to the Virgin. As the thirteenth century progressed, the two cults approached and sometimes merged into one another. In a characteristic medieval musical form, the polyphonic motet, a piece based on a fragment of plainsong from an antiphon to the Virgin might use the text of a French love song in the upper part. Furthermore, at a time when marriage was explicitly a matter of dynastic policy and brides were regarded as counters on the diplomatic chess board and wives as pieces of property, the notion of love was certainly not connected with the marital state. To some extent the cult was a game and known to be a game for, ironically, the objective of the poets, who were almost exclusively men and usually landless younger sons, was to win a rich and landed wife and thus join the system they were supposed to be fighting.

In some ways, the cult of courtly love was an ideal rationalization of a society centered upon the castle

Brutality and murder typical of the Albigensian crusade.

of a great lord thronged by landless adventurers and presided over during the lord's many absences by the great lady. But the game was taken to extraordinary lengths; for example, at the court of Eleanor of Aquitaine. First at Angers then at Poitiers, Eleanor held courts of love, presided over by the ladies. The cult even had its own bible or legal code in the shape of the Code of Love in thirty-one articles. Written for Eleanor's daughter by her chaplain, the Code of Love was regarded by the orthodox members of the old society as one of the most subversive, as it was certainly one of the most influential, books of the time.

We have seen Eleanor on crusade with her husband, Louis VII of France. The crusade, attended by many great ladies and their troubadours, was itself something of a romantic episode. Yet, angered by his wife's infidelity and disturbed by her inability to produce sons, the French king finally yielded to the urgings of St. Bernard to rid himself of this "she devil" and sought a dissolution of the marriage. The Pope, himself persuaded by Bernard, granted the dispensation. For Eleanor—who said of her husband "I thought to have married a king but found I am wed to a monk"—the event could only be considered as a "happy release." But the divorce had disastrous consequences for France and the history of Western Europe. Five years later she married Henry Plantagenet, heir to England and the duchy of Normandy.

Heresy and separation

We have already touched on the impact of the Catharist heresy in

Europe; by 1167 it had reached such proportions that the Cathari (their name comes from the Greek word meaning "pure") held their own ecclesiastical council. Sixty years later, the whole rich flowering of Provençal culture was obliterated in the bloody and vindictive Albigensian crusade launched with the Church's blessing and conducted by soldiers and adventurers from the north. The Cathars, like many reforming sects since, held that the Church had been corrupted by its involvement in the world ever since its adoption by Constantine in the fourth century. Only their own pure and simple living, they held, came close to that of the primitive Church. To the rebellious and aristocratic society of the south, it had a double appeal, both as the religious equivalent of that society's political separatism and as a truly aristocratic religion. The small elite of the Catharist *Perfecti*, for instance, exerted a deep fascination on the aristocratic ladies who dominated Provençal society. Indeed many of these ladies publicly embraced Catharism.

The Cathars proclaimed the wickedness as well as the irrelevance of war and even of the crusades. The Church was thus obliged to produce apologists of its own who advanced the argument of the just war. Yet the crusades had in their favor the facts that they hastened the Christianization of the worst excesses of the martial element in feudal society and fostered the evolution of the concept of Christian chivalry. After the twelfth century warfare was as bloody and brutal as ever, but the concept that war was subject to the laws of God and civilized behavior had arisen, and the code of knightly chivalry had been born.

135

The Palace of the Virgin

With its clusters of columns, its soaring arches, its superb stone carvings and its matchless stained-glass windows, the cathedral of Notre-Dame de Chartres is perhaps the finest achievement of the Gothic movement that swept Europe in the thirteenth century. A disastrous fire of 1194 left little more of Chartres' old cathedral than the western towers and the crypt. In a great burst of energy and artistic creativity, the reverent people of the small French town rebuilt their "palace of the Virgin" in the remarkably short span of twenty-five years—and for this reason Chartres Cathedral shows more unity of design than most Gothic cathedrals. Notre-Dame de Chartres has been called a Bible for those who cannot read : the saints appear immortalized in stone at the portals ; the glorious windows present Old and New Testament stories ; and the arches and columns carry men's eyes—along with their thoughts—heavenward.

On June 10, 1194, the cathedral of Notre-Dame de Chartres, rebuilt in the eleventh century by Bishop Fulbert, was destroyed by fire. Only the crypt, the narthex, the two western towers and the Portail Royal—built early in the twelfth century—were spared in the disaster, which also engulfed a great part of the small city, some fifty miles southwest of Paris. From this catastrophe there arose a cathedral that, in its architectural design, its sculptures and its stained glass windows, constitutes one of the outstanding proofs of the Gothic genius and one of its most original in expression.

Thanks to the religious faith of the Middle Ages, Notre-Dame de Chartres was largely rebuilt in a quarter of a century. The *Book of the Miracles of Notre-Dame* tells us of the enthusiasm of the enormous number of staunch Christians who took part in the rebuilding of the cathedral. They transported the materials across the flat country of Beauce, and even harnessed themselves to the heavy wagons of lime, timber and stone.

Everything favored the immediate rebuilding of the cathedral, which was achieved through the generosity both of anonymous believers in the diocese of Chartres and the whole of northern France, as well as the munificence of French and foreign rulers. Among the royal patrons of Chartres was Richard Coeur-de-Lion who, although he was at war with Philip Augustus, was eager to make his offering and to contribute to the restoration of this famous cathedral dedicated to the Virgin Mary. Christian unity was not yet an empty phrase.

From 1210 onwards, services could be held in the new nave. On January 1, 1221, the choir was handed over to the cathedral chapter. Between 1230 and 1235 the transepts were finished, and in 1260, with the solemn consecration of the rebuilt cathedral, the work had virtually been completed.

Perhaps the brilliant but anonymous architect responsible for the plan of the new cathedral came originally from Laon or Soissons, that is to say, from northern France, where Gothic art had recently emerged with such striking innovations. The consecration of the abbey church of Saint-Denis on June 11, 1144, had ensured the transmission of the Gothic style to the whole of France, and its influence at Chartres can be seen in the transverse ribbing of the cathedral towers, and even more in the Portail Royal, which was inspired by Saint-Denis and escaped the fire of 1194.

The second half of the twelfth century had been an age of rich and promising architectural experiments. Cathedrals were planned and built with widely differing plans—Laon with its single aisles, Paris with its double aisles, Sens with no transepts, Noyon with the ends of the transepts semicircular in form, and Senlis with an ambulatory surrounded by chapels. With the exception of Sens, all these cathedrals have great galleries or triforia above their aisles, and all of them, including Sens, have sexpartite nave vaults.

The architect of Chartres had no wish to copy these designs, splendid as they were. To understand his intentions, one must bear in mind the existence of the great crypt built in the eleventh century by Bishop Fulbert, and the considerable limitations this imposed on the ground plan. But the architect was sufficiently ingenious to overcome all these practical problems—in fact they provided him with inspiration. The interior of the building, which is some four hundred and thirty feet long, has a complete unity of conception because of the speed with which it was built, apparently with no second thoughts or regrets. The nave, fifty-four feet across, is wider than that of any other cathedral because of the Romanesque foundations of the existing crypt. It is divided into seven bays, not counting those between the two towers on the west front, and is flanked by single aisles which are repeated again in the transepts. The transepts, over two hundred feet long, almost form a second cathedral at the center of this vast church. The choir has four

The Angel of Chartres looks out from its pinnacle on the east end of the choir.

Opposite The cathedral of Notre-Dame de Chartres, rebuilt after its destruction by fire in 1194. The cathedral is a symbol of the medieval Christian unity, and is one of the greatest expressions of the Gothic genius.

Below The diagram of Gothic architectural development shows: (1) barrel vaulting; (2) the development of the pointed arch and rib vaulting; (3) the stress taken by a buttress; (4) the Gothic development of the flying buttress; (5) a section of a Gothic cathedral to show buttresses supporting the roof and the thin tracery of windows and pillars.

rectangular vaults and a semicircular apse with seven bays. It has also a double ambulatory with seven shallow apsidal chapels.

Had it not been for the exceptional width of the main structure, the architect would almost certainly have given the cathedral greater height. As it is, the main vault is about one hundred and twenty feet high, surpassing those of Senlis, Laon and Paris. Chartres itself was soon to be surpassed by Reims, Amiens and, above all, Beauvais—the most daring structure ever attempted by Gothic architects. Thanks to the unknown architect of Chartres at the end of the twelfth century, the way was opened up for a new style which most of Europe eventually embraced.

It was a vital turning point both from the esthetic and the spiritual point of view, a decisive flowering that was to dominate all others. It was the master

builder of Chartres who designed the pure Gothic style. He discarded excessively wide spans covered by sexpartite vaults and built the main structure with rectangular quadripartite vaults. He abandoned the triforia, which reduced the amount of light in other buildings. At Chartres, the simple and graceful arcades are above the great archways of the nave and choir, and in the clerestory he replaced the small, timid windows of the early Gothic period with two large vertical windows surmounted by a rose, thus reducing the wall at this point almost entirely to glass. He also replaced the cylindrical columns such as may be seen at Laon, Durham or Paris by shafts divided into small columns which foreshadowed the later column clusters of Amiens, Reims and Beauvais. Finally, on the exterior he was the first architect to devise a systematic use of the flying buttress, to withstand and counterbalance the forces exerted by the vaults.

The whole building was as sound as it was daring. This new predominance of void over solid was used in an equally masterly fashion on the façades of the transepts, which were pierced with five large lancet windows surmounted by glowing rose windows. This feature was derived from Laon, developed at Chartres, and soon afterwards brought to even greater magnificence in Paris. It was from Laon, too, that the architect of Chartres took the idea of a multiplicity of towers. He had inherited from the Romanesque period the two towers on the western façade, but this was not enough. He began the construction of further towers on either side of the façades of the transepts. In addition, and following a Carolingian tradition, two further towers were erected at the springing of the apse. Both are incomplete. If one adds the lantern doubtless intended above the crossing, there would eventually have been nine towers soaring above the city. No one had the courage to complete this imposing project. "Cathedrals," said Auguste Rodin in a later age, "inevitably remain unfinished. . . ."

Nevertheless, the "Classic" cathedral had been born and now imposed itself on the Christianity of the thirteenth century. The ceaseless craving for light sprang into life at Chartres, and what Chartres symbolizes above all—with boldness, but not recklessness—is the victory of the spiritual over the material. The time was not yet ripe for the next leap forward: time was, in every accepted sense of the term, at a stop, a divine moment within which the whole spirit of the century of St. Louis was embraced.

More than any other cathedral, that of Chartres is the living proof of the magnificence which the Church of the thirteenth century wished to confer upon the house of God. The Abbé Suger, a century before, had declared his intentions without ambiguity at the time of the reconstruction of Saint-Denis; and in this he was faithful to the explicit instructions which he had been given by the Order of St. Benedict to which he belonged, and even more precisely to the policy laid down by Hugues de Cluny. "The spirit in its blindness strives towards the truth through the medium of material things, and upon seeing the

Gothic Architectural Style

Jerusalem from the Saracens

talented brother John was also unhealthily ambitious, and during Richard's absence on crusade intrigued for the throne. Finally, troubles at home were compounded by threats abroad. Philip Augustus of France, who laid the foundations of his country's greatness in the later Middle Ages, was determined to recover the Angevin lands in France. He had exploited both the conflict between Henry II of England and his sons, and John's disloyalty to Richard, to good effect. But in five years Richard won back almost all Philip's gains, and confirmed England's presence in France with the building of the mighty fortress of Château Gaillard in Normandy. The art of military

A courtly tournament.

fortification had advanced considerably during the twelfth century and Richard was perhaps the greatest military architect of his age. With his death in 1199 and the growing discontent of the English barons with fighting the dynastic wars of the Angevins abroad, the kingdom was greatly imperiled. Compared to the disaster on the Bosphorus in the same year, the capture of Château Gaillard by the French in 1204 was of marginal significance in European affairs, yet it precipitated the loss of most of the English possessions in northern France to the French king.

Chivalry in the West

Richard I's defects as a man and as a ruler have been forgiven him by posterity for the aura of military glamour that surrounds his name. In these terms, his career was the fitting conclusion to a century in which the concept of knightly chivalry began to emerge from the bloody business of self-interested warfare. In the face of the slowly developing sophistication of society at large, the turbulent nobility of Europe—whose scope for private warfare was in any case being limited as the feudal monarchies

grew in power—began to accept the idea of rules to govern warfare. More and more, they channeled their aggressive urges into the causes of their sovereign, into the religious crusade, or into the military sport of the tournament.

At first, tournaments had been little more than wars to the death between friends, so to speak. In theory the vanquished were taken prisoner, but the weapons and conduct of the fight were genuine and men were often killed. Those who were captured could expect to pay heavy ransoms and the world of the tournament provided the opportunity for many a landless younger son to make his fortune. William the Marshal, the elder statesman of John's England, was the prime example; but even before his death the institutions were changing. Royal authority saw itself threatened by these violent gatherings of its vassals, and the wealthy landowner was less and less willing to chance his fortune to this military lottery. Furthermore, such old-world piracy hardly accorded with the new aura surrounding the chivalry of the institution of knighthood.

The idea of the Christian warrior in the service of the just war was partly inspired by the ideals that continued to cling to the crusade. Still more important were the romantic legends surrounding that greatest of all Christian warriors, the Celtic hero King Arthur.

Profits in the East

The Byzantine Empire was restored to an aggressive posture by Alexius I (d. 1118), who had not only recovered much of Anatolia from the Seljuk Turks after the disaster of his predecessor at Manzikert, but had also contained the ambitions of the first crusaders and restored the finances of the Empire. His successor, John II, successfully held the position; but Byzantium was embattled against strong and determined enemies. The Turkish victory at Myriocephalum in 1176 over the Emperor Manuel I, although it involved them in heavy losses, put an end to all hopes of a Byzantine recovery in Anatolia. At the moment, however, the real threat lay in Europe. Successive Norman rulers of Sicily had attempted to conquer the Christian Empire in the East, and in 1195 the Emperor Henry VI had prepared an expedition which only his death

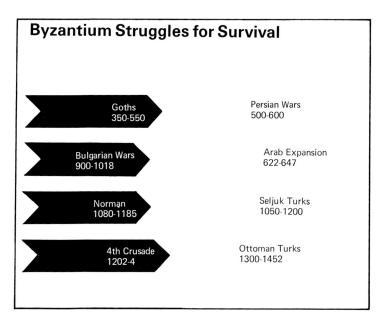

Byzantium Struggles for Survival

Goths 350-550	Persian Wars 500-600
Bulgarian Wars 900-1018	Arab Expansion 622-647
Norman 1080-1185	Seljuk Turks 1050-1200
4th Crusade 1202-4	Ottoman Turks 1300-1452

prevented. But quite apart from these military threats was the running sore of Venetian trading privileges within the Empire.

These privileges had been granted by Alexius I in his alliance with Venice against the Normans. They gave the merchants of Venice an even more privileged position in Constantinople than the Greek traders themselves. The Empire lost the carrying trade of its own merchandise and the revenue of the former tolls. The attempts of the Emperors to break loose (in 1171 Manuel I had all Venetians imprisoned and their goods impounded) only provoked a determined counterattack; and the Fourth Crusade has been called the greatest commercial coup of all time. But despite the declining political situation from the middle of the century, Byzantine art and letters enjoyed a remarkable flou-

The Christ mosaic in Hagia Sophia, mid-twelfth century, one of the supreme works of Byzantine art.

rishing during this period, including a marked revival in classical Greek scholarship and literature which paralleled the brilliance of the twelfth-century "renaissance" in Europe.

Seeds of autocracy

A rapid survey of twelfth-century society impresses us first with its vitality and second with the clear signs of new institutions in embryo. The town evolved systems of internal government and inter-city federations, but the guilds and the Hanseatic League later developed protective and monopolistic tendencies which hampered rather than directed growth. Chivalry, an excellent means for the taming and civilizing of aggression, soon became a meaningless game, and even in the realm of the intellect the same process can be observed. Vitality and restless inquiry were gradually institutionalized. The statutes drawn up by a papal legate for the University of Paris in 1215 heralded an age when the great centers of intellectual activity, once so free, not only gained powers for governing their own members but also became more easily subject to the control of outside authorities. The old universal institutions of empire and papacy were challenged not only by the emergence of new, more tightly knit political units but also by powerful "lobbies" for the interests of separate social groups. In the event of conflict with Church or king, such institutionalization made the target of official displeasure easier to identify.

The Fall of Constantinople

The crusaders from the West had taken an oath to free the Holy Land from the Moslems, but now they were stranded at Constantinople—unable to pay the Venetians for the ships that were carrying them eastward. Easily deflected from their religious mission, the knights and nobles of the Fourth Crusade agreed to help the deposed Byzantine Emperor regain his throne. And thus, in the spring of 1204, the walls of Constantinople—never before breached by an enemy —fell to the crusaders. The sack of the city, culmination of this senseless war of Christian against Christian, lasted for three days and when it was over Christendom's most splendid city lay in ruins. All Europe was shocked by this rapacious diversion of the crusading movement, and the breach between Eastern and Western Christianity widened to a permanent split. In the succeeding centuries, this fatal division could only work to the advantage of the Moslem Turks advancing from the East.

A portrait of the Emperor John II Comnenus, twelfth-century Byzantine Emperor.

Opposite A crusading knight mounted and in full armor.

During the winter of 1203–4, a large army of crusading knights, brought by a Venetian fleet, was encamped around the city of Constantinople. Their ultimate purpose was to reconquer the Holy Land, but since they did not have the necessary money to pay the Venetians for the ships, it had been agreed that the crusaders should postpone their conquest of the Holy Land and first use their armed might to accomplish a task dear to Venice: that was to place Alexius, the son of Isaac Angelus, on the throne of Byzantium. Alexius and his father had been the victims of a palace revolution: the Emperor Isaac was dethroned by his brother—another Alexius— and blinded, in the Byzantine fashion, to render him helpless. He was then thrown into prison with his son. But the son, Alexius, managed to escape and make his way to the court of his brother-in-law, Philip of Swabia, King of Germany. He made good use of his connections and when it became known that the crusading army, for lack of money, was stranded in Venice, Alexius seized his opportunity. He promised to pay the crusaders' debt to the Venetians if he were placed on the throne of his father in Constantinople.

The Venetians and crusaders had carried out their side of the bargain. In July, 1203, they laid siege to Constantinople. The usurper, Alexius III, fled and his officials released the old Emperor from his prison. On August 1, his son was solemnly crowned as Alexius IV in the church of Hagia Sophia.

Installed on the throne, Alexius IV soon discovered that he could not pay the Venetians. The crusaders were therefore still stranded in Constantinople. As time went by, their relations with the Byzantines became more and more strained, and when the crusaders presented an ultimatum in February, 1204, another palace revolution took place and Alexius IV was deposed. The crusaders now decided to install one of their own leaders as emperor. They stormed the city and in the middle of April made their first

successful landing on the Golden Horn. A fire in the city, started by accident or treachery, made defense impossible. The members of the imperial family, many nobles and the Patriarch fled, and before long Enrico Dandolo, the Doge of Venice, and the other leaders of the crusaders entered the Great Palace. The rank and file were allowed to sack the city.

The sack lasted for three days. Neither the Venetians nor the crusaders, coming from the West, had seen such riches before. Drunk with greed and lust they let themselves go. They seized everything that seemed precious and carried it away; the rest they destroyed. They ransacked palaces and dwellings; they killed, raped and looted; and countless books and works of art were destroyed—until Christendom's largest and most splendid city lay in ruins. On May 16, Count Baldwin IX of Flanders and Hainault was made Emperor of Romania, as the Latins chose to call it, but his power was negligible. Constantinople was in ruins and his power over the princes who established themselves in the western parts of old Byzantium became nebulous, for they only owed him some kind of feudal allegiance, whereas many of the outlying parts of the old Empire rallied to various members of the former imperial family.

The plan to continue the crusade, meanwhile, was abandoned and the papal legate, Peter of Saint-Marcel, absolved all crusaders from their oath to fight for the delivery of the Holy Land from the Moslems.

The city of Constantinople had been founded by the Roman Emperor Constantine in A.D. 328–37. It had been consecrated on May 11, 330, as the new Rome, a city that contained no traces of ancient paganism. The site was chosen for its strategic importance, at the spot where Asia and Europe meet on the Bosphorus—the significance of which had been obvious to Herodotus in the fifth century B.C. A great many churches were built and the city was

richly endowed with fountains and statues and soon became the administrative and commercial center of the Eastern Roman Empire.

Less than a hundred years after the founding of the new Rome, the city on the Tiber was sacked by the barbarian invaders of the Western Empire and, from then on, Constantinople alone carried on the traditions of Roman government.

The transfer of the capital to Constantinople was, of course, an explicit admission of the fact that the ancient Roman Empire was becoming orientalized. In the East, the Greek language was predominant, and eventually the reigning culture of Constantinople and its Empire became an amalgam of Oriental and Greek influences. It was inevitable that in the eastern half of the old Roman Empire the form and content of Christianity should develop along lines different from those followed in the West. And the Patriarch of Constantinople, presiding over his Church under the immediate eye of the Emperor, in a city vastly richer and more alive than medieval Rome, naturally became the head of the Eastern Church and became more and more reluctant to concede any claims the Bishop of Rome advanced as the successor of St. Peter. It is impossible to define the differences between Eastern and Western Christendom in one single principle; but in the East, Semitic traditions of uncompromising monotheism and of objection to religious imagery frequently came to the fore, and there were strong Oriental currents of cosmic mysticism apparent in the shape of the liturgy and even in the shape of the Cross, which in the East came to have four equal arms.

When the imperial center was shifted to Constantinople, the threat from central Europe was only peripheral. When it became stronger in the fifth century, Byzantine diplomats took steps to direct the invaders westward, away from Constantinople, into Italy and Spain. But when Byzantine influence in the West was completely extinguished in the seventh and eighth centuries, it became apparent that a threat far greater than that of the Teutonic invaders was about to engulf the Eastern Empire. The Teutonic invaders had not only displayed a certain respect for Roman traditions but had actually accepted Christianity. Their invasions of the Roman Empire therefore laid the foundations for an eventual assimilation. But in the eighth and ninth centuries, the Arabs—newly converted to Islam—erupted from the interior of their peninsula into the Mediterranean regions and swiftly conquered Egypt, Syria and Palestine—seriously weakening the power of Byzantium.

Islam was a religion even more fiercely prophetic and missionary than Christianity, and there was no possibility of assimilation. The Emperors in Constantinople had to watch their dominions shrink; they fought valiantly, however, and as long as they

A twelfth-century fresco in the church of Crenac depicts a crusading knight, visor down and lance poised, charging into the fray.

straddled the Bosphorus they kept a firm hold on Greece in the west and Asia Minor in the east. But in the course of the eleventh century another wave of Asian invaders came forward: the Seljuk Turks—a horde of nomads from the steppes of Turkestan—seeking their fortune by pillage. They conquered Syria and Palestine, and though they dealt a heavy blow to the power of the Moslem caliphs, they soon accommodated themselves with their Arabic subjects because they, too, embraced Islam. They advanced into Asia Minor and were confronted by a Byzantine army—which they defeated decisively on the field of Manzikert in Armenia in 1071. The whole eastern wing of the Byzantine Empire immediately collapsed.

Ten years later, a palace revolution in Constantinople brought to power Alexius I Comnenus, an intelligent and enterprising new Emperor—the first of a dynasty that was to rule for over a century. As part of his program of internal as well as external restoration, he wrote a letter to Pope Urban II asking for military help from the West in order to assist with the defense of Eastern Christendom against the Moslems. At that time the papacy was experiencing the full swing of the Gregorian reform movement; Urban eagerly welcomed this opportunity of leadership and promptly appealed to the newly stimulated religious fervor of the masses.

Naturally enough, the papal invitation to go on a crusade—issued at Clermont, France, in November, 1095—was not intended to rescue Alexius I Comnenus and support the tottering edifice of Byzantium.

The purpose of the crusade launched by Urban's appeal in 1095 was, therefore, different from Alexius' purpose when he had written for help. The crusaders were to fight the Moslems, not to save the dynasty at Constantinople but to conquer the Holy Land. The two purposes were, of course, not necessarily incompatible. But the differences in emphasis were strong enough to lead to deep mistrust and to ultimate dissension between Alexius and the crusaders.

As it was, the papal appeal met with enthusiastic response from all classes of people. Christians in Europe had never before experienced the liberating zest of religious evangelism. Religion had meant, if it was not an invitation to monasticism, the worship of relics and a certain amount of communal ceremonial in the shape of the Mass. There was hardly any clergy capable of giving spiritual nourishment and no popular edification of any kind. Hence the papal appeal, carried by countless preachers into every corner of Christendom, stimulated the pent-up religious enthusiasm; and people rushed to save Jerusalem. The reconquest of the Holy Land was indeed a stimulating goal; but it received substance from the papal idea that to go on a crusade meant to "take the Cross" and was, therefore, an act of penance: a crusader's vow would assure eternal salvation.

The idea of a pilgrimage to the Holy Land in expiation of sins was a very old Western tradition, even though the Moslem conquest of Jerusalem had made such pilgrimages very hazardous. Now the tradition

A crusading knight doing homage; an English miniature, c. 1250.

The Golden Gate and the walls of Constantinople around which the Venetian army encamped and laid siege to the treasure-laden city in 1203.

received not only a new vitality, but a new emphasis. The crusading pilgrim was also a fighter for God and the old pilgrimage was turned into a holy war.

The First Crusade, which departed for Jerusalem in 1096, made its way down the Balkans. It was a large number of poor people following an inarticulate religious sentiment. There were camp-followers and beggars, vagabonds, brigands, harlots and last, but not least, a large number of professional warriors—knights newly educated in the ideals of chivalry which now received a religious sanction. But religious fervor does not provide by itself much of a basis for a military expedition. The trains of people that set out eastwards were without provisions, without leadership and without discipline. The

enthusiasm of the poor tended to diminish as they were apprehended and set upon by people from whom they had pillaged. Their sufferings were enormous and most of them died on the way. The knights were in a more advantageous position, but they were subject to an odd mixture of religious fervor and material greed: they clearly bore in mind the possibility of carving out landed estates for themselves in the East, and the violence they displayed in foreign parts came to be a mixture of acquisitiveness and religious intoxication.

All in all, it is surprising that the First Crusade achieved its purpose. In crossing Asia Minor, the crusaders reconquered the littoral from the Turks and allowed Alexius to repossess himself of some of

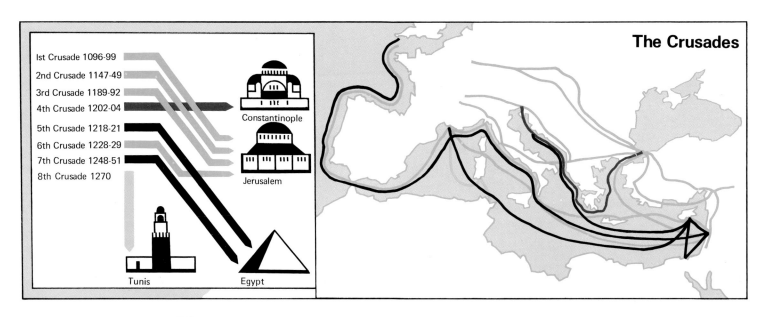

The Crusades

Ist Crusade 1096-99
2nd Crusade 1147-49
3rd Crusade 1189-92
4th Crusade 1202-04
5th Crusade 1218-21
6th Crusade 1228-29
7th Crusade 1248-51
8th Crusade 1270

Constantinople

Jerusalem

Tunis   Egypt

the major cities. Eventually, the knights invaded Syria and Palestine: they captured first Antioch and finally, in 1099, Jerusalem. With the opening of the Levantine ports to Christian trade, Italian ships started to arrive. The Mediterranean was once again opened to merchants from Christian lands.

But the relations with Byzantium went from bad to worse. Alexius owed a debt to the crusaders. But, alternately, they owed a debt to him for supplies, advice and guidance. Once established in Jerusalem, however, the Western knights refused to hand back the regained territories to Alexius. Instead, they set up the Latin kingdom of Jerusalem, received a papal legate, and obliged the Christian inhabitants of their new kingdom to withdraw from the Greek ritual. If Alexius felt relieved at the cessation of Moslem pressure, he soon realized that the expedition had not really helped to restore his Empire. On the contrary, owing to the close personal relations of many of the crusading knights with the Norman knights who, in the preceding century, had invaded southern Italy, he was now forced to resign himself to the loss of territory in Italy, and to recognize the independence of the kingdom of Jerusalem and several other principalities which the crusading knights had carved out for themselves in the East.

Apart from the political and ecclesiastical ill will prevailing on all sides, there were also powerful social and cultural forces at work in promoting tension. The crusaders had carried to Jerusalem their primitive military and political feudalism. The kingdom they set up in Palestine and Syria resembled England after the Norman Conquest much more than it did the centralized bureaucracy of Byzantium. And the theological and liturgical differences served to underline the rift. Early in the twelfth century, the Latin West was as yet largely innocent of dialectics and scholasticism; and the theological assertiveness of the Roman Church struck the Byzantine theologians, trained in the subtler traditions of Greek scholarship, as mere boorish presumption.

Eventually, however, the nemesis of power began to overtake everybody. The Christian knights in their Jerusalem kingdom eagerly availed themselves of the Oriental luxury that surrounded them. They tended to become acclimatized. At the same time, Moslem power began to recover from the shock of its first defeats. The crusaders' victory had been the stimulus needed for reorganization. Zanghi of Mosul conquered Aleppo and Edessa; his son, Noureddin, Damascus and Egypt. And Saladin finally won the victory of Hattin in 1187 and

Above A coin from Constantinople shows the personification of the city holding a cornucopia or horn of plenty.

Detail of the Pala d'Oro, the altarpiece at St. Mark's in Venice, which incorporates part of the looted treasure that the crusaders brought back from the sack of Constantinople.

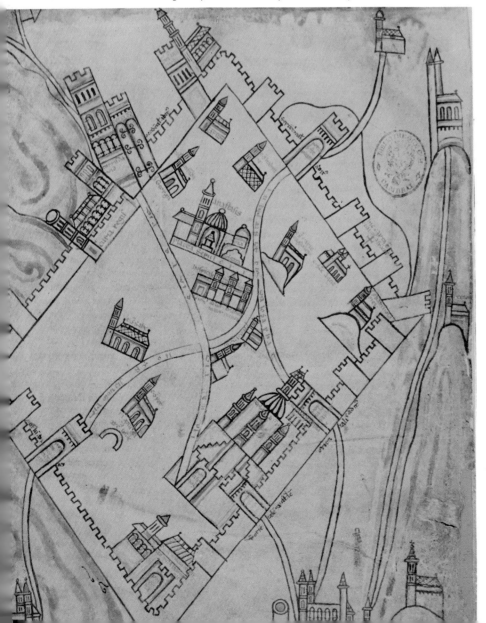

Above The crusader castle of Krak des Chevaliers in Lebanon. Many crusader fortifications are still standing today.

Below A crusader's map of Jerusalem marking the holy places of the city.

regained Jerusalem for Islam from the Christians.

Appeals for more aid were sent to the West. The Emperors of Byzantium became more and more reluctant to help, because they reckoned that they had been duped by the crusaders. Italian merchants were willing to provide ships—at a price. But the new crusading recruits who came over from the West were shocked to find their relatives and companions installed in palaces of Oriental splendor, with food and spice , incense and precious clothes, which were neither reminiscent of their austere castles in Flanders and Lorraine nor particularly expressive of religious zeal.

If the Byzantines were displeased with the outcome, they at least benefited for the time being because the attention of the Moslems was directed against the Kingdom of Jerusalem instead of against their Empire. In Europe itself, the growing threat to that kingdom stimulated further efforts which in turn were nourised by the Apocalyptic fears current in the twelfth century. In 1147, St. Bernard of Clairvaux preached a new crusade and fired people's imagination by fanatical sermons that exhibited a curious combination of bloodthirsty aggressiveness and a desire for moral purification. The immediate effect of his activities was the Second Crusade led by the Emperor Conrad III and by King Louis VII of France. The expedition was a complete failure; and most knights perished in Asia Minor before they even reached the endangered Holy City. After the battle of Hattin and the fall of Jerusalem, the Emperor Frederick Barbarossa set out in 1189 on a third crusade and was supposed to be joined in the Holy Land by Richard the Lion Heart of England and Philip Augustus, King of France. This time the most elaborate preparations were made. Crusaders were recruited in order to serve their Lord Jesus as vassals—a marked departure from the earlier, indiscriminate religious enthusiasm and the blank promise of eternal salvation for taking the Cross.

After a long march down the Danube, the crusaders crossed safely into Asia Minor during Easter, 1190. But Frederick himself was drowned in the Saleph River and a great many crusaders died from hunger and thirst as well as from fighting the Turks. Only a remnant of the army reached Antioch, and they failed to reconquer Jerusalem.

If the new organization and official royal leadership had introduced a more serious kind of military planning, it had also shifted the perspective. With kings in the lead, a crusade was more clearly a political than a religious venture. And kings, in the nature of things, had dynastic ambitions. Already, in 1190, when forced to spend the winter in southern Greece, Frederick Barbarossa had been under great pressure to conquer Constantinople. Many of his knights felt that it was better to have a bird in the hand than two in the bush. It had taken all of Frederick's determination to force them to desist, and his own determination drew great strength from his conviction that his expedition to Jerusalem was a necessary part of the Apocalyptic vision of the universe according to which, at the end of time, the last Emperor had to go to Jerusalem in order to hang up his shield and lance on the barren tree on the Mount of Olives.

After Frederick's death and the removal of his influence, dynastic ambitions gained the upper hand. Richard the Lion Heart was an irresponsible adventurer and Philip Augustus had concerns closer to home: the mutilated trunk of the Kingdom of Jerusalem received no help from either of them. In the early years of the thirteenth century, Pope Innocent III, full of his own prestige, sought to revive the idea of a crusade. But though his appeal met with an enthusiastic response and a large army of knights assembled in Venice to take ship to the East, the political issues had gained the upper hand. Lack of money for the passage placed the crusaders at the Venetians' mercy. And since King Philip of Germany was married to the sister of Alexius, the fugitive claimant of the Byzantine throne, the whole expedition—as we have seen—was eventually diverted to the conquest of Constantinople with the avowed aim of placing Alexius IV on the imperial throne. Alexius himself had played cleverly on the crusaders' lack of money: he promised ample rewards from the coffers of Byzantium. But the crusaders' rewards did not come in the manner envisaged by Alexius.

The fall of Constantinople and the installation of the Latin kingdom of Romania there fatally weakened the great bastion that had sheltered Europe from the East. None of the Byzantine successor states in Asia Minor, nor the restored dynasty of the Paleologi in Constantinople in 1261, were militarily viable. As a result of the enfeebled state in which Constantinople was left, the Turks advanced from strength to strength. By the middle of the fifteenth century, they had surrounded the imperial city on the Golden Horn and pushed forward into the Balkans as well as into the Aegean Sea. Finally, in 1453, Constantinople itself fell, and the Turks were at last poised to strike at the heart of Europe.

PETER MUNZ

Mosaic pavement in the Basilica of St. John the Evangelist at Ravenna, 1213, depicting episodes from the Fourth Crusade.

Tomb of a crusader in Dorchester abbey. Medieval England, like the other nations of Christendom considered a crusader killed in battle worthy of the highest honors of the Church.

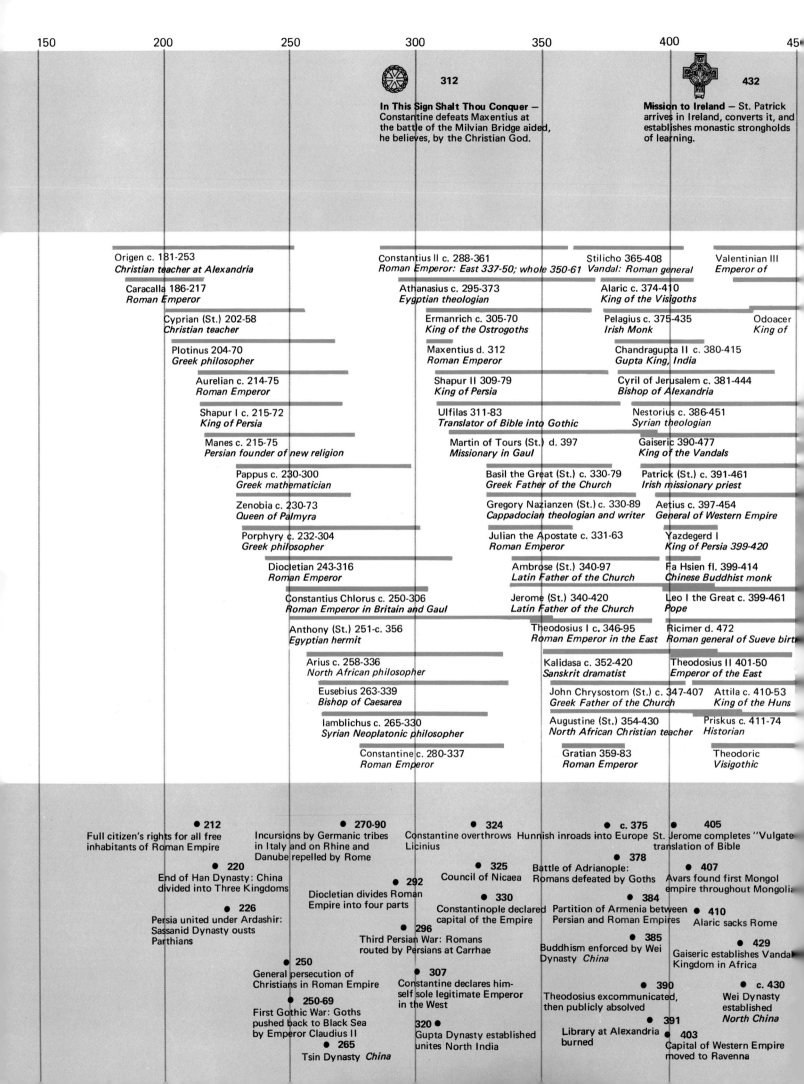

312

In This Sign Shalt Thou Conquer — Constantine defeats Maxentius at the battle of the Milvian Bridge aided, he believes, by the Christian God.

432

Mission to Ireland — St. Patrick arrives in Ireland, converts it, and establishes monastic strongholds of learning.

Origen c. 181-253
Christian teacher at Alexandria

Constantius II c. 288-361
Roman Emperor: East 337-50; whole 350-61

Stilicho 365-408
Vandal: Roman general

Valentinian III
Emperor of

Caracalla 186-217
Roman Emperor

Athanasius c. 295-373
Eygptian theologian

Alaric c. 374-410
King of the Visigoths

Cyprian (St.) 202-58
Christian teacher

Ermanrich c. 305-70
King of the Ostrogoths

Pelagius c. 375-435
Irish Monk

Odoacer
King of

Plotinus 204-70
Greek philosopher

Maxentius d. 312
Roman Emperor

Chandragupta II c. 380-415
Gupta King, India

Aurelian c. 214-75
Roman Emperor

Shapur II 309-79
King of Persia

Cyril of Jerusalem c. 381-444
Bishop of Alexandria

Shapur I c. 215-72
King of Persia

Ulfilas 311-83
Translator of Bible into Gothic

Nestorius c. 386-451
Syrian theologian

Manes c. 215-75
Persian founder of new religion

Martin of Tours (St.) d. 397
Missionary in Gaul

Gaiseric 390-477
King of the Vandals

Pappus c. 230-300
Greek mathematician

Basil the Great (St.) c. 330-79
Greek Father of the Church

Patrick (St.) c. 391-461
Irish missionary priest

Zenobia c. 230-73
Queen of Palmyra

Gregory Nazianzen (St.) c. 330-89
Cappadocian theologian and writer

Aetius c. 397-454
General of Western Empire

Porphyry c. 232-304
Greek philosopher

Julian the Apostate c. 331-63
Roman Emperor

Yazdegerd I
King of Persia 399-420

Diocletian 243-316
Roman Emperor

Ambrose (St.) 340-97
Latin Father of the Church

Fa Hsien fl. 399-414
Chinese Buddhist monk

Constantius Chlorus c. 250-306
Roman Emperor in Britain and Gaul

Jerome (St.) 340-420
Latin Father of the Church

Leo I the Great c. 399-461
Pope

Anthony (St.) 251-c. 356
Egyptian hermit

Theodosius I c. 346-95
Roman Emperor in the East

Ricimer d. 472
Roman general of Sueve birt

Arius c. 258-336
North African philosopher

Kalidasa c. 352-420
Sanskrit dramatist

Theodosius II 401-50
Emperor of the East

Eusebius 263-339
Bishop of Caesarea

John Chrysostom (St.) c. 347-407
Greek Father of the Church

Attila c. 410-53
King of the Huns

Iamblichus c. 265-330
Syrian Neoplatonic philosopher

Augustine (St.) 354-430
North African Christian teacher

Priskus c. 411-74
Historian

Constantine c. 280-337
Roman Emperor

Gratian 359-83
Roman Emperor

Theodoric
Visigothic

● **212**
Full citizen's rights for all free inhabitants of Roman Empire

● **270-90**
Incursions by Germanic tribes in Italy and on Rhine and Danube repelled by Rome

● **324**
Constantine overthrows Licinius

● **c. 375**
Hunnish inroads into Europe

● **405**
St. Jerome completes "Vulgate translation of Bible

● **220**
End of Han Dynasty: China divided into Three Kingdoms

● **325**
Council of Nicaea

378
Battle of Adrianople: Romans defeated by Goths

● **407**
Avars found first Mongol empire throughout Mongolia

● **292**
Diocletian divides Roman Empire into four parts

● **226**
Persia united under Ardashir: Sassanid Dynasty ousts Parthians

● **330**
Constantinople declared capital of the Empire

● **384**
Partition of Armenia between Persian and Roman Empires

● **410**
Alaric sacks Rome

● **296**
Third Persian War: Romans routed by Persians at Carrhae

● **385**
Buddhism enforced by Wei Dynasty *China*

● **429**
Gaiseric establishes Vandal Kingdom in Africa

● **250**
General persecution of Christians in Roman Empire

● **307**
Constantine declares himself sole legitimate Emperor in the West

● **390**
Theodosius excommunicated, then publicly absolved

● **c. 430**
Wei Dynasty established *North China*

● **250-69**
First Gothic War: Goths pushed back to Black Sea by Emperor Claudius II

320 ●
Gupta Dynasty established unites North India

Library at Alexandria burned

● **391**

● **403**
Capital of Western Empire moved to Ravenna

● **265**
Tsin Dynasty *China*

450	500	550	600	650	700	750

451

The Scourge of God
At Campus Mauriacus (Chalons) Aetius turns back Attila at the gates of the Empire; but Western unity is shattered.

520

The Rule of St. Benedict — It provided a framework in which monasteries became self-sufficient communities where learning could survive.

622

The Flight to Medina —
The establishment of the Moslem religion brings with it a unifying Islamic civilization, new yet preserving ancient scholarship.

419-54
the West

Zeno c. 426-9l
Emperor of the East

c. 433-93
the Heruli

Theodoric the Great c. 455-526
Ostrogothic King

Romulus Augustulus c. 459-98
Last Roman Emperor

Clovis 466-511
King of the Salian Franks

Kavadh I c. 470-531
King of Persia

Mazdak c. 475-531
High Priest of Zoroastrianism

Tribonian c. 475-545
Eastern jurist

Narses c. 478-567
Byzantine courtier

Boethius c. 480-524
Philosopher

Benedict of Nursia (St.) c. 480-547
Italian monk

Justinian I 482-565
Eastern Emperor

Procopius c. 490-562
Eastern historian

Belisarius c. 505-65
Eastern general

Theodora 508-48
Eastern Empress

Chosroes I c. 511-79
Persian King

King 419-51

Totila c. 513-52
King of the Ostrogoths

Columba of Iona (St.) c. 520-97
Irish missionary to N. Scots

Gregory of Tours c. 538-94
Frankish historian

Gregory I the Great 540-604
Pope

Columbanus (St.) c. 540-615
Irish missionary to Gaul

Augustine of Canterbury (St.) d. 604
Roman apostle of England

Alboin c. 541-72
King of the Lombards

Aethelbert c. 560-616
King of Kent

Isidore of Seville c. 560-636
Bishop and man of letters

Yang Ti 560-618
Founder of Sui Dynasty

Mohammed 570-632
Founder of Moslem religion

Li Yuan 570-636
First T'ang Emperor, China

Shotoku Taishi 572-621
Ruler of Japan

Abu Bakr 573-634
First Moslem Caliph

Heraclius I 575-641
Byzantine Emperor

Omar 582-644
Arabian Caliph

Chosroes I c. 511-79
Persian King

Uthman c. 588-656
Caliph

Chosroes II d. 628
King of Persia

Harsha c. 590-647
Ruler of N. Indian Empire

Theodore of Tarsus c. 602-90
Archbishop of Canterbury

Ali c. 602-61
Caliph, Mohammed's son-in-law

Aidan (St.) d. 651
Apostle of England

Rothari 605-52
King of the Lombards

Fujiwara Kamatari c. 605-80
Japanese statesman

Hsuan-tsang 605-64
Chines Buddhist traveller in India 625-48

Moawiyah c. 609-80
First Ummayad Caliph

Caedmon c. 617-82
English Christian poet

Tenji 626-72
Emperor of Japan

Pepin of Heristal 635-714
Mayor of Austrasia and Neustria

Musa c. 640-716
Moslem general

Oswy d. 670
King of Northumbria

Isperich c. 652-700
Khan of Bulgaria

Recceswinth d. 672
Catholic King of Visigoths

Reccared
Visigothic King 586-601

Willibrord (St.) 657-739
English missionary

Boniface (Winfrid) 673-754
Anglo-Saxon missionary

Bede 673-735
English historian

Leo III 675-740
Byzantine Emperor

Abd al Malik
Caliph 685-705

Charles Martel c.688-741
Ruler of Austrasia and Neustria

John of Damascus 690-754
Orthodox theologian

Liutprand
Lombard King 712-44

Pepin the Short 714-68
Frankish king

● **455**
Rome sacked by Vandal Gaiseric

● **476**
End of the Western Empire

● **486**
Clovis defeats Syagrius at Soissons: end of Roman rule in Gaul

● **493**
Theodoric defeats Germans, kills Odoacer

● **c. 500**
Talmud receives definitive form *Babylon*

● **449**
Britain occupied by Angles, Saxons and Jutes

● **c. 450**
Skandagupta beats back White Huns (Ephthalites) *India*

● **507**
Clovis drives Visigoths out of Gaul at Battle of Vouille

● **534**
Vandal kingdom in North Africa overthrown by Belisarius

● **546**
Rome ravaged by Totila the Ostrogoth

● **563**
Hagia Sophia cathedral consecrated at Constantinople

● **c. 585**
St. Columbanus sets out from Ireland to Gaul

● **597**
King Aethelbert converted by Augustine at Canterbury *England*

● **606**
Civil service examination system established *China*

● **614**
Capture of the True Cross in Jerusalem by Persians *Palestine*

● **534**
Justinian's legal code Corpus Juris Civilis

● **616**
Compulsory baptism of Jews *Spain*

● **618**
T'ang Dynasty founded *China*

● **627**
Persia defeated by Heraclius

● **630**
Mecca captured by Mohammed *Arabia*

● **637**
Ctesiphon captured by Islamic armies *Mesopotamia*

● **658**
Moawiyah establishes Ummayad Dynasty at Damascus *Syria*

● **664**
Synod of Whitby

● **720**
Arabs cross Pyrenees into Aquitaine *France*

● **732**
Battle of Poitiers: Franks defeat Arabs *France*

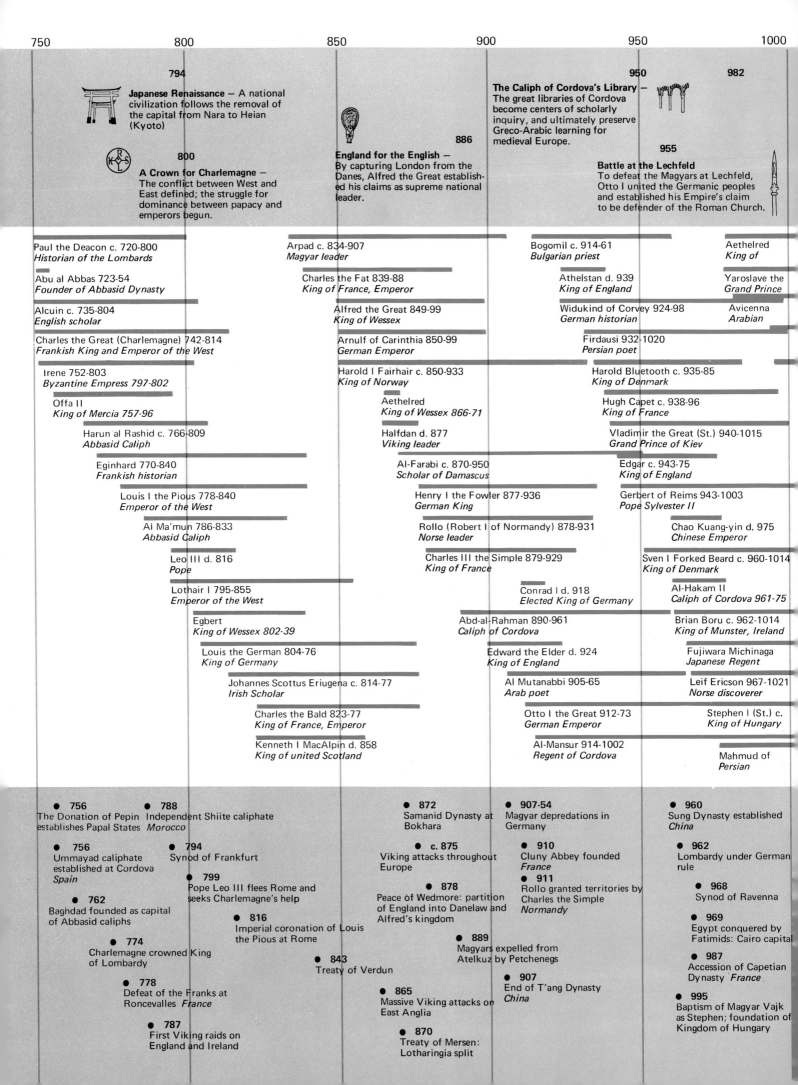

| 750 | 800 | 850 | 900 | 950 | 1000 |

794

Japanese Renaissance — A national civilization follows the removal of the capital from Nara to Heian (Kyoto)

800

A Crown for Charlemagne — The conflict between West and East defined; the struggle for dominance between papacy and emperors begun.

886

England for the English — By capturing London from the Danes, Alfred the Great established his claims as supreme national leader.

950

The Caliph of Cordova's Library — The great libraries of Cordova become centers of scholarly inquiry, and ultimately preserve Greco-Arabic learning for medieval Europe.

982

955

Battle at the Lechfeld — To defeat the Magyars at Lechfeld, Otto I united the Germanic peoples and established his Empire's claim to be defender of the Roman Church.

Paul the Deacon c. 720-800
Historian of the Lombards

Abu al Abbas 723-54
Founder of Abbasid Dynasty

Alcuin c. 735-804
English scholar

Charles the Great (Charlemagne) 742-814
Frankish King and Emperor of the West

Irene 752-803
Byzantine Empress 797-802

Offa II
King of Mercia 757-96

Harun al Rashid c. 766-809
Abbasid Caliph

Eginhard 770-840
Frankish historian

Louis I the Pious 778-840
Emperor of the West

Al Ma'mun 786-833
Abbasid Caliph

Leo III d. 816
Pope

Lothair I 795-855
Emperor of the West

Egbert
King of Wessex 802-39

Louis the German 804-76
King of Germany

Johannes Scottus Eriugena c. 814-77
Irish Scholar

Charles the Bald 823-77
King of France, Emperor

Kenneth I MacAlpin d. 858
King of united Scotland

Arpad c. 834-907
Magyar leader

Charles the Fat 839-88
King of France, Emperor

Alfred the Great 849-99
King of Wessex

Arnulf of Carinthia 850-99
German Emperor

Harold I Fairhair c. 850-933
King of Norway

Aethelred
King of Wessex 866-71

Halfdan d. 877
Viking leader

Al-Farabi c. 870-950
Scholar of Damascus

Henry I the Fowler 877-936
German King

Rollo (Robert I of Normandy) 878-931
Norse leader

Charles III the Simple 879-929
King of France

Abd-al-Rahman 890-961
Caliph of Cordova

Edward the Elder d. 924
King of England

Al Mutanabbi 905-65
Arab poet

Otto I the Great 912-73
German Emperor

Al-Mansur 914-1002
Regent of Cordova

Bogomil c. 914-61
Bulgarian priest

Athelstan d. 939
King of England

Widukind of Corvey 924-98
German historian

Firdausi 932-1020
Persian poet

Harold Bluetooth c. 935-85
King of Denmark

Hugh Capet c. 938-96
King of France

Vladimir the Great (St.) 940-1015
Grand Prince of Kiev

Edgar c. 943-75
King of England

Gerbert of Reims 943-1003
Pope Sylvester II

Chao Kuang-yin d. 975
Chinese Emperor

Sven I Forked Beard c. 960-1014
King of Denmark

Al-Hakam II
Caliph of Cordova 961-75

Brian Boru c. 962-1014
King of Munster, Ireland

Fujiwara Michinaga
Japanese Regent

Leif Ericson 967-1021
Norse discoverer

Stephen I (St.) c.
King of Hungary

Conrad I d. 918
Elected King of Germany

Aethelred
King of

Yaroslave the
Grand Prince

Avicenna
Arabian

Mahmud of
Persian

● **756**
The Donation of Pepin establishes Papal States

● **756**
Ummayad caliphate established at Cordova *Spain*

● **762**
Baghdad founded as capital of Abbasid caliphs

● **774**
Charlemagne crowned King of Lombard

● **778**
Defeat of the Franks at Roncevalles *France*

● **787**
First Viking raids on England and Ireland

● **788**
Independent Shiite caliphate *Morocco*

● **794**
Synod of Frankfurt

● **799**
Pope Leo III flees Rome and seeks Charlemagne's help

● **816**
Imperial coronation of Louis the Pious at Rome

● **843**
Treaty of Verdun

● **865**
Massive Viking attacks on East Anglia

● **870**
Treaty of Mersen: Lotharingia split

● **872**
Samanid Dynasty at Bokhara

● **c. 875**
Viking attacks throughout Europe

● **878**
Peace of Wedmore: partition of England into Danelaw and Alfred's kingdom

● **889**
Magyars expelled from Atelkuz by Petchenegs

● **907**
End of T'ang Dynasty *China*

● **907-54**
Magyar depredations in Germany

● **910**
Cluny Abbey founded *France*

● **911**
Rollo granted territories by Charles the Simple *Normandy*

● **960**
Sung Dynasty established *China*

● **962**
Lombardy under German rule

● **968**
Synod of Ravenna

● **969**
Egypt conquered by Fatimids: Cairo capital

● **987**
Accession of Capetian Dynasty *France*

● **995**
Baptism of Magyar Vajk as Stephen; foundation of Kingdom of Hungary

Voyagers West — Eric the Red's discovery of Greenland like the conquests of Normandy, England and Sicily, an example of Norse expansionism.

1066
William the Conqueror — under a strong monarchy England fully enters the orbit of the European world.

1100
Abelard in Paris — The Council of Sens confirmed Church resistance to Abelard's application of Aristotelian logic to matters of faith.

1204
The Fall of Constantinople — By sacking the Byzantine capital and setting up there the Latin Kingdom of Romania, the knights of the Fourth Crusade fatally weakened the greatest bastion against the Turks.

1077
Humiliation at Canossa — By humiliating Henry IV and making the conflict an open one, Gregory VII ultimately strengthened the independence of medieval monarchies.

1194
The Palace of the Virgin — Chartres Cathedral as rebuilt after the fire of 1194 was intended as an epitome of the wonders of the world and served as torch-bearer for medieval humanism.

the Redeless
England 978-1016

Somadeva c. 1035-82
Indian poet

Nur ed Din 1·118-74
Ruler of Syria

Henry VI 1165-97
German Emperor

Wise 978-1054
of Kiev, ruler of Russia

Urban II 1042-99
Pope

Manuel I Comnenus c. 1120-80 ·
Byzantine Emperor

Philip II Augustus 1165-1223
King of France

980-1037
scholar

Alexius I Comnenus 1048-1118
Byzantine Emperor

Louis VII c. 1120-80
King of France

Dominic (St.) c. 1170-1221
Castilian preacher

Ibn Hazm 994-1063
Spanish statesman and writer

Henry IV 1050-1106
German Emperor

Frederic I Barbarossa c. 1122-90
German Emperor

Francis of Assisi (St.) c. 1182-1226
Italian itinerant preacher

Canute 995-1035
King of Denmark and England

Philip I 1052-1108
King of France

Eleanor of Aquitaine c. 1122-1204
Wife of Henry II of England

Frederick II of Sicily 1194-1250
German Emperor

Berengar of Tours 1000-89
French theologian

Bohemond I c. 1056-1111
Norman Prince of Antioch

Averroes c. 1126-98
Spanish Moslem scholar

Ferdinand III 1199-1252
King of Castile and Leon

Leo IX (St.) 1002-54
Pope and Church Reformer

Henry I 1068-1135
King of England

Ibn Tufayl c. 1127-85
Spanish Moslem scholar

Edward the Confessor 1002-66
King of England

Peter Abelard 1079-1142
French Scholar

Waldemar I the Great 1131-82
King of Denmark

Robert Guiscard c. 1013-85
Norman conqueror of S. Italy

Avempace (Ibn Bajja) d. 1138
Spanish Arabic philosopher

Henry II 1133-89
King of England

Henry III 1017-56
German Emperor

Suger c. 1081-1151
Abbot of St. Denis

Maimonides 1135-1204
Jewish scholar in Spain

Gregory VII (Hildebrand) 1020-85
Pope 1073-85

Louis VI the Fat 1081-1137
King of France

Saladin c. 1137-93
Sultan of Egypt

Wang An-shih 1021-86
Chinese minister

Bernard of Clairvaux (St.) c. 1090-1153
French churchman

Eric IX (St.)
King of Sweden 1150-60

Harold Godwinsson c. 1022-66
King of England

Arnold of Brescia c. 1095-1155
Italian Church reformer

Yoritomo Minamoto c. 1147-99
Japanese military dictator, Shogun

966-1028

William I the Conqueror c. 1027-87
King of England

Roger II 1097-1154
Norman Count of Sicily

Alfonso VIII the Noble 1155-1214
King of Castile

Alfonso VI 1030-1109
King of Leon and Castile

Genghis Khan 1155-1227
Mongol ruler

972-1038

Roger I c. 1031-1101
Norman Count of Sicily·

John of Salisbury c. 1115-80
English political philospher

Richard Coeur-de-Lion 1157-99
King of England

Anselm 1033-1109
Archbishop of Canterbury

Thomas Becket 1118-70
Archbishop of Canterbury

Innocent III 1161-1216
Pope

Ghazni 976-1030
conqueror of Punjab

● c. 1000
Leif Ericson sails to North America ("Vinland")

● 1046
Emperor Henry III deposes Pope Gregory VI in favor of reform popes

● 1106
Henry I settlement with the papacy
England

● 1167
Oxford University founded
England

● 1000
Poland converted: allegiance direct to Rome

● 1071
Battle of Manzikert: Byzantium loses Asia Minor to Seljuk Turks
Turkey

● 1122
Kitan territory seized by Kin tribes *China*

● 1169
Kiev conquered by Andrei Boguliubski of Suzdal ·
Russia

● 1001
Mahmud of Ghazni begins plunder and conquest of Punjab *India*

● 1122 Concordat of Worms
Holy Roman Empire

● 1187
Saladin defeats crusaders at Battle of Hattin *Palestine*

● 1004
Sung Empire buys off Kitans with annual tribute
China

● 1085
Toledo recaptured from Moors *Spain*

● 1144
Franks expelled from Edessa by Zanghi of Mosul

● 1192
Feudal military rule under shogunate: Kamakura period
Japan

● 1013
Fall of Caliphate of Cordova
Spain

● 1086
Almoravids annex Moorish Spain

● 1145
Almohades conquer Moorish Spain

● 1042
End of Danish rule in England

● 1099
Capture of Jerusalem by First Crusade
Palestine

● 1167
The Taira seize power from the Fujiwara
Japan

Acknowledgments

The authors and publishers wish to thank the following museums and collections by whose kind permission the illustrations are reproduced. Page numbers appear in bold, photographic sources in italics:

1 (1) *Hirmer Verlag* (2) *Green Studio* (4) Vatican Library, Rome
2 (1) British Museum (property of R. Pinder-Wilson), London (2) *Benrido Co. Ltd.* (3) *Giraudon*
3 (1) Ashmolean Museum, Oxford (2) *Wim Swaan, Elek Books* (3) Castello Sforzesco, Milan : *Scala*
4 (1) Universitetets Oldsaksamling, Oslo (2) *Boudot-Lamotte* (3) Vatican Library, Rome
5 (1) *Bildarchiv Foto Marburg* (2) *Michael Holford* (3) British Museum
12 Palazzo dei Conservatori, Rome : *Curtis G. Pepper*
13 *Alinari*
14 (1) *Scala* (2) Palazzo dei Conservatori : *Commune di Rome*
15 (1) *Scala* (2) Museo delle Terme, Rome : *Pont. Comm. di Arch. Sacra*
16 (1, 2) *Alinari*
17 *Alinari*
18 (1) *Scala* (2) *Anderson*
19 (1) *Scala* (2) *Zentrale Farbild Agentur*
20 (1) *Abe Čapek* (2) *Ian Graham* (3) Freer Gallery of Art, Washington
21 (1) *Arthaud* (3) British Museum (4) *Alinari*
22 *Green Studio*
23 *Irish Tourist Board*
24 (1, 2) *Irish Tourist Board* (3) Commissioners of Public Works for Ireland
25 (1) *Northern Ireland Tourist Board* (2) National Museum of Ireland, Dublin
26 (1, 2) *Green Studio* (3) *Irish Tourist Board*
27 (1) National Museum of Ireland (2) Trinity College, Dublin : *Green Studio*
28 (1) British Museum (2) City Museum, Gloucester (3) *Irish Tourist Board*
29 (1) *Ministry of Public Building and Works, Edinburgh, Crown* ©
(2) Kuntsgeschichtliche Sammlungen, Vienna : *Werner Forman*
30 Cathedral Treasury, Monza
31 Academia di Storia, Madrid : *Scala*
32 (1) Museum, Troyes (3) Musei Civici, Brescia
33 British Museum
35 (1, 2) *Scala* (3) Bargello, Florence : *Scala*
36 (1) Landemuseum für Vorgeschichte, Halle (2) Coll. Joan Lamotte, Tortosa-Tarragona : *Mas*
37 (1) Musei Civici (3) *Alinari* (4) Museo delle Terme : Deutches Archäologisches Institut, Rome
38 Stiftsbibliothek, St Gallen
39 *Scala*
40 (1) *Alinari* (2) *Leonard von Matt*
42 (1) Vatican Library
(2) Laurentian Library, Florence : *Scala*
43 Library, Montecassino : *Scala*
44 (1) *Anderson* (2) *Hirmer Verlag*
(3) *Josephine Powell*

45 (1) *Brogi* (2) *Werner Forman* (3) *Ian Graham*
46 *Werner Forman*
47 *Alinari*
48 *Elek Books*
49 (1, 2) University Library, Edinburgh (3) *David Harris*
50 (1) British Museum (property of R. Pinder-Wilson) (2) Bodleian Library, Oxford : MS. Laud Or. 317, fols. 9V, 10R.
51 '*The Times*'
52 *Bernd Lohse, Prestel Verlag*
53 (1) *Ian Graham* (2) *Werner Forman*
54 (1) British Museum (2) *J. E. Dayton* (3) *Ronald Sheridan* (4) Gulbenkian Museum, Durham
55 (1) Private Collection, Prague : *Werner Forman* (2) *Benrido Co. Ltd.*
(3) *Boudot-Lamotte*
56 *Benrido Co. Ltd.*
57 *Werner Forman*
58 (1) *Ian Graham* (2) *De Antonis*
59 (1) National Museum, Tokyo
60 (1) *Zauho Press-Ziolo* (2) *Werner Forman*
61 (1) *Ian Graham* (2) National Museum, Tokyo : *De Antonis*
62 (1) National Museum, Tokyo (2) Cathedral Treasury, Monza (3) *Gabinetto Fotografico Nazionale*
63 (1) Cathedral Treasury, Monza : *Alinari* (2) *Bildarchiv Foto Marburg* (3) Bibliothèque Nationale, Paris
64 Louvre, Paris : *Giraudon*
65 *Ann Münchow*
66 (1) *Ann Münchow* (2) *Scala* (3) *Ann Münchow*
67 (1) Byzantine Institute, Dumbarton Oaks Field Committee (2) *André Held*
68 (1) Staatlichen Museen-Münzkabinett, Berlin : *Ann Münchow* (2) *Bürgerbibliothek, Bern*
69 (1) Victoria and Albert Museum, London : *Ann Münchow* (2) University Library, Utrecht
70 Archives Nationales, Paris : *Douet D'Arcq*
71 (1) Bibliotheque Municipale, Epernay : *Giraudon* (2) Biblioteca Nacional, Madrid : *Ann Münchow* (3) *Ann Münchow*
72 (1) Nationalbibliotheck, Vienna (2) Abbey, Kremsmünster (3) University Library, Utrecht
73 (1) British Museum (2) Bibliothèque Nationale (3) British Museum
74 Ashmolean Museum
75 (1, 2) British Museum (2) British Museum : *John Freeman*
76 (1, 2) Bodleian Library (3) London Museum
77 *Courtauld Institute*
78 *Reece Winstone*
79 (1) Victoria and Albert Museum (2) British Museum
80 (1) Bodleian Library (2) British Museum (3) Bibliothèque Nationale : *Giraudon*
81 (1) *Ian Graham* (2) British Museum
82 *Wim Swaan, Elek Books*
83 *Wim Swaan, Elek Books*
84 (1) *Mas* (2) *Wim Swaan, Elek Books*
85 (1) *Wim Swaan, Elek Books*
(2) British Museum : *Courtauld Institute*

86 (1) *Edición Rafael Garzón* (2) *Elek Books*
88 (1) British Museum
(2) Nationalbibliothek, Vienna
89 (1) *Scala* (2) *Wellcome Foundation* (3) India Office Library, London (4) *Wellcome Foundation*
90 Stiftsbibliothek, St Gallen
91 (1) *Kenneth John Conant* (courtesy of the Mediaeval Academy of America) (2) *Jean Roubier* (3) Staatlichen Museen —Münzkabinett (4) Staatliche Bibliothek, Bamberg
92 *Inge Karlewki*
93 Castello Sforzesco : *Scala*
94 (1) Kuntshistorisches Museum, Vienna (2) University Library, Utrecht
95 *Alinari*
96 Metropolitan Museum of Art (gift of George Blumenthal), New York
97 (1) *Bildarchiv Foto Marburg* (2) Bayerische Staatsbibliothek, Munich : *Hirmer Verlag*
98 (1) *Bildarchiv Foto Marburg* (2) *Abe Čapek* (3) Gulbenkian Museum
99 (1) Universitetets Oldsaksamling (2) British Museum
100 *Werner Forman*
101 *Werner Forman*
102 (1) Universitetets Oldsaksamling (2) Nationalmuseum, Copenhagen (3) *Werner Forman*
103 (1) *Werner Forman* (2) Antikvarsk-Topografiska Arkivet, Stockholm : *Werner Forman*
104 (1, 2, 3) *Werner Forman*
105 *Michael Holroyd*
106 (1) Universitätets Oldsaksamling (2) Nationalmuseum, Copenhagen (3) *Werner Forman*
107 (1) Antikvarisk-Topografiska Arkivet (2, 3) *Werner Forman*
108 (1) Bibliothèque Nationale (2) British Museum
109 (1) Metropolitan Museum of Art (2, 3) British Museum (4) Musée, Bayeux
110 *British Museum*
111 (1, 2) Musée, Bayeux : *Giraudon*
112 Musée, Bayeux : *Victoria and Albert Museum*
113 (1) Musée, Bayeux : *Michael Holford* (2) *Boudot-Lamotte*
114 (1) *Edwin Smith* (2) *Courtauld Institute*
115 *Gabinetto Fotografico Nazionale*
116 (1) *British Travel Association*
117 (1, 2) *British Travel Association* (2) Public Record Office, London
118 (1) *Edwin Smith* (2) *Boudot-Lamotte* (3) *A. F. Kersting*
119 (1) Musée, Le Mans : *Boudot-Lamotte* (2) *Alinari*
120 Vatican Library
121 Wawel, Biblioteka Kapitularna, Cracow : *A. Wierzda*
122 (1, 2) *Franz Klimm* (3) *Lala Aufsberg*
123 (1) *Ann Bredol-Lepper* (2) Universitäts Bibliothek, Jena
124 (1) Archivio Segreto, Vatican, Rome (2) Escorial, Madrid : *Scala*
125 (1) Deutsche Staatsbibliothek, Berlin (2) *Courtauld Institute*
126 (1) Archivio Segreto (2) *Roger-*

Viollet (3) Nationalbibliothek, Vienna
127 (1) Bibliothèque Municipale, Dijon (2) *Jean Roubier*
128 Clare College, Cambridge : *John Marmaras*
129 *I. Bandy*
130 *Archives Photographiques*
131 (1, 2, 3) *I. Bandy*
132 (1) *Bildarchiv Foto Marburg* (2) Bodleian Library : *Penny Tweedie* (3) *Photothèque Editions Robert Laffont*
133 (1) Gonville and Caius College, Cambridge : *John Marmaras* (2) *I. Bandy* (3) Musée Condé, Chantilly : *Photothèque Editions Robert Laffont*
134 (1) *Janine Niepce* (2) Musée de Cluny, Paris (3) *Leonard von Matt*
135 (1) Bibliothèque, Reims (2) Musée de Cluny : *Leonard von Matt* (3) Fogg Art Museum, Harvard University, Cambridge (Mass.) (4) Bibliothèque Nationale
136 *Michael Holford*
139 (1, 2, 3, 4) *Courtauld Institute*
140 (1, 2, 3) *Scala*
141 (1) *James Austin* (2) *Scala* (3) *Michael Holford*
142 *Courtauld Institute*
143 (1) *ND-Viouet* (2) *Bildarchiv Foto Marburg*
144 (1) Biblioteca Nacional (3) Bürgerbibliothek, Bern
145 (1) *Alinari* (2) *Hirmer Verlag*
146 *Ian Graham*
147 Bargello : *Scala*
148 (1) *Giraudon* (2) Vatican Library : *Giraudon* (3) *Giraudon*
149 (1) *Archives Photographiques* (2) British Museum
150 *Wim Swaan, Elek Books*
151 (1) Castello Sforzesco : *Scala* (2) *Josephine Powell*
152 (1) *Bernd Lohse, Prestel Verlag* (2) Bibliothèque Muncipale, Cambrai : *Giraudon*
153 *British Travel Association*

Acknowledgments

The authors and publishers wish to thank the following museums and collections by whose kind permission the illustrations are reproduced. Page numbers appear in bold, photographic sources in italics:

1 (1) *Hirmer Verlag* (2) *Green Studio* (4) Vatican Library, Rome
2 (1) British Museum (property of R. Pinder-Wilson), London (2) *Benrido Co. Ltd.* (3) *Giraudon*
3 (1) Ashmolean Museum, Oxford (2) *Wim Swaan, Elek Books* (3) Castello Sforzesco, Milan : *Scala*
4 (1) Universitetets Oldsaksamling, Oslo (2) *Boudot-Lamotte* (3) Vatican Library, Rome
5 (1) *Bildarchiv Foto Marburg* (2) *Michael Holford* (3) British Museum
12 Palazzo dei Conservatori, Rome : *Curtis G. Pepper*
13 *Alinari*
14 (1) *Scala* (2) Palazzo dei Conservatori : *Commune di Rome*
15 (1) *Scala* (2) Museo delle Terme, Rome : *Pont. Comm. di Arch. Sacra*
16 (1, 2) *Alinari*
17 *Alinari*
18 (1) *Scala* (2) *Anderson*
19 (1) *Scala* (2) *Zentrale Farbild Agentur*
20 (1) *Abe Čapek* (2) *Ian Graham* (3) Freer Gallery of Art, Washington
21 (2) *Arthaud* (3) British Museum (4) *Alinari*
22 *Green Studio*
23 *Irish Tourist Board*
24 (1, 2) *Irish Tourist Board* (3) Commissioners of Public Works for Ireland
25 (1) *Northern Ireland Tourist Board* (2) National Museum of Ireland, Dublin
26 (1, 2) *Green Studio* (3) *Irish Tourist Board*
27 (1) National Museum of Ireland (2) Trinity College, Dublin : *Green Studio*
28 (1) British Museum (2) City Museum, Gloucester (3) *Irish Tourist Board*
29 (1) *Ministry of Public Building and Works, Edinburgh, Crown* © (2) Kuntsgeschichtliche Sammlungen, Vienna : *Werner Forman*
30 Cathedral Treasury, Monza
31 Academia di Storia, Madrid : *Scala*
32 (1) Museum, Troyes (3) Musei Civici, Brescia
33 British Museum
35 (1, 2) *Scala* (3) Bargello, Florence : *Scala*
36 (1) Landemuseum für Vorgeschichte, Halle (2) Coll. Joan Lamotte, Tortosa-Tarragona : *Mas*
37 (1) Musei Civici (3) *Alinari* (4) Museo delle Terme : Deutches Archäologisches Institut, Rome
38 Stiftsbibliothek, St Gallen
39 *Scala*
40 (1) *Alinari* (2) *Leonard von Matt*
42 (1) Vatican Library (2) Laurentian Library, Florence : *Scala*
43 Library, Montecassino : *Scala*
44 (1) *Anderson* (2) *Hirmer Verlag* (3) *Josephine Powell*

45 (1) *Brogi* (2) *Werner Forman* (3) *Ian Graham*
46 *Werner Forman*
47 *Alinari*
48 *Elek Books*
49 (1, 2) University Library, Edinburgh (3) *David Harris*
50 (1) British Museum (property of R. Pinder-Wilson) (2) Bodleian Library, Oxford : MS. Laud Or. 317, fols. 9V, 10R.
51 'The Times'
52 *Bernd Lohse, Prestel Verlag*
53 (1) *Ian Graham* (2) *Werner Forman*
54 (1) British Museum (2) *J. E. Dayton* (3) *Ronald Sheridan* (4) Gulbenkian Museum, Durham
55 (1) Private Collection, Prague : *Werner Forman* (2) *Benrido Co. Ltd.* (3) *Boudot-Lamotte*
56 *Benrido Co. Ltd.*
57 *Werner Forman*
58 (1) *Ian Graham* (2) *De Antonis*
59 (1) National Museum, Tokyo
60 (1) *Zauho Press-Ziolo* (2) *Werner Forman*
61 (1) *Ian Graham* (2) National Museum, Tokyo : *De Antonis*
62 (1) National Museum, Tokyo (2) Cathedral Treasury, Monza (3) *Gabinetto Fotografico Nazionale*
63 (1) Cathedral Treasury, Monza : *Alinari* (2) *Bildarchiv Foto Marburg* (3) Bibliothèque Nationale, Paris
64 Louvre, Paris : *Giraudon*
65 *Ann Münchow*
66 (1) *Ann Münchow* (2) *Scala* (3) *Ann Münchow*
67 (1) Byzantine Institute, Dumbarton Oaks Field Committee (2) *André Held*
68 (1) Staatlichen Museen-Münzkabinett, Berlin : *Ann Münchow* (2) *Bürgerbibliothek, Bern*
69 (1) Victoria and Albert Museum, London : *Ann Münchow* (2) University Library, Utrecht
70 Archives Nationales, Paris : *Douet D'Arcq*
71 (1) Bibliotheque Municipale, Epernay : *Giraudon* (2) Biblioteca Nacional, Madrid : *Ann Münchow* (3) *Ann Münchow*
72 (1) Nationalbibliotheck, Vienna (2) Abbey, Kremsmünster (3) University Library, Utrecht
73 (1) British Museum (2) Bibliothèque Nationale (3) British Museum
74 Ashmolean Museum
75 (1) British Museum (2) British Museum : *John Freeman*
76 (1, 2) Bodleian Library (3) London Museum
77 *Courtauld Institute*
78 *Reece Winstone*
79 (1) Victoria and Albert Museum (2) British Museum
80 (1) Bodleian Library (2) British Museum (3) Bibliothèque Nationale : *Giraudon*
81 (1) *Ian Graham* (2) British Museum
82 *Wim Swaan, Elek Books*
83 *Wim Swaan, Elek Books*
84 (1) *Mas* (2) *Wim Swaan, Elek Books*
85 (1) *Wim Swaan, Elek Books* (2) British Museum : *Courtauld Institute*

86 (1) *Edición Rafael Garzón* (2) *Elek Books*
88 (1) British Museum (2) Nationalbibliothek, Vienna
89 (1) *Scala* (2) *Wellcome Foundation* (3) India Office Library, London (4) *Wellcome Foundation*
90 Stiftsbibliothek, St Gallen
91 (1) *Kenneth John Conant* (courtesy of the Mediaeval Academy of America) (2) *Jean Roubier* (3) Staatlichen Museen—Münzkabinett (4) Staatliche Bibliothek, Bamberg
92 *Inge Karlewki*
93 Castello Sforzesco : *Scala*
94 (1) Kuntshistorisches Museum, Vienna (2) University Library, Utrecht
95 *Alinari*
96 Metropolitan Museum of Art (gift of George Blumenthal), New York
97 (1) *Bildarchiv Foto Marburg* (2) Bayerische Staatsbibliothek, Munich : *Hirmer Verlag*
98 (1) *Bildarchiv Foto Marburg* (2) *Abe Čapek* (3) Gulbenkian Museum
99 (1) Universitetets Oldsaksamling (2) British Museum
100 *Werner Forman*
101 *Werner Forman*
102 (1) Universitetets Oldsaksamling (2) Nationalmuseum, Copenhagen (3) *Werner Forman*
103 (1) *Werner Forman* (2) Antikvarsk-Topografiska Arkivet, Stockholm : *Werner Forman*
104 (1, 2, 3) *Werner Forman*
105 *Michael Holroyd*
106 (1) Universitätets Oldsaksamling (2) Nationalmuseum, Copenhagen (3) *Werner Forman*
107 (1) Antikvarisk-Topografiska Arkivet (2, 3) *Werner Forman*
108 (1) Bibliothèque Nationale (2) British Museum
109 (1) Metropolitan Museum of Art (2, 3) British Museum (4) Musée, Bayeux
110 *British Museum*
111 (1, 2) Musée, Bayeux : *Giraudon*
112 Musée, Bayeux : *Victoria and Albert Museum*
113 (1) Musée, Bayeux : *Michael Holford* (2) *Boudot-Lamotte*
114 (1) *Edwin Smith* (2) *Courtauld Institute*
115 *Gabinetto Fotografico Nazionale*
116 (1) *British Travel Association* (2) Public Record Office, London
117 (1, 2) *British Travel Association*
118 (1) *Edwin Smith* (2) *Boudot-Lamotte* (3) *A. F. Kersting*
119 (1) Musée, Le Mans : *Boudot-Lamotte* (2) *Alinari*
120 Vatican Library
121 Wawel, Biblioteka Kapitularna, Cracow : *A. Wierzda*
122 (1) *Franz Klimm* (3) *Lala Aufsberg*
123 (1) *Ann Bredol-Lepper* (2) Universitäts Bibliothek, Jena
124 (1) Archivio Segreto, Vatican, Rome (2) Escorial, Madrid : *Scala*
125 (1) Deutsche Staatsbibliothek, Berlin (2) *Courtauld Institute*
126 (1) Archivio Segreto (2) *Roger-*

Viollet (3) Nationalbibliothek, Vienna
127 (1) Bibliothèque Municipale, Dijon (2) *Jean Roubier*
128 Clare College, Cambridge : *John Marmaras*
129 *I. Bandy*
130 *Archives Photographiques*
131 (1, 2, 3) *I. Bandy*
132 (1) *Bildarchiv Foto Marburg* (2) Bodleian Library : *Penny Tweedie* (3) *Photothèque Editions Robert Laffont*
133 (1) Gonville and Caius College, Cambridge : *John Marmaras* (2) *I. Bandy* (3) Musée Condé, Chantilly : *Photothèque Editions Robert Laffont*
134 (1) *Janine Niepce* (2) Musée de Cluny, Paris (3) *Leonard von Matt*
135 (1) Bibliothèque, Reims (2) Musée de Cluny : *Leonard von Matt* (3) Fogg Art Museum, Harvard University, Cambridge (Mass.) (4) Bibliothèque Nationale
136 *Michael Holford*
139 (1, 2, 3, 4) *Courtauld Institute*
140 (1, 2, 3) *Scala*
141 (1) *James Austin* (2) *Scala* (3) *Michael Holford*
142 *Courtauld Institute*
143 (1) *ND-Viouet* (2) *Bildarchiv Foto Marburg*
144 (1) Biblioteca Nacional (3) Bürgerbibliothek, Bern
145 (1) *Alinari* (2) *Hirmer Verlag*
146 *Ian Graham*
147 Bargello : *Scala*
148 (1) *Giraudon* (2) Vatican Library : *Giraudon* (3) *Giraudon*
149 (1) *Archives Photographiques* (2) British Museum
150 *Wim Swaan, Elek Books*
151 (1) Castello Sforzesco : *Scala* (2) *Josephine Powell*
152 (1) *Bernd Lohse, Prestel Verlag* (2) Bibliothèque Muncipale, Cambrai : *Giraudon*
153 *British Travel Association*

Voyagers West — Eric the Red's discovery of Greenland like the conquests of Normandy, England and Sicily, an example of Norse expansionism.

1066
William the Conqueror— under a strong monarchy England fully enters the orbit of the European world.

1100
Abelard in Paris — The Council of Sens confirmed Church resistance to Abelard's application of Aristotelian logic to matters of faith.

1204
The Fall of Constantinople — By sacking the Byzantine capital and setting up there the Latin Kingdom of Romania, the knights of the Fourth Crusade fatally weakened the greatest bastion against the Turks.

1077
 Humiliation at Canossa — By humiliating Henry IV and making the conflict an open one, Gregory VII ultimately strengthened the independence of medieval monarchies.

1194
The Palace of the Virgin — Chartres Cathedral as rebuilt after the fire of 1194 was intended as an epitome of the wonders of the world and served as torch-bearer for medieval humanism.

---

the Redeless
England 978-1016

Somadeva c. 1035-82
Indian poet

Nur ed Din 1·118-74
Ruler of Syria

Henry VI 1165-97
German Emperor

Wise 978-1054
of Kiev, ruler of Russia

Urban II 1042-99
Pope

Manuel I Comnenus c. 1120-80
Byzantine Emperor

Philip II Augustus 1165-1223
King of France

980-1037
scholar

Alexius I Comnenus 1048-1118
Byzantine Emperor

Louis VII c. 1120-80
King of France

Dominic (St.) c. 1170-1221
Castilian preacher

Ibn Hazm 994-1063
Spanish statesman and writer

Henry IV 1050-1106
German Emperor

Frederic I Barbarossa c. 1122-90
German Emperor

Francis of Assisi (St.) c. 1182-1226
Italian itinerant preacher

Canute 995-1035
King of Denmark and England

Philip I 1052-1108
King of France

Eleanor of Aquitaine c. 1122-1204
Wife of Henry II of England

Frederick II of Sicily 1194-1250
German Emperor

Berengar of Tours 1000-89
French theologian

Bohemond I c. 1056-1111
Norman Prince of Antioch

Averroes c. 1126-98
Spanish Moslem scholar

Ferdinand III 1199-1252
King of Castile and Leon

Leo IX (St.) 1002-54
Pope and Church Reformer

Henry I 1068-1135
King of England

Ibn Tufayl c. 1127-85
Spanish Moslem scholar

Edward the Confessor 1002-66
King of England

Peter Abelard 1079-1142
French Scholar

Waldemar I the Great 1131-82
King of Denmark

Robert Guiscard c. 1013-85
Norman conqueror of S. Italy

Avempace (Ibn Bajja) d. 1138
Spanish Arabic philosopher

Henry II 1133-89
King of England

Henry III 1017-56
German Emperor

Suger c. 1081-1151
Abbot of St. Denis

Maimonides 1135-1204
Jewish scholar in Spain

Gregory VII (Hildebrand) 1020-85
Pope 1073-85

Louis VI the Fat 1081-1137
King of France

Saladin c. 1137-93
Sultan of Egypt

Wang An-shih 1021-86
Chinese minister

Bernard of Clairvaux (St.) c. 1090-1153
French churchman

Eric IX (St.)
King of Sweden 1150-60

Harold Godwinsson c. 1022-66
King of England

Arnold of Brescia c. 1095-1155
Italian Church reformer

Yoritomo Minamoto c. 1147-99
Japanese military dictator, Shogun

966-1028

William I the Conqueror c. 1027-87
King of England

Roger II 1097-1154
Norman Count of Sicily

Alfonso VIII the Noble 1155-1214
King of Castile

Alfonso VI 1030-1109
King of Leon and Castile

Genghis Khan 1155-1227
Mongol ruler

972-1038

Roger I c. 1031-1101
Norman Count of Sicily·

John of Salisbury c. 1115-80
English political philospher

Richard Coeur-de-Lion 1157-99
King of England

Anselm 1033-1109
Archbishop of Canterbury

Thomas Becket 1118-70
Archbishop of Canterbury

Innocent III 1161-1216
Pope

Ghazni 976-1030
conqueror of Punjab

● **c. 1000**
Leif Ericson sails to North America ("Vinland")

● **1000**
Poland converted: allegiance direct to Rome

● **1001**
Mahmud of Ghazni begins plunder and conquest of Punjab *India*

● **1004**
Sung Empire buys off Kitans with annual tribute *China*

● **1013**
Fall of Caliphate of Cordova *Spain*

● **1042**
End of Danish rule in England

● **1046**
Emperor Henry III deposes Pope Gregory VI in favor of reform popes

● **1071**
Battle of Manzikert: Byzantium loses Asia Minor to Seljuk Turks *Turkey*

● **1085**
Toledo recaptured from Moors *Spain*

● **1086**
Almoravids annex Moorish Spain

● **1099**
Capture of Jerusalem by First Crusade *Palestine*

● **1106**
Henry I settlement with the papacy *England*

● **1122**
Kitan territory seized by Kin tribes *China*

● **1122** Concordat of Worms
Holy Roman Empire

● **1144**
Franks expelled from Edessa by Zanghi of Mosul

● **1145**
Almohades conquer Moorish Spain

● **1167**
The Taira seize power from the Fujiwara *Japan*

● **1167**
Oxford University founded *England*

● **1169**
Kiev conquered by Andrei Boguliubski of Suzdal *Russia*

● **1187**
Saladin defeats crusaders at Battle of Hattin *Palestine*

● **1192**
Feudal military rule under shogunate: Kamakura period *Japan*

Index